UNDERSTANDING THE HIGH-FUNCTIONING ALCOHOLIC

Professional Views and Personal Insights

SARAH ALLEN BENTON

The Praeger Series on Contemporary Health and Living
Julie Silver, M.D., Series Editor

PRAEGER

Westport, Connecticut
London

Library of Congress Cataloging-in-Publication Data

Benton, Sarah Allen, 1976–
    Understanding the high-functioning alcoholic : professional views and personal insights /
Sarah Allen Benton.
    p.   cm.–(The Praeger series on contemporary health and living, ISSN 1932–8079)
    Includes bibliographical references and index.
    ISBN 978–0–313–35280–5 (alk. paper)
    1. Alcoholics.   2. Alcohol–Physiological effect.   3. Alcoholism.   I. Title.
    RC565.B463   2009
    616.86'1–dc22   2008040393

British Library Cataloguing in Publication Data is available.

Library of Congress Catalog Card Number: 2008040393
ISBN: 978–0–313–35280–5
ISSN: 1932–8079

First published in 2009

Praeger Publishers, 88 Post Road West, Westport, CT 06881
An imprint of Greenwood Publishing Group, Inc.
www.praeger.com

Printed in the United States of America

The paper used in this book complies with the
Permanent Paper Standard issued by the National
Information Standards Organization (Z39.48–1984).

10 9 8 7 6 5 4 3 2 1

UNDERSTANDING
THE HIGH-FUNCTIONING
ALCOHOLIC

To all the men and women who battle the disease of alcoholism on a daily basis.

CONTENTS

SERIES FOREWORD

Over the past hundred years, there have been incredible medical break-throughs that have prevented or cured illness in billions of people and helped many more improve their health while living with chronic conditions. A few of the most important twentieth-century discoveries include antibiotics, organ transplants, and vaccines. The twenty-first century has already heralded important new treatments including such things as a vaccine to prevent human papillomavirus from infecting and potentially leading to cervical cancer in women. Polio is on the verge of being eradicated worldwide, making it only the second infectious disease behind smallpox to ever be erased as a human health threat.

In this series, experts from many disciplines share with readers important and updated medical knowledge. All aspects of health are considered including subjects that are disease-specific and preventive medical care. Disseminating this information will help individuals to improve their health as well as researchers to determine where there are gaps in our current knowledge and policymakers to assess the most pressing needs in health care.

Series Editor Julie Silver, M.D.
Assistant Professor
Harvard Medical School
Department of Physical Medicine and Rehabilitation

PREFACE

Understanding the High-Functioning Alcoholic represents the untold story of millions of alcoholics. The goal of this book is to allow society to see that alcoholics all suffer from the same disease, but that it may manifest in different ways. The homeless person and the high-powered executive can both be alcoholics—alcoholism does not differentiate among socioeconomic class, education level, and appearance. However, because the high-functioning alcoholic (HFA) has the ability to perform and succeed, the treatment often comes too late or not at all. Each and every alcoholic should be diagnosed and treated—because denial kills.

The term *high-functioning alcoholic* is one that most people seem to understand or identify with, but ironically, it has yet to be formally defined or examined. Although millions of HFAs exist, and most individuals can say they know one personally, there is a surprising gap in the addiction and research fields in this area. This book challenges the traditional criteria used by clinicians for diagnosing alcohol dependence and abuse, as defined by the American Psychiatric Association's *Diagnostic and Statistical Manual of Mental Disorders* (DSM-IV TR), because many HFAs fall through the cracks of assessment and treatment. In addition, rampant societal denial and stereotypes surround the alcoholic. It is imperative that a new image of alcoholism emerges—and that it includes HFAs.

This book combines research, interviews with addiction experts, interviews with sober HFAs, and personal reflections of the author. Although minimal research has been done on the specific topic of HFAs, related research has been integrated into each chapter. A variety of addiction and mental health experts were interviewed and their experience and varying points of view incorporated. The HFAs interviewed have been identified with pseudonyms or are referred to by their gender, profession, or length of sobriety (when relevant) to protect their confidentiality. Each has become sober through the help of a Twelve-Step Recovery Program. At the end of each chapter, a section titled

"'Hindsight' Reflections of the Author" is included and comprises actual entries from the author's past journals, along with present-day personal insights. These sections illustrate the author's understanding of this topic from a personal as well as professional perspective.

ACKNOWLEDGMENTS

I want to express deep gratitude to my Twelve-Step Recovery Program—without my sobriety, this book and the life that I have today would never have been possible. To my fellow members: you are a network of individuals who can truly empathize with the challenges of recovery. I am eternally grateful to the sober alcoholics whom I interviewed—your voices are the heart and soul of this book. Because of your honesty, many individuals will be helped by your experiences. Thank you to my sponsors for the example you have set for me and for sharing your wisdom. To those whom I have had the honor of being a sponsor to: it has been a joy to walk with you on your path toward recovery.

I am deeply appreciative to the experts interviewed—your knowledge and expertise are invaluable to this book. I would like to acknowledge the following individuals: Dr. Herbert Benson, Richard Caron, Teresa Bullock Cohen, LICSW, Joanna Duda, RN, MS, CS, Dr. Ana Kosok, Dr. Michael Levy, Maura Mulligan, LICSW, Dr. Alfred C. Peters, MSW, Melanie Renaud, LICSW, Dr. Luis T. Sanchez, Dr. James Scorzelli, Ryan Travia, MEd, and Dr. David C. Treadway.

I am profoundly indebted to the supervisors, mental health professionals, and colleagues who have come into my life. Your insights and guidance have enhanced my own ability to counsel others. I feel fortunate to have the opportunities I received through the Harvard Medical School Department of Continuing Education course Publishing Books, Memoirs, and Other Creative Non-Fiction, under the direction of Dr. Julie Silver. To Debora Carvalko and Praeger: you have allowed me the opportunity to help others through my writing and life experiences—I will be forever grateful. To my editor, Dr. Susan Aiello: you were not only invaluable in your official capacity, but also unofficially as my "therapist." To my research assistant, Terra Kallemeyn: your passion and talent for finding information were most helpful when I found myself stuck.

I am honored to be walking this path of recovery hand in hand with my remarkable husband. I want to thank you for your unconditional love and the peace of mind that you offered me during the process of writing this book and always. Thank you for your patience in spending our first year of marriage with me constantly sitting at my computer and ordering take-out food. You stood by me through the darkest periods of my recovery with hope and faith, even when I felt discouraged and fearful. I admire the man who you are, and I am blessed to be able to share my life with you.

I have been graced with parents who have given me unwavering love throughout my life and the encouragement to pursue my lifelong dreams. You have been instrumental in my recovery efforts and have always encouraged me to live in my truth. To my father, who has inspired me to express myself through the written word: thank you for believing in me. To my mother, who has had the strength to fight off parental denial and to acknowledge my alcoholism both to herself and to me: I will be forever grateful for your empathy and compassion. I have learned that you are more remarkable as my mother than as my wannabe editor!

Thank you to my friends near and far who have been there for me through the years—your friendships have touched me deeply. I believe we were meant to cross paths, and you have each brought meaning and your own unique light into my life. It is clear that God truly works through people. My appreciation to Tricia Anderson for enthusiastically reading and giving feedback on each chapter—you helped me immensely.

I am grateful to God for giving me the strength to handle all of life's experiences—the joyful and the painful. I am the person I am today mostly because of the struggles, for they have led me deeper into my faith. I experience serenity in my life as I continue to grow and maintain my spiritual connection. Finally, to my cats, Leela and Tulku, you are precious gifts from God.

PART I
ACTIVE ALCOHOLISM

1

Introduction: High-Functioning Alcoholics

Of course, active alcoholics love hearing about the worse cases, we cling to stories about them. Those are the true alcoholics: the unstable and the lunatic: the bum in the subway drinking from the bottle: the red-faced salesman slugging it down in a cheap hotel. Those alcoholics are always a good ten or twenty steps farther down the line than we are, and no matter how many private pangs of worry we harbor about our own drinking, they always serve to remind us that we're ok, safe, in sufficient control.

—Caroline Knapp, *Drinking: A Love Story*[1]

Personal Stories

Tracy is a thirty-one-year-old librarian at a prestigious Catholic college in New England. She was eleven years old when she first drank as much as she could and then passed out. She didn't go to parties while she was in high school because she was extremely focused on getting into a good college. Tracy went to her first party during her freshman year in college. She remembers having one beer and then waking up in a shower with a male stranger. Following this scare, she decided to drink only on "safe" occasions, during which she would binge drink and then pass out. She graduated from college and made friends with people who frequented bars. At this point, she began to drink daily. She feared that she was beginning to drink like her alcoholic father. Armed with this self-knowledge, she attempted to control her drinking, but failed. Tracy decided that moving across the country to attend graduate school would cure her "drinking issue." She began to dabble in Twelve-Step Recovery Program meetings and became convinced that she could control her drinking. This included hiding her drinking lapses during graduate school and justifying them because "no one else was getting hurt." She successfully completed her master's degree and was then hired at the college. Her drinking binges were occurring "out of the blue" every few months. She maintained her job but continued to break her promises to herself of never drinking again.

Jacob is a forty-two-year-old doctor at a family practice in New England. He began drinking occasionally in high school by himself and did not like to socialize. He graduated salutatorian, was a presidential scholar, and received a full scholarship to an engineering school. In college, he began to drink three to four nights a week, graduated with a 3.6 grade point average, and considered himself "well rounded." He was then accepted at an elite music conservatory and worked nights, which left him little time to drink. Jacob got married when he was twenty-seven and began to hide his drinking from his wife. He was divorced at age thirty and feeling depressed. He decided that medical school would "cure me of something" and spent four years trying to get in. He began medical school at age thirty-four and was living alone in a new city. He was drinking daily and promised himself each day that "this is the last day of my drinking." However, Jacob continued to drink throughout medical school and managed to complete his classes with above average grades. He finished both his clinical rotations and residency while drinking daily and rarely called in sick.

Elizabeth is sixty-three years old and took her first drink at age twenty-one. She drank socially for about ten years, having five drinks or less a week. She drank only white wine. Elizabeth earned her master of fine arts degree at age twenty-four, and in her thirties, she moved in with her husband and her lifestyle changed. They both used alcohol for stress relief and as a reward for their hard work. She experienced her first blackout in her early thirties, and at age thirty-three, she began to drink wine daily. Elizabeth had children and drank throughout her pregnancies and while nursing. She experienced blackouts for about nine years and decided to go to a Twelve-Step Recovery Program meeting. She attended five meetings in three years and remained abstinent. She recalls that her therapist told her, "Maybe you are not an alcoholic; you don't have an addictive personality," and then suggested that she was "depriving" herself of alcohol because of her religious upbringing. Therefore Elizabeth taught herself to like wine again, and within a year and a half, her drinking picked up where it had left off. She spent the 1990s trying to control her alcohol consumption, and her husband began to worry about her drinking. She then decided to join other twelve-step self-help groups that she felt had less of a stigma than those for alcoholism. She felt that "people with my education, my class, my standing in the community, and my successful husband could not be alcoholic."

Matthew is thirty-three years old and began drinking when he was in high school. He felt that alcohol took his anxiety away. He had minimal access to alcohol because of parental constraints. When he left home and attended a well-respected business school, he was then able to drink the way that he wanted to. Matthew felt that grades were a competition and would determine how much money he would make after graduating. He was drinking daily at this point and now feels that his drive to prove he was "as good as everyone on the outside" motivated him to do well. He managed to have a girlfriend throughout college as well as a social network. Just after graduating, he was arrested for driving under the influence (DUI). Matthew was scared and felt that being arrested went against the way he was brought up and the image he had for his life "with a white picket fence." As a young professional, he drank daily but was never drunk at work. He found it hard to "hold it all together." However, he rationalized that work was a time to prove that he was "still OK" and was in "overachiever mode."

The term *high-functioning alcoholic* (HFA) sounds like an oxymoron, but it is not. Tracy, Jacob, Elizabeth, and Matthew are all HFAs. They do not fit the stereotype of the skid row or low-bottom drunks who have lost their jobs, family, friends, and housing. Instead, their alcoholism presents in different ways. This may lead them as well as their families, friends, and colleagues to deny that they are actually alcoholics.

FACTS AND NATIONAL STATISTICS ABOUT ALCOHOLISM

It is estimated that there are about 18 million people in this country who meet the diagnostic criteria for alcohol abuse and alcohol dependence.[2] A study published in May 2007 by the U.S. Department of Health and Human Services National Institute on Alcohol Abuse and Alcoholism (NIAAA) reported that only 9% of these alcoholics are chronic severe alcoholics. It is this small percentage that has created the image of "the falling down booze-hound: an older person, usually male, staggering down the street and clutching a brown paper bag. A pathetic image, hopeless and depraved."[3] It is this stereotype that has left an impression in our minds preventing so many from ever knowing the truth about alcoholism. Other findings of this research study stated that young adults comprise over 30% of alcoholics, and another 20% are "highly functional and well-educated with good incomes"[4] indicating that up to 50% of alcoholics may be high functioning.

Dr. Michael Levy is the director of clinical treatment services at CAB Health and Recovery Services in Massachusetts and author of a newspaper column about addiction in the Gloucester area titled "Take the First Step." He believes that a majority of the alcoholics in this country are high functioning. He observes that they often "squeak by" and function well enough so that they and others do not become concerned. Joanna Duda, RN, CS, MS, another addiction expert who set up an inpatient and outpatient alcohol detox facility in the mid-1980s, continues to do therapy with alcoholics and estimates that 90% of alcoholics are high functioning. Melanie Renaud, LICSW, an addiction specialist at Brigham and Women's Hospital in Boston, Massachusetts, estimates that 75% of all alcoholics are high functioning.

Given the estimated number of HFAs in this country, the lack of research on this condition is surprising. Countless research studies have been conducted on alcoholics and alcoholism in general, but information on HFAs is minimal. When asked, even the manager of the Hazelden Foundation Library struggled to find research specific to HFAs. One relevant study focused on alcohol abuse in medical school,[5] and another study evaluated how high-functioning middle-aged men labeled their drinking patterns.[6] Several memoirs and books have been written by people who can be considered HFAs, including *Drinking: A Love Story* by Caroline Knapp, which was a *New York Times* best seller.[7] Regardless, so many aspects of HFAs remain unexplored.

When asked why this gap in alcoholism research exists, experts such as Renaud and Duda surmise that HFAs don't tax government systems and are not a societal problem, as are chronic-relapsing, low-bottom alcoholics. Therefore research grants are more apt to go toward research on those alcoholics who cost the government more money to treat. Maura Mulligan, LICSW, is the current director of counseling services at Wentworth Institute of Technology in Boston, Massachusetts, and former director of Habit Management, Boston, an outpatient substance abuse treatment organization. She speculates that this lack of research on HFAs may be due to the fact that they have evaded treatment by keeping their jobs and staying out of the legal system. On the flip side, she wonders if researchers have not wanted to differentiate different types of alcoholics because they don't want to imply that some are not as sick as others. Dr. David C. Treadway, author of several books, including *Before It's Too Late: Working with Substance Abuse in the Family*, has treated alcoholic individuals and their families for over thirty years. He believes that lower-functioning alcoholics are treated in the public sector and therefore are more apt to be researched, while HFAs are usually treated in the private sector. Treadway also suggested that HFAs may be less willing to participate in research.

FAMOUS HIGH-FUNCTIONING ALCOHOLICS

Throughout history, there have been HFA celebrities, political figures, and high-profile executives who have been able to maintain their professional and personal lives. In 1978, one year after Betty Ford became the first lady, members of her family staged an intervention to get her help for alcoholism. She went on to cofound the Betty Ford Center with her good friend Ambassador Leonard Firestone in 1982. This nonprofit treatment center emphasizes the special needs of women, although 50% of its space is reserved for men.[8] Actress Elizabeth Taylor acknowledged going to the Betty Ford Center for alcoholism treatment.[9] In 1984, actress Mary Tyler Moore checked into the Betty Ford Center for treatment after she experienced several losses and had been a caregiver for family members.[10] In 2001, astronaut Buzz Aldrin admitted to seeking help for alcoholism through a Twelve-Step Recovery Program.[11] Teen heartthrob and Backstreet Boys singer A. J. McLean entered rehab while the music group was on tour in July 2001.[12] Celebrity host Pat O'Brien spent years covering stories for the television shows *Access Hollywood* and *The Insider*. In 2005, he acknowledged his alcoholism and checked himself into a forty-day rehab facility in Los Angeles.[13]

More recently, in May 2006, Representative Patrick Kennedy admitted to suffering from alcoholism as well as drug addiction.[14] Actor Robin Williams, who has acknowledged that he was a recovering alcoholic, relapsed in October 2006 after first getting sober in 1982.[15] In November 2006, football legend Joe Namath admitted to his lifelong "bout with the bottle." After being visibly intoxicated on national television, he decided to seek professional help.[16] Miss USA 2007, Tara Conner, admitted, "I suffer from the disease of alcoholism," and entered rehab to save her crown.[17] At thirty-nine years of age, country music singer and Grammy winner Keith Urban completed a three-month stint in rehab for alcoholism in May 2007.[18] Eric Clapton disclosed in *Clapton: The Autobiography,* released in 2007, that he "suffered through a lengthy, epic battle with alcoholism."[19] In January 2008, President George Bush publicly acknowledged that "the term *addiction* had applied to him." He admitted to getting a DUI in 1976 and that he eventually quit drinking in 1986 after his heavy-drinking fortieth birthday celebration. In a speech to adolescents in recovery, he admitted, "I had to quit drinking, and addiction competes for your affection. . . . You fall in love with alcohol." He went on to explain that his Christian faith has helped him to remain sober.[20] This list only scratches the surface of well-known individuals who have publicly admitted that they sought treatment for alcoholism and/or were alcoholic. In addition, there are far more people in the public eye who have either not received treatment for their alcoholism or have kept the information quiet.

DEFINING ALCOHOLISM

To define the characteristics of HFAs, the symptoms of alcoholism must first be identified. There are two main schools of thought regarding the categorization and symptoms of alcoholism. The first is found in the *Diagnostic and Statistical Manual of Mental Disorders* (DSM-IV TR), created by the American Psychological Association. The DSM-IV TR is used by mental health professionals in diagnosing patients and has established diagnostic criteria for two alcohol use disorders: *alcohol dependence* and *alcohol abuse*.[21] The second perspective can be found in the general text used by the Alcoholics Anonymous (A.A.), titled *Alcoholics Anonymous*, commonly referred to as the *Big Book*.[22] This nonclinical approach allows individuals to identify and acknowledge their own alcoholism.

For an individual to be diagnosed with alcohol dependence, he or she must also meet the diagnostic criteria for substance dependence (see Appendix A). In the field of psychology, the term *alcohol dependence* is synonymous with *alcoholism*. The following is a summary of the DSM-IV TR diagnostic criteria for alcohol dependence:

- Physiological dependence on alcohol is indicated by evidence of tolerance or symptoms of withdrawal. Withdrawal is characterized by physical symptoms that develop 4–12 hours after heavy alcohol ingestion.
- Individuals may continue to consume alcohol, despite adverse consequences, often to avoid or to relieve symptoms of withdrawal.
- Once a pattern of compulsive alcohol use develops, individuals may devote substantial periods of time to obtaining and consuming alcohol.
- Individuals often continue to use alcohol despite evidence of adverse psychological or physical consequences (eg, depression, blackouts, liver disease).[23]

Alcohol abuse requires fewer symptoms and is considered less severe than alcohol dependence, and the diagnostic criteria focus mostly on the negative consequences of an individual's alcohol usage. The main difference between alcohol abuse and alcohol dependence is that someone who abuses alcohol is not physiologically addicted to it. In physiological addiction, an individual's body has become dependent on the substance. When he or she stops drinking, the individual begins to experience physical withdrawal symptoms (e.g., nausea, sweating, racing heart).[24] For a person to be diagnosed with alcohol abuse, he or she must also meet the diagnostic criteria for substance abuse (see Appendix B). The following is a summary of the DSM-IV TR diagnostic criteria for alcohol abuse:

- School and job performance may suffer from drinking on the job or the after-effects, and work absences may occur.
- Child care or household responsibilities may be neglected.
- The person may use alcohol in physically hazardous circumstances (e.g., driving drunk).
- Legal difficulties may arise because of use (e.g., arrests).
- Individuals may continue to consume alcohol despite the knowledge that continued consumption leads to significant social or interpersonal problems (e.g., child abuse).[25]

The perspective of the *Big Book* used in A.A. is based on the disease concept of alcoholism, and it differs in terminology and diagnostic criteria from the DSM-IV TR. According to the NIAAA, alcoholism is considered a disease and, like many other diseases, is chronic and lifelong. It follows a predictable course and has symptoms,[26] and there is scientific evidence that documents changes in the brain.[27] The descriptions of the symptoms of alcoholism in the *Big Book* are meant for the general public and give an individual the information and tools needed to conclude that "I am an alcoholic." In contrast, a professional may or may not diagnose that same individual as alcohol-dependent, which, translated, means "you are an alcoholic":

1. The physical cravings of the disease are described in "The Doctor's Opinion" chapter of the *Big Book*. This chapter includes a letter written by Dr. William D. Silkworth, in late 1935, after years of specializing in the treatment of alcoholism. He theorized that alcoholics have an allergy or sensitivity to alcohol that normal drinkers do not. Once a person takes a drink, the allergy is set off, and the individual then continues to drink to "overcome a craving beyond their mental control."[28]
2. The alcoholic experiences a "sensation so elusive" from a drink that differs from the feeling that normal drinkers experience.[29] This then leads to a mental obsession about the next time they will be able to drink and feel the effects of alcohol.
3. The alcoholic may also have the desire to stop drinking; however, "this is the baffling feature of alcoholism as we know it—this utter inability to leave it alone, no matter how great the necessity or the wish."[30] Although an alcoholic may have negative and dangerous consequences of his or her drinking, the alcoholic will drink again.
4. When the alcoholic drinks, he or she behaves in uncharacteristic ways: "He does absurd, incredible, tragic things while drinking. He is a real Dr. Jekyll and Mr. Hyde."[31]

The progression of alcoholism leads people to give in to the mental obsession of taking the first drink, which then sets off the phenomenon of craving. They then experience drinking sprees, after which they feel remorse but continue to repeat the cycle, unless they receive help. The *Big Book* also describes five types of alcoholics: (1) the "psychopaths who are emotionally unstable" and try to abstain for periods of time; (2) "the type of man who is unwilling to admit that he cannot take a drink" and changes types of drink or environment; (3) "the type who believes that after being entirely free from alcohol for a period of time he can take a drink without danger"; (4) "the manic-depressive type"; and (5) "the type entirely normal in every respect except in the effect alcohol has upon them. They are often able, intelligent, friendly people."[32]

These differing viewpoints have caused a divide between portions of the therapeutic community and Twelve-Step Recovery Programs, in addition to treatment facilities that are twelve-step based. Many doctoral and master's-level graduate programs for psychology and social work educate their students to conceptualize alcoholism through the lens of the DSM-IV TR diagnostic criteria. Dr. James Scorzelli is a professor of a graduate-level substance abuse class at Northeastern University in Boston and has been doing therapy with mainly low-bottom alcoholics for over thirty years. He spends about two hours on discussions of alcohol in his sixteen-week course. He doesn't believe that there needs to be more discussion about HFAs in his class because "whether or not you are high-functioning or low-functioning, it is all the same disease."

Dr. Luis Sanchez is the president of the Federation of State Physician Health Programs and the director of Physician Health Services in Massachusetts, and has been a Harvard-trained addiction psychiatrist for the past thirty years. He believes that the medical community is at a "crossroads and transition period" in its acceptance of the disease concept of alcoholism. He explains that the concept of illness has only been around for about fifty years. Adding that it has only been in the past ten years that medicine has moved into "exploring and examining the complexity of the brain and neurotransmitters etc. that are substance prone . . . now the disease concept, from my point of view, is making much more sense." In addition, Sanchez observes that it is going to take a while for acceptance of the disease concept because addictive behaviors can be "so problematic to society and so criminal in nature" that law enforcement officials and others have difficulty accepting alcohol and drug addiction as a disease. Dr. Alfred C. Peters, MSW, has done extensive work increasing awareness of alcoholism in the dental and medical community. He feels that many psychiatrists refuse to accept that alcoholism is a disease, and instead, they see it as the manifestation of underlying psychopathology.

Treadway suggests that the disease model, from a scientific perspective, is considered flawed and that the use of the word *disease* as a medical term applied to this condition has some holes. Specifically, he indicates that there is no scientific evidence that alcoholism progresses even if the alcoholic does not drink. Therefore the world of therapy has tended to be judgmental and dismissive about the world of the Twelve Steps. He went on to state that the

Twelve Steps have a remarkably high success rate—in some respects, better than traditional psychotherapy. The net result is that despite the success of the Twelve-Step Recovery Programs, they are still not fully embraced by graduate schools and mental health professionals in general. Richard Caron is a former board member and son of the founder of Caron Treatment Services (formerly Chit Chat Farms and the Caron Foundation), one of the first drug and alcohol treatment centers in the country. He theorizes that the main reason why alcoholism became classified as a disease was so that insurance companies would pay for alcohol treatment programs. He adds that the alcohol treatment programs "lobbied for this designation because they thought it would work to the advantage of the alcoholic." He personally believes that the disease model of alcoholism "leaves the door open for all involved not to accept responsibility" for the alcoholic's drinking. Caron goes on to say, "It ignores the cause of the addiction—the sadness and the interior emptiness felt so deeply in the heart of the addict."

HFAs experience most or all of the symptoms described by the *Big Book.* However, they may not meet the diagnostic criteria for alcohol abuse in that they may have the ability to manage their lives by maintaining their jobs, providing child care, and avoiding major legal trouble. Dr. Mark L. Willenbring, director of the Division of Treatment and Recovery Research at the NIAAA, reports that "people can be dependent and not have abuse problems at all. They're successful students. They're good parents, good workers. They watch their weight. They go to the gym. Then they go home and have four martinis or two bottles of wine. Are they alcoholics? You bet."[33]

In terms of alcohol dependence, HFAs may or may not be physiologically addicted to alcohol, but instead, are psychologically dependent. In psychological dependence, an individual may or may not be physiologically addicted, but he or she will mentally obsess about the next time he or she will drink alcohol or feel that he or she "needs" to drink alcohol in certain settings. The term *psychological dependence* is not mentioned in the DSM-IV TR criteria. In addition, HFAs may not experience true withdrawal beyond a hangover, and they also may not drink to avoid the withdrawal (e.g., drinking in the morning). For these reasons, they may not meet the criteria for alcohol dependence. In many ways, they can "slide through the cracks" of this model. One recovering alcoholic is a mental health professional who has worked in psychiatric hospital units with mentally ill alcoholics (dual-diagnosis), alcoholic veterans, and alcoholics with chronic medical conditions. He feels that there is a tendency within the psychology field not to diagnose individuals as alcoholic because they are not physiologically addicted; however, they are psychologically addicted. One recovering HFA dentist concludes that it doesn't matter if an individual is physiologically or psychologically addicted to alcohol or drugs because "it has got you."

According to Dr. Howard B. Moss, NIAAA associate director for clinical and translational research, the recent study published in May 2007 by the NIAAA "should help to dispel the popular notion of the typical alcoholic."[34] This study found that most of the data samples used in studies on alcohol dependence are obtained from individuals in treatment. However, the National Epidemiological Survey on Alcohol and Related Conditions suggests that only 25% of alcoholics ever receive treatment. Therefore the current DSM-IV TR diagnostic categories of alcohol abuse and alcohol dependence may be based on cases that are more severe or that have clinical features that lead to treatment facility admission and may not generalize well to other individuals. The NIAAA study was done in an effort to stimulate changes in the future DSM-V classification system for alcohol dependence. The five subtypes of alcohol dependence summarized from this study are as follows:

1. The *young adult subtype*, which comprises 31.5% of U.S. alcoholics, has low rates of mental illness or other substance abuse. These individuals rarely seek help for their drinking and have low rates of alcoholism in their families.
2. The *young antisocial subtype* represents 21% of U.S. alcoholics. They tend to be in their mid-twenties, and about half have a diagnosis of an antisocial personality disorder. Many have mental illness and substance abuse issues, and more than one-third of these individuals seek help for their drinking.
3. The *functional subtype*, which constitutes 19.5% of U.S. alcoholics, are "typically middle-aged, well-educated, with stable jobs and families."[35]
4. The *intermediate familial subtype*, which makes up 19% of U.S. alcoholics, can be described as middle-aged with mental illness. About 25% of these individuals seek treatment for their problem drinking.
5. The *chronic severe subtype*, which represents 9% of U.S. alcoholics, may fit the stereotype of the low-bottom alcoholic. Typically, these individuals are middle-aged and have high rates of being diagnosed with antisocial personality disorders and criminality. About two-thirds of these alcoholics seek help in treatment centers, and 80% have a family history of alcoholism.[36]

CHARACTERISTICS OF HIGH-FUNCTIONING ALCOHOLICS

Considering the potential number of high-functioning alcoholics nationally as well as the lack of diagnostic accuracy and research available, it is crucial to acknowledge and define the characteristics of HFAs. If mental health professionals and other individuals can identify HFAs, ultimately, people will receive appropriate treatment sooner, and the level of denial and colluding that surrounds many HFAs will decrease. It will then be possible to lift the mask of this hidden epidemic of alcoholism. The characteristics of HFAs have been identified through research and interviews with both addiction experts and a wide range of HFAs.

The following lists are meant to be applied to people who have either been diagnosed by a mental health/health care professional according to the DSM-IV TR diagnostic criteria or who have admitted that they are alcoholics through the symptoms listed in the *Big Book* (see Appendix C for an alcohol use questionnaire). The traits listed represent the most common behavioral patterns, but they are by no means the only ones. This list is intended to be used as a guide and not as strict diagnostic criteria. The range of behaviors listed demonstrates how alcoholism penetrates into so many aspects of the lives of HFAs.

Denial
- Have difficulty viewing themselves as alcoholics because they don't fit the stereotypical image
- Believe that they are not alcoholics because their lives are still manageable and/or successful
- Avoid recovery help
- Label their drinking as "a habit," "a problem," "a vice," or as "abuse"
- Compare themselves to alcoholics who have had more wreckage in their lives to justify their drinking
- Make excuses for drinking or feel entitled to drink because they have worked or studied hard (use alcohol as a reward)
- Think that drinking expensive brands of alcohol or at sophisticated events implies they are not alcoholic
- Experience strong and lasting denial by themselves, their loved ones, and their social set

Double Life
- Appear to the outside world to be managing life well
- Skilled at living a compartmentalized life
- Set up lifestyles in such a way that negative feedback from others can be avoided
- Appearances contradict the alcoholic stereotype (e.g., fashionable, physically attractive, elegant, refined mannerisms)
- Hide alcohol consumption by methods such as drinking alone or sneaking alcohol before/after a social event

Drinking Habits and Behaviors
- Experience cravings for alcohol
- Have immediate or increased levels of tolerance
- Drink despite adverse consequences (emotional, physical)
- Experience blackouts (memory lapses)
- Feel shame and remorse from drunken behavior
- Attempts to control drinking
- Have the ability to abstain for month(s)/year(s)
- Lack of interest or ability to drink moderately
- Compulsion to finish alcoholic drinks, even someone else's
- Deceiving themselves and/or others about the portion and alcohol content of their drinks
- Increased sex drive and promiscuity when drinking

Employment and Academics
- Capable of showing up for work and/or school and having above average attendance
- Able to maintain consistent employment and/or gain education
- May excel at job and/or school
- Succeed financially and academically
- Well respected for job/academic performance and accomplishments

Financial Status
- Pay bills on time (e.g., rent, mortgage, car lease, utilities)
- Do not have significant debt
- Have not filed for bankruptcy
- Avoid financial problems because of obtaining money from job, family, inheritance, marriage, or luck
- May have above average credit

Interpersonal Relationships
- Sustain friendships and family relationships
- Have romantic relationships (but may struggle to stay faithful because of drunken behavior)
- Can maintain a social life
- Are involved in the community
- Have difficulty being sexually intimate without the use of alcohol

Legal Matters
- Often break the law but do not get caught
- Drive drunk and may have DUIs
- May get stopped for drunk driving, but through connections, luck, social status, or appearance, are treated more leniently
- Can afford proper legal representation, and charges are often dismissed (when cited)
- Often given second and third chances by the legal system

Hitting Bottom
Hitting bottom is defined as the point to which an alcoholic's life and/or emotions must sink before he or she is willing and able to admit that he or she has a problem and is receptive to getting help.
- Their lives depart from their personal standards in terms of emotional losses, loss of dignity, loss of moral standards, and negative effect on relationships
- Their lives are negatively impacted by drinking
- Experience few tangible losses and consequences from their drinking (again, by luck)
- Often hit bottom(s) and are unable to recognize it
- Experience recurrent thoughts that because they have not "lost everything," they have not hit bottom

Level of Functioning
- Able to function in society
- Engage in some self-care: eat healthily and regularly, exercise, sleep, maintain personal hygiene
- Appear physically well groomed (sometimes meticulous)

"HINDSIGHT" REFLECTIONS OF THE AUTHOR

I am a Licensed Mental Health Counselor at a college in Boston and have worked for several years as a community residence counselor at a prestigious psychiatric hospital. I graduated with honors from undergraduate school and earned my master of science degree in counseling psychology in 2003. I have excelled in numerous extracurricular activities, held professional positions, and maintained close relationships throughout each phase of my life. I consider myself a happy person, one who has lived a wonderful existence. My name is Sarah, and I am an alcoholic.

My connection to the topic of HFAs is at both a professional and a personal level. After admitting that I was an alcoholic, my friends and family still had trouble viewing me as one. Many times, I heard comments like "but you don't start drinking at noon," "but you weren't always drunk," "you're not as messed up as those other people in the Twelve-Step Recovery Program." These statements were meant to comfort me, but instead, they haunted me as I clung to them in my denial.

As a high-functioning individual, I found many aspects of acknowledging my alcoholism, getting treatment, and feeling part of a Twelve-Step Recovery Program extremely difficult. Even after my graduate school education—which included a substance abuse course—I struggled to rid myself of the stereotype of the skid row alcoholic.

Having outside accomplishments led me and others to excuse my drinking and avoid categorizing me as an alcoholic. My success was the mask that disguised the underlying demon and fed my denial. In fact, I don't recall that I learned about the disease concept of alcoholism in my counseling psychology master's degree program. I was taught about the DSM-IV TR symptoms of alcohol dependence and alcohol abuse, and my denial led me to believe that I did not fit into either of those diagnoses. It wasn't until I joined a Twelve-Step Recovery Program myself that I was able to understand and admit that I am an alcoholic. Finally, my drinking behaviors and thought processes began to make sense. Society, school, and loved ones didn't teach me—a recovery program did.

As a mental health professional and a recovering alcoholic, I understand alcoholism on many levels. Throughout my drinking years, I kept a journal that has provided me with clear tangible evidence of the alcoholic battle within my mind, body, and soul. Some of these entries have saved me from having an even deeper denial of my addiction, for in the end, I could not argue with my own journal writings. I am choosing to share some of these writings and other reflective pieces to find meaning in my own struggle to recover from alcoholism and to help others realize that they are not alone.

Past Journal Entry: December 9, 1998, Age 22

How many times did I have to wake up in the morning learning about my evil actions the night before from other people? It was humorous at first, but eventually it became hurtful to all involved.

For the first time in my life, I needed to control myself. My parents were not there punishing me. I was punishing myself in my own way. No one could teach me the lessons that I was learning. I had to go through them myself. I pushed my own safety to the limit and knew subconsciously that it was a rebellion. How many close calls did I have to survive, how many mornings did I need to wake up with fragmented memories of the night before?

I didn't even feel guilt. I blew it off and continued to get good grades. To me having good grades would compensate for anything stupid that I did drunk. Good grades would keep my parents quiet and make me feel as though my life was in control.

After this past journal entry, I went on to drink for six more years. The longer I have been in recovery, the more I change my perspective on my past. I often wonder how I couldn't see certain truths about my alcoholism through the twelve years that I drank. Now, I know that my inability to see this truth was yet another symptom of alcoholism. The longer that I am in recovery, the more I am able to see the insanity of my drinking. I feel the need to tell aspects of my story because it is not that of the stereotypical alcoholic. The story of the HFA is seldom told, for it is not one of obvious tragedy, but that of silent suffering.

2

IN THE BEGINNING: HIGH-FUNCTIONING ALCOHOLICS IN HIGH SCHOOL

My dance with the enchantress began at the tender age of 14. I was a scared, timid Native kid from a small town in Saskatchewan, who was practically without a friend in the world, thrown into a metropolis setting for which I was not prepared. When I finally found peers, I wanted to fit in so badly that I took the bottle of whiskey passed to me and took a draught from it. Like molten ore being poured down my throat, my first taste of alcohol burned the entire way down until it settled in my stomach. I was coughing, sputtering, gagging . . . and already craving more. The courtship between the bottle and me began.

—John Adrian McDonald[1]

"Alcohol remains the most heavily abused substance by America's youth," according to Acting Surgeon General Kenneth Moritsugu, MD, MPH.[2] The U.S. Department of Health and Human Services reported that there are 11 million underage drinkers nationally: 7.2 million are considered binge drinkers, and about 2 million can be classified as heavy drinkers. *The Surgeon General's Call to Action to Prevent and Reduce Underage Drinking*, released in March 2007, indicated the severity of this issue. The concern regarding high school drinking is that 40% of individuals who report drinking before the age of fifteen meet the criteria for alcohol dependence at some point in their lives—whether or not there is a family history of alcoholism.[3] Levy stated that these problems with alcohol generally arise within ten years of when the teenager started drinking. In fact, 5.5% of adolescents twelve to seventeen years old currently meet the diagnostic criteria for alcohol abuse or dependence.[4]

Abusing alcohol in high school can be a rite of passage in our culture, according to Treadway. However, testing boundaries and asserting independence are typical during the adolescent phase of life, and drinking is not always a red flag that a teenager is an alcoholic.[5] Thus it is challenging to distinguish teenagers who are going through the normal developmental stage that includes learning how to handle alcohol from those who are in serious trouble. For teenagers who experience anxiety, anger, and/or have low self-esteem, alcohol can take away these feelings and consequently make it easier for them to become addicted.[6]

For high-functioning alcoholics (HFAs), making this distinction is even more challenging because they appear to be holding their lives together well. It is easy for their loved ones to excuse their drinking as a phase that they will grow out of. Indeed, a problem drinker, as opposed to an alcoholic, will pass through this phase and go on to drink in moderation or not at all. In the case of HFAs, these drinking patterns remain constant or increase throughout later phases of their lives.

Patrice Selmari, manager of the Chemical Dependency Unit at the Hazelden Center for Youth and Family, believes that girls, in particular, tend to "slip through the cracks," being diagnosed with mood disorders, while alcoholism is overlooked. Other experts concur that scores of excuses are used to justify girls' drinking. This denial is possibly a result of society, as a whole, not wanting to believe that young women can be heavily involved with alcohol.[7] The reality is that national surveys indicate that teenage girls now equal or even exceed teenage boys in terms of their alcohol consumption. Deborah Prothrow-Stith, a professor of public health at Harvard University, explains this trend, stating, "If society offers girls and boys the same opportunities, that means they're exposed to the good as well as the bad.... Why wouldn't you expect girls to behave [like boys]? Girls and women are closing all the other gaps."[8]

The typical high school student with an alcohol use disorder does not have a lot to lose in terms of a spouse, home, career, and so on. Therefore it is easier for him or her to be considered functioning at a high level. Even some low-bottom alcoholics are able to hold their lives together while in high school, although eventually, their lives begin to unravel. It is important to recognize that HFAs are able to continue functioning beyond their high school years.

DRINKING PATTERNS AND PERSONALITY CHARACTERISTICS

I didn't drink more than my peers, got honor roll grades, and was a three-varsity-sport athlete and on two state honorary teams. I constantly reminded myself that it wasn't a problem and that alcoholics were homeless men drinking booze from paper bags.

—Jennifer, HFA, age 26

I got really drunk for the first time, vomited, sick, and swore that I'll never do it again.

—Brian, HFA, age 28

The first time I was drunk was when I was fourteen years old. After taking the first drink, I couldn't stop drinking. By the end of the evening, I managed to almost get myself killed, and humiliated myself and my friends.

—Mary, HFA, age 30

There do not appear to be specific statistics on the percentages of high school students who are HFAs or on the most common age that HFAs begin drinking. In fact, some adult HFAs didn't begin drinking until after high school. So it is evident that drinking patterns differ. However, most HFAs have some common personality traits.

The average age that adolescents take their first drink is fourteen for boys and fourteen and a half for girls. Most of the HFAs interviewed reported having had their first drink between the ages of thirteen and fifteen. For many HFAs, their first time drinking involved binge drinking, blacking out, vomiting, and/or other embarrassing behavior. Some HFAs reported drinking only on occasion because of "parental constraints" and because they wanted to ensure success both academically and in extracurricular activities. Their drinking frequency ranged from "infrequently" to "about three times a week, and summer was a free-for-all." One consistent pattern among these HFAs seemed to be that when they did drink during their high school years, the drinking tended to be extreme. One man reflected that he began to "have problems right away: fights, arrests, and car accidents. But I played on the high school hockey team and was an A student." Depression and anxiety have been found to be risk factors for alcohol problems during the teenage years. Some teenagers use alcohol to self-medicate.[9] One HFA reported that "alcohol took away anxiety and made me feel OK." In general, teenagers may suffer from mental illness and/or any number of insecurities, but those who do not have alcoholic tendencies find other ways to cope.

Adolescents who are heavy drinkers or have alcohol use disorders often have personality traits in common. These include "high levels of impulsiveness, aggression, conduct problems, novelty seeking, low harm avoidance and other risky behaviors."[10] Although HFAs may exhibit some of these traits, other aspects of their personality enable them to succeed throughout high school in between drinking episodes. The following are some of the terms and phrases that HFAs used in describing these traits and tendencies:

- Perfectionist
- Overachiever
- Good student
- People pleaser
- Need for other's approval
- Fear of other's opinions
- Motivated by praise
- Belief that doing well will lead to positive feelings of self
- Ability to hide true feelings
- High standards of personal achievement
- An innate ability to manipulate other's perceptions

HFAs in high school also have the beginning signs of compartmentalized lives, or divided sides of their personalities. One teenage recovering alcoholic author from Canada writes, "I soon realized that I had two different personalities. There was a persona of myself that I showed to my family of a clean-cut, nerdy, sober individual who played by the rules and never did a thing that would be in any way negative. It was a facade that I kept up throughout this time."[11]

FAMILY DYNAMICS

Each HFA has a unique story and family. However, addiction experts who treat HFAs have observed some common family patterns. Most experts and HFAs agree that alcoholism has a genetic component. The Surgeon General's report states that more than three decades of research have established that genes account for over half of the risk for alcoholism. However, it is the environment that appears to influence the initiation of alcohol use.[12] Scorzelli believes that alcoholism is 60% genetic and 40% environmental. Renaud has observed that about 90% of the alcoholism cases with which she is familiar have a family history of the disease. Over 80% of the HFAs interviewed reported a family history of alcoholism.

Experts have observed some trends within the families of HFAs. Renaud notes that some parents have high expectations of their children, and the children are constantly trying to gain their parents' approval. In contrast, she has also observed families in which there is little parental supervision or involvement. In her practice, Duda concludes that there is often another alcoholic relative, divorce, and/or mental illness within the HFA's family. Levy notices that these families often dance around their children's issues. In many ways, he sees a level of family frustration because the HFA isn't totally "falling down." The families struggle to find concrete problems to address with their children. Overall, Levy feels that "if you put 20 HFAs in a room then you will have 20 very different people" with varying types of families. Treadway works specifically with families of alcoholics and concludes that "if someone's getting A's, is on the cheerleading squad and is writing for the school newspaper, then they can basically be a raging alcoholic and the family won't know and nobody will." He went on to state that this creates conflict within HFAs about what they are really doing versus how they appear to be.

Common trends as well as differences were found within the families of the HFAs interviewed. About two-thirds of the HFAs who drank in high school came from intact families. Most reported that they were not able to open up emotionally with their parents, especially regarding their drinking. One HFA stated that she "hid a lot to maintain the image of the good daughter," and another HFA reported that "lying was pretty standard and I was proud of what I could get away with." Those HFAs who were open with their parents about their drinking tended to come from families in which one parent was also an alcoholic (either recovering or active). Most reported that there was family pressure to do well academically and athletically and to succeed in general. Those HFAs who came from broken homes and were lacking adult role models used their academic success as a way to feel in control and validated.

There is not much research specific to the families of HFAs. However, general research has been done in the area of family influences on the alcohol usage of adolescents fourteen to eighteen years old. The National Center on Addiction and Substance Abuse (CASA) at Columbia University released the results of the "National Survey of American Attitudes on Substance Abuse XII: Teens and Parents" in August 2007. The findings indicate that teens are much more likely to drink when their parents do not monitor what their child is exposed to through movies, television, music, and the Internet. The results also indicated that teens are more apt to experiment with alcohol if their parents believe that their child will likely drink or try drugs.[13] A past study conducted in a town in Ireland supported research findings that high school teenagers are more likely to use alcohol if their fathers are employed, their parents drink alcohol, their parents give them more freedom, their fathers are not close to their daughters, and if their siblings drink alcohol.[14]

A study conducted through Columbia University concluded that high school students from affluent, suburban communities are at a high risk for alcohol and drug problems as well as mental health issues. Achievement pressures, common in these communities, led these students to acquire "maladaptive perfectionism," which led to increased distress levels and delinquency. One suburban high school student states, "We work so hard during the week because of college pressure that by the weekends we're totally, like, *Let the games begin.*"[15] Prior evidence has suggested that suburban children often experience "overscheduling," which decreases the amount of time spent having "suppertime conversations and family outings."[16] The Columbia study indicates that closeness, particularly with mothers, was found to be one of the strongest links with lower levels of alcohol and drug usage—emphasizing the need for family bonding time. Parents' demanding careers were also found to have a negative effect in that those adolescents who were unsupervised by adults after school had an increase in alcohol and drug usage.[17]

The most common theme within the families of HFAs appears to be denial by the family members. Denial is powerful and impenetrable at times. Toren Volkmann and his mother, Chris Volkmann, coauthored the book *From Binge to Blackout: A Mother and Son Struggle with Teen Drinking* (2006), in which they describe the role of denial in their family. Toren graduated from high school with a 3.63 grade point average. He did receive several minor possession charges, but after such incidents, his parents "thought Toren had finally wised up. And he was still a joy—a respectful kid who talked about social injustice, world causes, sonnets." He reflects on his family dynamic, stating, "I just lied my way through everything. An adolescent's biggest weapon is his parents' denial."[18]

HFAs project a facade of normalcy through their accomplishments, appearance, and secrecy. Some parents may suspect that their child is drinking, but they tend to ignore the issue. One female HFA observed that "in my family, if you don't acknowledge something, then it isn't real." Another female HFA stated that her parents were very concerned with outward images and that alcoholism would have tarnished that picture.

According to the National Survey on Drug Use and Health, alcohol usage and binge drinking (five or more drinks on the same occasion) for individuals twelve to seventeen years old had a negative effect on their academic performance.[19] This study confirms the belief many people hold regarding the image that a good student doesn't drink to excess. HFAs defy the results of this study in that they are often good students and well-rounded individuals. Therefore parents and many others may overlook or be unaware of their drinking habits.

Family denial can serve several purposes, including preventing parents from feeling guilt about the way they raised their child. In many ways, it is easier for parents to have a positive view of their child. One HFA described her parents' beliefs, stating, "Look at our daughter, she's responsible, we didn't mess up as parents." Another HFA stated that his parents believed that because he was getting As in school but getting into trouble from his drinking, that "it wasn't my drinking, but the friends I was hanging around with." For many families, recognizing their child's alcoholism may lead them to feel that they failed in some way. However, through interviews with HFAs and addiction experts, it is clear that there is not just one cause. Although there are some family patterns, HFAs come from all types of families and backgrounds.

PEER PRESSURE

High school students contend with a variety of pressures. The adolescent period is characterized by an increase in time spent with peers, a strong need for social approval, group membership, and close friends.[20] Navigating through social networks is a challenging but necessary part of teenage development. Parents may attempt to be the greatest influence on their children's values and behaviors, but earning the approval of their peers is a prevailing force in the life of most teenagers. Inevitably this peer pressure sways decisions regarding alcohol. Research has clearly shown that teenagers influence their peers' alcohol usage. In fact, over time, peers in groups often begin to behave more and more like each other.[21] Many alcoholics agree that throughout their lives, including during high school, they migrated toward forming friendships with peers who drank like they did. These groups of friends allowed the alcoholics to believe that their drinking habits were normal and that their drinking was not a problem in comparison with that of others in the group.

Joseph A. Califano Jr. is CASA's president and chairman and the former U.S. Secretary of Health, Education, and Welfare. He referenced the CASA 2007 study, which explored the attitudes of teens and parents regarding substance abuse, stating, "This fall, more than 16 million teens will return to middle and high schools where drug dealing, possession, use, and students high on alcohol or drugs are part of the fabric of the school."[22] This study found that at least once a week, high school students observe other students drunk. The study found that compared to teens in drug-free schools, teens in high schools without an alcohol policy are six times likelier to get drunk at least monthly.[23] It appears that being exposed to peers drinking alcohol leads teens to drink as well.

Various studies have found that beginning to drink, in particular, is likely to be affected by being around peers. In one research study that looked at adolescent best friends and alcohol consumption, friendship dyads tended to have similar drinking habits in early and middle adolescence. However, a friend's drinking had limited impact on another individual over time.[24] Some alcoholics report that they may have started drinking similarly to their friends. Yet, over time, they continued or increased their intake and frequency, while their nonalcoholic friends moderated their drinking.

Popularity has also been found to influence teenage behavior regarding alcohol. CASA results indicate that teens in general are three times more likely to say that the popular peers at their school have a reputation for drinking a lot.[25] This implies that many teens perceive drinking as an activity that will lead them to be viewed as popular or that drinking will help them fit in with the popular crowd.

CONSEQUENCES OF HIGH SCHOOL DRINKING

High school is often a carefree time in life. It is also a period of exploration, sensation seeking, high-risk behaviors, bonding with peers, and rebellion—so much so that teenagers do not view themselves as vulnerable to any negative consequences, including accidents or becoming dependent on alcohol. In the case of the HFA, these feelings of invincibility are exaggerated by alcoholic drinking.

HFAs in high school are usually drinking in more extreme ways than normal teenagers who are experimenting with alcohol. One consequence of their drinking is that they are likely putting themselves and others in danger. According to the Surgeon General's 2007 Call to Action report, alcohol frequently plays a major role in tragedies for underage drinkers. Some of the negative consequences of underage drinking listed in this report, along with specifics of how they relate to HFAs, are as follows:

- Underage drinking is the leading contributor to deaths of underage people. About five thousand people under age twenty-one die from alcohol-related injuries; about 38% of these involve motor vehicle crashes.[26] Many HFAs lose control of their actions when they are drinking and admit to drunk driving. Even though they feel guilty, they continue to drink and repeat their behaviors. In contrast, normal or problem drinkers may drive drunk, feel extreme remorse, and learn their lesson. The latter drinkers resolve to limit their drinking and not to drive when under the influence of alcohol.
- Underage drinking often leads to risky sexual behavior.[27] HFAs often report that they black out and wake up lying next to someone with whom they

do not remember being intimate. Contraceptives are not always used, so the risk of pregnancy is greater. When drunk, female alcoholics have an increased risk of physical and sexual assault. Also, both men and women are at a greater risk of contracting a sexually transmitted disease.

- For many teenage girls in particular, alcohol and sex are linked. Professors Sharon Wilsnack and Richard Wilsnack of the University of North Dakota School of Medicine and Health Sciences have been studying female drinking for twenty years. They estimate that two-thirds of women who used alcohol were drinking to "get into the party mood" by breaking down their inhibitions to have sex. If these young women are drinking to have sex, then they may be having mixed feelings about their actions.[28]

- Underage drinking leads to an increased risk of alcohol poisoning, which may even lead to death.[29] Alcohol poisoning has several signs: (1) an unconscious or semiconscious state; (2) breathing fewer than ten times per minute or irregular breathing; (3) cold, clammy, pale skin; (4) inability to be awakened by pinching, prodding, or shouting; and (5) vomiting without waking up.[30] Some high school drinkers experience a bout of alcohol poisoning and learn to limit their drinking. HFAs may be hospitalized for alcohol poisoning and, despite promising themselves or others that they will not make that mistake again, inevitably lose control and find themselves in the same situation multiple times.

- Underage drinking can alter the structure and function of the developing brain, leading to lasting consequences.[31] In addition, underage drinking is a risk factor for drinking heavily later in life,[32] which leads to increased chances of having future medical problems.[33] HFAs may know or learn about these risks, but the allure of alcohol is so powerful that they are unable to resist the craving to drink again.

- Underage drinking also creates secondhand effects that put other people at risk of harm: violence, property destruction, and, potentially, death. About 45% of fatal car crashes involve a drunk driver who is younger than twenty-one.[34] Underage HFAs often behave in dangerous and embarrassing ways that negatively affect those around them. They and their friends may use drunken behavior (such as fights) as opportunities to brag or joke. They also may be lucky and can avoid taking responsibility for their actions. As a result, HFAs may not truly understand the impact that their drunken actions have on other people.

WARNING SIGNS

HFAs often set drinking patterns and arrange their lives so that their problem can remain hidden for years. It is especially easy for teenagers to conceal their drinking and convince loved ones that they are all right. The typical warning signs for HFAs may be subtle. Selmari suggests that adolescents may need treatment when their initial experimentation with alcohol evolves into regular use and when they drink specifically to alter their mood.[35] The challenge is knowing when these individuals are using alcohol and how much they consume when they do.

Family members and friends of teenagers can watch for the following warning signs for potential alcohol problems in teens:

- Change in peer group
- Unwillingness to have friends meet their parents
- Significant mood swings
- Unwillingness to accept authority and rules (e.g., curfew)
- Major disturbances in sleep and eating patterns
- Loss of interest and involvement in typical high school social activities (e.g., going to the movies)
- An excessive need for money
- Withdrawal from participation or interest in family life[36]
- Chewing gum or eating candy to mask alcohol on the breath
- Repeated breaking of family rules after promises not to
- Being secretive about social plans
- Going to friends' houses (and/or sleeping over) instead of inviting friends home[37]
- Smoking cigarettes[38]
- Defensive attitude when asked if they were drinking
- Excessive preoccupation with "socializing"
- Extreme fatigue and/or sleeping late (e.g., 1:00 or 2:00 P.M.) the day after going out at night with friends
- Unexplained bruises
- Random dents and scratches on the vehicle driven by the teenager

If a loved one recognizes some of these signs and suspects that a teenager has an alcohol problem, he or she should consider several additional points. Teenagers, especially if high functioning, are very often in denial. They do not see how their alcohol usage is harming them because they are still able to do well in school, play sports, maintain friendships, and so on. Often, a negative consequence of drinking must occur before teenagers are open at all to others' concern for them. Encouraging the teenager to talk to a qualified professional is always a good option.

The more that a parent tries to set alcohol limits, the greater the chance that the son or daughter will rebel. In some ways, the reaction that a teenager has to these limits is a good test of his or her relationship to alcohol. The greater the protest, the greater the likelihood that the teen may have a problem. Sometimes, the most helpful thing that a loved one can do is to keep the lines of communication open and be there for support, regardless of the situation. Many times, teenagers fear telling their parents about their drinking because they are afraid of being punished or grounded. If a parent provides reassurance that it is more important to know the truth, there is a greater chance that the child will open up to them.

"HINDSIGHT" REFLECTIONS OF THE AUTHOR

High school was an experience that starkly contrasted with the experiences of my earlier school years. I had attended a private academy in a wealthy neighboring town from first through eighth grades. This small school provided a sheltered environment in a predominantly white, middle- to upper-class institution. By eighth grade, I had tired of the homogenous nature of the student body and was eager to attend the very large local public high school, full of racial and socioeconomic diversity.

After the initial discomfort of my first week, I recall meeting countless friends and having what I consider to be an ideal high school existence. However, in many ways, my innocence was lost while in this high school culture. I was exposed to fights on an almost daily basis at school and at most parties. Drugs and alcohol were everywhere, and my junior high school resolve not to drink disappeared after I got drunk for the first times. I found myself in dangerous areas of the city and, occasionally and by accident, amid drug deals. I began to thrive on this excitement and eventually made my way into the popular crowd of students, who partied and lived for danger. I was drawn toward friendships with people who drank like I did, and so I didn't feel that I had a problem.

Both of my parents are well-educated professionals and productive members of society who have been married to each other for over thirty years. I am an only child, and my parents provided me with emotional and financial security, including unconditional love and affection. Their parenting style was attentive, strict, and overprotective. I had an extremely close relationship with my mother and an argumentative but loving relationship with my father. I truly believe that there is nothing that my parents could or should have done to prevent my alcoholic drinking. Alcoholics can always find a reason to drink and anyone to blame their drinking on. My parents both drink alcohol, but to my knowledge, they are not alcoholics (although alcoholism runs in my mother's side of the family).

Although my parents set strict rules to try to shelter me, during high school, I found myself right in the thick of all the dangerous situations from which they tried to protect me. This was an exciting time for me. I excelled academically and graduated with honors, ranking 25 out of over 650 students. My life was full of extracurricular activities, including drama club, chorus, outdoor track, tennis, television club, and debate club. I even held leadership positions such as junior class secretary and tri-captain of the varsity field hockey team. These external accomplishments fed both my parents' denial as well as my own. However, good grades, school involvement, and friends could not stand between me and alcohol. In the beginning of high school, I drank less frequently, but I would binge drink when I did. By senior year, I was drinking with friends once every few weeks—a fact I hid from my parents by sleeping over at my friends' houses.

Past Journal Entry: August 13, 1991, Age 14
Three days ago I slept over at Jane's house. We got home from cruising around the city—to West Island, "The Ave.," Accu-Billiards and some other hang-outs. We ended up picking up Don and A.J. and then they slept over the house. We decided to pull out some drinks. Jackie and I mixed the drinks, mine was Tropicana Twister with almost three shots of gin in it. The second was Kool-Aid

and vodka. I peed my pants twice and the second time, I couldn't feel the wetness. I kept crashing into walls. People hit me and I didn't feel it! I was so gone that I probably would have regretted it if someone was the taking advantage type. I fell asleep to a spinning room. I never got sick. The next morning I was pretty hung over. Things still spun and I was light headed and drowsy. This was my first time getting drunk. I had drunk some in New Mexico at my cousins' party, at home with Susan (orange juice and vodka) and with Jackie at her house—a lot of gin and orange juice—I got a large buzz from that time!!!

Past Journal Entry: January 24, 1992, Age 15

My friends and I all went to Ted's B-day party and his parents weren't home. They had a keg and I had a few big cups of beer. I got buzzed and realized that my ride home never showed up at the party. Some guy ended up bringing me home, he was flying at 90 miles per hour and I didn't even notice. My parents didn't even know that I had been drinking—cool eh!?!

Past Journal Entry: May 23, 1992

I went out with Robin and her two male cousins. We were driving around and one of the cousins had a fake ID, so he bought eight Bacardi Breezers and two pints of vodka. There was beer in the back of the car. So, I drank one beer in the car—then a cop passed by close—and I freaked out! Then we went to her cousin's house and I drank two wine coolers and about 5 shots of vodka—some of the wine coolers I mixed with vodka—I was fucked up. They drove me home and I walked in *so* gone! I had fallen so many times! I felt sick. So, I pulled the garbage can over to my bed and spit in it. The next morning I woke up lying in throw-up! It was so gross. I could have died! My mom thought that I had the 24-hour flu. I was hung over until 4 P.M. that day! I learned my lesson. The thought of drinking for the next month made me sick!

I actually remember adding vodka to the wine coolers because I was worried that they would not be strong enough to get me drunk. It seemed that right from the beginning, I had a dangerous relationship with alcohol. My casual comment "I could have died" exemplifies the detachment that I had regarding my behavior when I was drunk. This incident deterred me from drinking for a while. However, once the memory faded, fear slipped away, and I began drinking again. I most certainly had not learned my lesson.

Past Journal Entry: July 18, 1992

Two nights ago I went to Kelly's house for a party—her parents were out of town. I was there with friends from one town over. I had 9 shots: seven vodka and two whiskey. I was fucked up! This girl's ex-boyfriend wanted to kiss me and I did—I don't remember half of it. I said so many stupid things to him that I didn't know. When I got to my friend's house, I don't remember anything. She says that I threw up for 4 hours—including on her bed and stuffed animals and sheets, as well as in the toilet. She drank as much as me, but still took care of me. I passed out with my head in the toilet. The next morning I was in bed and I woke up so dizzy, I threw up again though—it was gross.

These brief entries describe the beginning of my drinking. Right from the start, I was blacking out, vomiting, and unable to recognize the danger I was in. These events felt ordinary to me, and I quickly began to live for them—in fact I felt the need to document them in detail. I was truly infatuated with alcohol from my first experiences. It just felt right—even when it made me sick. My love-hate relationship with alcohol had just begun.

3

FREEDOM: HIGH-FUNCTIONING ALCOHOLICS IN COLLEGE

> We often define "at-risk" youth as those who are failing out of school, but alcoholism and addiction do not discriminate.
>
> —Amy Kamm, LICSW[1]

College is a time of emotional growth, intellectual development, and identity formation. It is also a time for binge drinking, playing drinking games, and taking alcohol shots as rites of passage. For high-functioning alcoholics (HFAs) in particular, the opportunities to drink excessively without parental constraints are endless. In fact, given the present-day culture of college campus drinking, HFAs can often mask their drinking as normal, as they party with peers who currently binge drink but later phase out such behavior.

John D. Wiley, chancellor of the University of Wisconsin in Madison, has passionately stated that "unambiguously, alcohol abuse is the No. 1 health and safety problem on every college campus. I don't even know what would be No. 2. Just about every unpleasant incident, every crime, involves alcohol abuse."[2] Numerous studies have been done on college binge drinking, alcohol abuse, and alcohol dependence. However, none is specifically aimed at HFAs in college, including colleges with or without the Greek system (fraternities and sororities). The National Center on Addiction and Substance Abuse (CASA) at Columbia University reported in 2007 that 3.8 million full-time college students, or 49%, regularly binge drink or abuse drugs.[3] (Binge drinking can be defined as having five or more standard drinks[4] in one sitting for men and four or more for women.)[5] Even more alarming are CASA's recent findings that nearly 25% of the nation's college students meet the diagnostic criteria for alcohol and drug abuse or dependence.[6] Specifically, in 2002, the National Institute on Alcohol Abuse and Alcoholism (NIAAA) published a report stating that 31% of college students met the criteria for alcohol abuse and that 6% were alcohol-dependent.[7] For HFAs, college can be the safe haven away from their families for which they have been waiting to drink excessively with fewer restrictions. If high school is the runway for their disease, then college is the takeoff.

Drinking Patterns and Personality Characteristics

So I drank a few nights a week, peed a few beds and blacked out. Isn't that part of what happens in college?

—Joanne, HFA, age 25

I had the reputation as the guy who could party and still manage to not get kicked out of school.

—Joseph, HFA, age 46

I could do whatever I wanted, drinking became four to five times a week and I graduated with honors.

—Jennifer, HFA, age 26

I studied drunk and I was drunk once in class . . . I just got by.

—Matthew, HFA, age 33

Given the drinking culture of many college campuses, it is difficult to recognize which students are alcoholic and which are simply "having a good time." Most research on college drinking focuses on binge drinking in general and does not distinguish between which binge drinkers are also potential or active alcoholics. The drinking patterns of most HFAs in college change from their patterns in high school. Of the HFAs interviewed who went to college, 100% reported an increase in the frequency of their drinking. Those who had been drinking about once per week or "occasionally" increased to four or five days per week, and even more reported drinking daily. One student who attended a prestigious college in Boston felt that her college drinking was "just typical college partying" and that "it was always social, never by myself, because at school you can always find somebody to go to the pub with you."[8]

For an HFA, college is a slice of heaven filled with bars, parties, and peers who want to drink any day, any time. Living in a dorm, in a sorority or fraternity house, or in an off-campus apartment provides students the freedom they may not have had in high school, balanced by a sense of purpose in terms of course work and the goal of graduation. One male HFA reminisced that "I really enjoyed the lifestyle that I was living because there were no ramifications for the way that I was drinking." In fact, drinking heavily and acting belligerently become commonplace for HFAs and their circle of friends—so much so that many report laughing about their out-of-control drunk actions. Another typical college drinking practice is *preparrtying* or *pregaming*, which involves students drinking heavily before attending social or athletic events. One senior student at the College of William and Mary in Virginia explains that "we'd sit in our dorm rooms—eighteen- and nineteen-year-olds—and try to drink as much as possible before going out. I think it goes on at every college. No one cares, even when they get caught. They think a speeding ticket is worse."[9] Some college students claim that they preparty to save money before going to bars or that they are not old enough to drink at bars, while others may be attending sober functions and want to make sure they will have alcohol in their systems. Others prefer to show up at social drinking events already drunk, especially if everyone around them is encouraging them to drink.

Throughout college, HFAs demonstrate certain personality characteristics that allow them to complete homework assignments, take tests, and pass their classes, all while drinking alcoholically. These traits include being task oriented, a naturally good memory, a strong academic skill set, the ability to binge study, a tendency to be organized and associate good grades with high self-esteem, the drive to achieve, deep denial, extreme self-will, perfectionist tendencies, and a strong family support system. Mulligan has observed that HFAs often have parents who have high expectations of their children. This instills a belief system in the student that he or she has to maintain good grades and therefore do a "better job of managing their budding alcoholism" than students who are lower functioning or fail out of college.

One female HFA who reported drinking alcoholically four times a week throughout college stated, "I was on the honor roll again, had long-term boyfriends, never slept around, worked out regularly, never got arrested, and made it to class." She demonstrated that although her drinking was out of control, she was able to control other areas of her life. Another HFA stated that she was drinking daily, showing up to class half of the time, working a part-time job, and maintaining a 3.4 grade point average (GPA) at a well-respected college. She admits, "I told myself that I couldn't be an alcoholic, because I was in college, came from a good family, was very young, and was a woman." She went on to state that she would go to tanning beds excessively to compensate for the grayish and weathered physical effects of drinking. This was a true attempt to create an outside image of health, while internally, she was deteriorating. By achieving a high GPA, being involved in extracurricular activities, maintaining relationships, and appearing "put together" on the outside, HFAs feed their denial that they do not fit the image of an alcoholic. Other HFAs use drinking as a reward for their hard academic work, and one reported that she believed her accomplishments in high school gave her a "blank check to party hard" in college. Alcoholics can always find justification for their drinking.

For HFAs whose drinking in high school was limited because of parental constraints and/or lack of access, college is drinking heaven. HFAs show many signs of potential alcoholic drinking in college, including the following:

- Chronic blackouts
- Not knowing how they got home
- Not knowing how many drinks were consumed the night before
- Leaving their credit cards at bars
- Repeatedly losing personal items (e.g., cell phone, license, jacket, purse, keys) when drinking
- Feeling guilt, shame, and lowered self-esteem from their drunken actions
- Doing and saying things while drunk that hurt others emotionally or physically

- Making decisions while drunk that they would not make when sober
- Wetting beds while passed out
- Vomiting while drunk or hungover
- Not remembering making phone calls to people while drunk
- Going home with random people from parties and bars
- Getting drunk before actually arriving at parties/bars (prepartying)
- Engaging in risky sexual activity
- Taking breaks from drinking and then increasing alcohol consumption when they resume drinking
- Drinking daily
- Defiantly resisting friends' attempts to stay together and/or bring them home safely
- Tending to laugh about dangerous drinking behaviors and incidents
- Having college disciplinary actions filed
- Receiving charges such as minor in possession, disrupting the peace, lewd and lascivious behavior in public, and driving under the influence
- Driving drunk and, by sheer luck, not getting arrested or involved in a serious or fatal accident

During college, both male and female HFAs tend to develop certain drinking habits that allow them to follow through with their academic responsibilities. Some migrate toward extreme binge drinking on certain days of the week, for a certain number of days, or only after they have completed their assignments and/or studying. Others are daily maintenance drinkers who sustain a steady blood alcohol level. Some maintenance drinkers are deluded into thinking that because they tend to have some control over their actions while drinking and/or they don't black out, they are not alcoholic.

Some HFAs report having moments of clarity in which they sense they have some type of drinking problem. Treadway has observed that during college, HFAs begin to know that their relationship with alcohol may be different from that of their peers. One HFA expressed that by senior year, he realized that "everyone else was planning to graduate and go off into the business world, and I was still looking for the next party." He went on to say that he had problems related to his drinking such as "fights, broken bones, broken relationships, and disciplinary probation, but I still managed to show up to class." These glimpses of the negative consequences of drinking were then erased in his mind by attending class or having a good GPA.

During college, HFAs may begin to sense a void or spiritual emptiness within themselves after a drinking binge. Some begin to realize that drinking actually amplifies the feelings they are trying to mask. For example, if individuals are sad about something, they may end up crying for an extended time while or after drinking.

In addition, friends of HFAs may comment on their drinking, but as one male HFA experienced, "they would then rationalize that he shows up to class most of the time, and he gets pretty good grades, so it's not that big of a deal." Some HFAs hold their academic and personal lives together and convince both their peers and themselves that they are OK, while others are never even questioned about their drinking.

COLLEGE CULTURE

College campuses provide students with numerous resources, a generally sheltered environment, and a sense of community. In many ways, college is a protective bubble from the real world. Although many events do not revolve around alcohol, numerous ones do. Sporting events, formal dances, homecoming weekend, senior graduation week, and spring break are integral parts of many college students' experiences, and they often involve heavy drinking. Dr. Richard Kadison, the chief of the Mental Health Service at Harvard University Health Services in Cambridge, Massachusetts, is coauthor of the book *College of the Overwhelmed: The Campus Mental Health Crisis and What to Do about It.* He explains when heavy college drinking began: "In 1978, the movie *National Lampoon's Animal House* glamorized irresponsible college drinking as a rite of passage, and soon the college experience became culturally linked with drunken antics and alcohol binging. Since that time, college alcohol abuse has been declared a major public health problem, and alcohol prevention professionals have battled daily to undo the damage caused by this portrayal of college life."[10] Ryan Travia, MEd, director of alcohol and other drug services at Harvard University, reports that on average, generally, 40% to 50% of college freshmen abstain from drinking, and that at Harvard, 69% of incoming freshmen identify as nondrinkers before entering college. This is "an inordinately high percentage of freshman who have no prior experience with alcohol." However, after the "college effect kicks in," the percentage of students at Harvard who do not drink drops to 20% during sophomore year—a figure consistent with that of most colleges across the United States. He also adds that most of the Ivy League schools have about the same drinking rates, but the intensity of the drinking varies.

Research indicates that college students drink more than their high school peers who did not go to college.[11] Dr. Henry Wechsler of the Harvard School of Public Health (HSPH) conducted a study of 116 four-year colleges throughout the United States. The most startling statistics were obtained after studying the drinking habits of members of the Greek system. Two out of three members of the Greek system binge drink, and four out of five among those who live in fraternity or sorority houses binge drink. In another HSPH study, 86% of fraternity members binge drink—and this is 35% more than other male college students. Among the women, 80% of sorority members binge drink, about two times more than other female students. However, the results also indicated that Greek societies both attract and create binge drinkers. In fact, 60% of those who lived in fraternity houses were binge drinkers in high school, and over three-fourths of students in both fraternities and sororities who had not binged in high school became binge drinkers in college.[12] Given these statistics, it is clear why Califano criticizes the Greek system for "fostering an environment where heavy drinking is accepted or encouraged."[13] Several years ago, Travia ran the Dartmouth College Office of Alcohol and Other Drug Education Programs and acknowledged that the campus culture fostered student drinking behavior and was deeply rooted in social traditions. He affirmed that 65% of the students were part of the Greek system, which serves as the social hub on campus, and that contributed to heavy and frequent drinking.

A CASA report released in March 2007 observed a 22% increase in binge drinking among college women from 1993 to 2005. In addition, 37% of college women reported drinking on ten or more occasions in the past month.[14] It seems that the gender gap is closing regarding extreme college drinking.

Considering that the alcohol abuse and dependence rate of college students is three times that of the general population, it appears that the college atmosphere is conducive to excessive drinking.[15] According to *The Surgeon General's Call to Action to Prevent and Reduce Underage Drinking*, released in March 2007, the prevalence of alcohol dependence is highest in eighteen- to twenty-year-olds—more so than in twenty-one- to twenty-four-year-olds. These data emphasize the point that college-age individuals are more apt to engage in alcoholic drinking.[16] The question remains whether it is the college environment or the developmental age that leads individuals in this age group to have higher levels of alcohol dependence. The NIAAA published a report concluding that while noncollegiate individuals may drink more often, college students drink more heavily.[17] Another study found that heavy drinking patterns are common in the early twenties, regardless of college attendance. The findings indicate that the quantity and frequency of drinking as well as drinking problems are similar among college students and nonstudents but that college students matured out of drinking more quickly.[18] HFAs do not represent college students who grow out of drinking; they defy this statistic.

So what is it about certain college environments that lead students to drink in such extreme manners? NIAAA research has determined that certain campus characteristics reinforce heavy college drinking, including the presence of a dominant Greek system, colleges where sporting teams are important, and colleges located in the Northeast.[19] A college alcohol study conducted by HSPH suggests that "colleges create or perpetuate through selection, tradition, policy and other intended and unintended mechanisms, their own drinking cultures."[20] This study showed that drinking behaviors that may be viewed as alcohol abuse outside of college settings become the norm. For those who like to drink or have a drinking problem, there are always peers available to drink with or parties to go to. Many social functions revolve around drinking, and students are exposed to heavy drinking and peers who have more of a positive attitude toward alcohol than they did in high school.[21]

One female HFA drank heavily four times a week and still felt like she didn't stand out. Another stated that she was at a party and noticed a girl who was clearly the drunkest there and thought, "Great, she'll be the standard; I won't be the one who stands out." Alcoholics can hide within the depths of the drinking culture of college and feel normal. HFAs often report choosing friends who party like them and surrounding themselves with reinforcing feedback. Blackouts and kissing strangers all become a joke and the highlight of morning-after hangover conversations. Theresa Bullock Cohen, LICSW, a therapist in Harvard University's Health Services, finds that college students' denial consists of beliefs such as "I don't have a problem because everyone else does it." Travia adds that students believe they don't have alcohol problems "as long as they don't drink in the morning and as long as they don't drink alone." He finds that many students define social drinking as playing drinking games such as beer pong and maybe having fifteen beers, and that this is not a problem because "people are around." However, these students believe that "if you drink fifteen beers alone, then that's a problem."

Although research indicates that college environments encourage heavy drinking, ironically, it may be that the heavy drinkers create the culture. One study by the HSPH that focused on binge drinking in American colleges included 140 accredited public and private colleges in forty states around the country. In this study, those colleges with high binge drinking rates were more likely to attract students who were binge drinkers in high school. Therefore there may be confusion as to the factors that maintain the heavy drinking culture of colleges labeled as "party schools." The rates of binge drinking in this study varied considerably from campus to campus, from the lowest of 1% to the highest of 70%.[22] One study on drinking expectancies found that other college students may drink more because they believe that students are drinking more than they actually are.[23] Travia believes that some students are looking to go to college for the wrong reasons and are attracted to those schools with reputations for a party culture. He also acknowledges that the culture of alcohol abuse on many campuses contributes to "a wealth of the problems." One HFA reports that she was attending a reputable business school and her GPA slipped from a 4.0 to a 2.0 after she joined a sorority and began to party and drink more. In her sophomore year, she decided to transfer to a larger university where "I knew I could float by and party."

The nature of college, for those who live away from home, is a true separation of students from their parents, and the possible parental influence on drinking slowly disintegrates. Students are exposed to peer pressure in combination with a freedom they may not have had when living with their families. In time, the peer influences become more powerful than the parental influence.[24] The female HFA mentioned previously came from a long line of recovering alcoholic family members, and in high school, "it was drilled that I couldn't drink." Once she started college, she was "tired of being the good girl and doing everything everyone wanted," and she began to drink. In fact, during her first night of drinking, she behaved in ways that were uncharacteristic of her and compromised her morals. Students may be especially vulnerable during this period because of their need to form new friendships. They also may feel awkward at social events, and a drink can take away the feelings of discomfort. Many alcoholics, in general, report that they feel uncomfortable in their own skin, and when they drink alcohol, they gain confidence and the ability to talk to others. They may also observe others having a good time while drinking and then want to have that experience themselves.

Diagnosing the Problem

I was having a great night. I drank at least fifteen beers. Then I blanked out. This is not unusual for me. Another time, I became violent, smashed bottles, pushed [residence assistants], and got in tons of trouble.

—college student[25]

College drinking...to me it was all about getting drunk. I can actually recall being afraid that I wouldn't be "drunk enough" for a concert, or for a football game. I would drink almost frantically and of course in haste. Sometimes, this provided a great buzz...other times it would hit me like a ton of bricks and I would end up throwing up on my boyfriend's comforter. You never knew.

—Lauren, college graduate

Thursday, Friday, and Saturday nights I would black out, not know how I got home, and I would leave my credit card out.

—Andrea, college graduate

I went to three different frats during pledge class week, got drunk, and was almost run over by a car. I didn't realize how close (I came) until the next day. However, overall I had a great time.

—college student[26]

College partying consisted of drinking at parties/bars and continuing the binge drinking until I would run home by myself or throw up and go home.

—Tiffany, college graduate

It is hard to tell from these quotes which of these individuals are alcoholics and which are college binge drinkers who grew into normal drinking habits. They demonstrate the confusion that professionals may face in determining whether heavy college drinkers are alcoholics or problem drinkers who will phase out of these drinking habits. Recovering HFAs often have insight into their past drinking and can see signs of their drinking problems from the start of their drinking in high school or college. However, during the time of college binge drinking, these individuals may have a really difficult time knowing or admitting that they are alcoholic. Comparing their drinking habits with those of their binge-drinking friends allows them to instantly normalize their intake and justify their drinking habits.

Binge drinking is so common on college campuses that it can be difficult to know when it is actually pathological. Duda feels that alcohol use is so much a part of the culture of college life that it is hard to differentiate the alcoholic from the problematic, normative culture of binging. Other professionals view college binge drinking as a normal life stage phase that students generally grow out of when they have adult responsibilities such as a job and a family.[27] Chris Volkmann, the mother of an HFA who coauthored the book *From Binge to Blackout: A Mother and Son Struggle with Teen Drinking*, believes that "by explaining this behavior away as an adolescent stage, we act as accomplices to our youth's road to possible demise."[28]

Cohen has observed that college students with drinking problems usually come to therapy to discuss failing grades, romantic issues, or lowered functioning in some way. However, they are unable to see the connection of these negative issues in their lives to excessive drinking. For example, their denial may lead them to believe that "the reason my relationships aren't working has nothing to do with alcohol." Alcohol is rarely the presenting problem. Students may also come to therapy with concerns about alcoholic family members and avoid looking at their own issues with alcohol by focusing on others. Although the issue of the student's drinking may eventually come to the surface, college students are not generally ready to deal with their drinking issues, which complicates the diagnostic process. Cohen has also found that even when college students are ready to address their drinking problems, they only want to learn ways to reduce their consumption and cannot imagine completely cutting alcohol out of their lives. This type of thinking is actually symptomatic of alcoholism; that is, normal drinkers would simply cut alcohol out of their lives if they felt it was causing considerable problems for them.

Mulligan has observed that students often minimize the symptoms that they may experience from drinking and that their denial is so powerful that even some therapists may struggle to see it. She stated that a student can be alcoholic even if he or she has not experienced the shakes or other expected withdrawal symptoms. Students may experience subtle lethargy and depression when they stop drinking, but they dismiss these signs. They address their drinking problem with ambivalence, and it is crucial that a therapist help them to become honest with themselves. Mulligan asks students who are possibly alcoholic to identify in a measurable way how they will know if they have a problem. Some state, "When I get Cs instead of Bs" or "If my friends tell me," and together, they write out a contract with these statements, which they can revisit if the student crosses these lines.

One study published in the journal *Drug and Alcohol Dependence* suggested that a diagnosis of alcohol abuse made when an individual is eighteen to twenty-one years old may not be accurate when that same individual is twenty-one to twenty-five years old. However, the diagnosis of alcohol dependence for these age groups was more consistent. This suggests that young people with alcohol disorders may not be doomed to always have these disorders, but that they are at risk, and therefore early intervention is recommended.[29] Levy predicts that many young people who have alcohol problems around age eighteen will mature out of it, although for a significant percentage, alcohol problems will continue into adulthood. Travia concludes that having blackouts is the strongest predictor of having future alcohol problems. Willenbring reports that the NIAAA's recent research indicates that about 72% of people have a single period of heavy drinking that lasts an average of three to four years. This period often takes place in college and generally peaks during ages eighteen to twenty-four, and then "they mature out of it and get on with their lives."[30]

The Drug and Alcohol Dependence study may fuel the debate concerning the relevance of the American Psychiatric Association's *Diagnostic and Statistical Manual of Mental Disorders* (DSM-IV TR) alcohol dependence criteria for young people. One concern is that some young people do not intend to drink as much as they do when they go out socially. These behaviors are then being interpreted as "compulsions," when instead, the extreme alcohol intake may relate more to social influences than to an inability to stop drinking. Regardless of whether an alcohol use disorder can be diagnosed in an individual, drinking may still be a problem. DSM-IV TR diagnoses are a tool used for research, for communication between practitioners, and for the development of treatment plans. HFAs often slip through the medical and mental health system; therefore peers and family should not feel that they don't have the right to express concern over their loved one's drinking because of the lack of a formal diagnosis of alcohol dependence or alcoholism.

Many high-risk student drinkers reduce their alcohol consumption after leaving college. But HFAs are not the students whom research studies suggest are able to phase out of their risky drinking. They enter college with a predisposition to being alcoholic and are at special risk because of a combination of factors, including family influences, personality, their history of alcohol consumption in high school, and family histories of alcoholism. In fact, twenty-five percent of students come to college with a family history of alcoholism,[31] and research indicates that children of alcoholics are between four and ten times more likely to become alcoholics than children from families without adult alcoholics.[32] Others may have a history of trauma, low self-esteem, social anxiety, or an inability to handle academic pressure. They are then exposed to a variety of college drinking cultures. These forces may all combine to form the perfect storm within the individual. The female HFA, with most of her family members being recovering alcoholics, on taking her first drink in college, thought to herself, "I wonder how long it will take me to get to an alcohol recovery program meeting?" Travia adds that some students come to college with no noted family history of alcoholism, but that they are exposed to the drinking culture and have a hard time breaking the habit after graduation. Some HFAs report that their college drinking started off as fun, but that it may have led them, at times, to suffer. Another female HFA with a family history of alcoholism reported that after she turned twenty-one, she realized that she was alcoholic after drinking daily for four years and maintaining an excellent GPA. But not all alcoholics are able to see that they have a problem at this point because they are continuing to function well in life and believe that they are too young to be alcoholic.

In contrast, many classmates of HFAs are able to drink heavily, even put their lives in danger, but manage to move through this developmental stage and on with their lives.[33] One college binge drinker who is now a normal drinker stated that she "phased out of college drinking because the hangovers became unbearable as I got older. Also, as a function of environment, I began to drink less. I was not surrounded by the 'drink until you pass out' crowd. As I got older, it felt better to sip on wine and get a good buzz, and then go home and get a restful night's sleep and feel good the next day."

CONSEQUENCES OF COLLEGE DRINKING

Knowledge of the dangers of heavy drinking in college will not scare an HFA into drinking moderately. Dr. Paul Joseph Barreira, director of behavioral health and academic counseling at Harvard University Health Services, believes that giving students facts on alcohol dangers will not stop the problem.[34] In fact, these individuals often feel a sense of invincibility after drinking alcoholically so many times without paying any true consequences. The alcoholic or alcohol-dependent individual will continue to drink recklessly despite this information and the known risks. This individual has no desire to drink responsibly, and he or she often resents those who try to scare him or her into drinking normally or abstaining altogether. In contrast, the normal drinker, problem drinker, or alcohol abuser may experience negative consequences of his or her drinking or read about consequences and decide to control his or her drinking or not to drink at all.

All of the consequences listed for high school drinking in Chapter 2 also apply to college students. In addition, the following are relevant or unique to college-age drinking.

Drunk Driving

Over 2 million students between the ages of eighteen and twenty-four drove under the influence of alcohol in 2001.[35] The Centers for Disease Control and Prevention estimates, through a National College Risk Behavior Survey, that about 40% of college students reported riding with a drinking driver within the previous month.[36] HFAs often report driving drunk but not always getting caught.

Violent Sexual Acts

Over seventy thousand college students are victims of alcohol-related sexual assault or date rape.[37] On 90% of all campuses, rapes occur when alcohol has been used by either the victim or the perpetrator.[38] In the case of the sexual assault, the victim generally knows the perpetrator.[39]

Risky Sexual Behavior

About 70% of college students admit to having engaged in sexual activity because they were drinking or to having sex they would not have had if sober. Of college women who are infected with sexually transmitted diseases, 60% report that they were drinking when they had intercourse with the suspected infected person. At least one in five college students fails to use safe sex prac-tices when they are drunk, even if they do so when they are sober.[40] That means that nearly four hundred thousand college students nationwide have had unprotected sex as a result of drinking.[41] Some HFAs report reckless sex-ual behavior while intoxicated, and those who black out tend to be emotionally detached from these drunken actions. Sometimes the combination of drinking and risky sexual behavior becomes an addictive cycle.

Health Problems, Death, and Near-Death Experiences

About seventeen hundred college students between the ages of eighteen and twenty-four die each year from alcohol-related incidents, including drunk driving.[42] Most off-campus fires (59%) involved alcohol, and from 2000 to 2006, fifty-four college students died from fires.[43] Nearly 1.2% to 1.5% of students indicate that they tried to commit suicide because of drinking or drug use.[44] Those who have suicidal tendencies, and even those who do not when sober, have an increased risk of acting on such an impulse when intoxicated.[45] Luck is involved for HFAs who survive drinking and driving accidents as well as suicide attempts. This false sense of invincibility allows HFAs to continue drinking even after such close calls with death.

Injuries

Approximately five hundred thousand college students unintentionally in-jure themselves while intoxicated, and over six hundred thousand students are assaulted by other students who have been drinking.[46] Fights, minor in-juries, and mystery bruises may become bragging and laughing material for HFAs.

Mental Health

Binge drinking during college may also be associated with mental disorders such as compulsiveness, depression, anxiety, and deviant behavior.[47] Those who suffer from these disorders may then drink for relief, and a dangerous cycle has begun.

Brain Development

The Surgeon General reports that animal studies signify that binge drinking in adolescence affects memory and impairs motor skills as well as damages frontal-anterior cortical regions of the brain.[48] Somehow, HFAs sometimes defy these results in the short term by performing well academically, both after and when drinking alcoholically. The frontal cortex is also crucial in the development of judgment, reasoning, and impulse control. These findings also indicate that alcohol consumption before and during adolescence leads individuals to increased alcohol consumption in adulthood.[49] These results are consistent with the responses of HFAs interviewed who reported that they started drinking in high school and continued this pattern into college and afterward.

School Performance

The NIAAA reports that about 25% of college students report negative effects on their academics as a result of drinking. These effects include missing class, falling behind in assignments, doing poorly on exams or papers, and lower grades in general.[50] It can be inferred from research that heavy weekly drinking by some athletes could decrease their physical abilities.[51] Again, HFAs often defy these statistics and may overcompensate for their drinking by performing well academically or athletically. These successes allow them to further convince themselves and others that they must not have an alcohol problem.

Alcohol and Eating Issues

Eating disorders, disordered eating, and dieting are rampant on college campuses. Alcohol exacerbates the medical complications common to those students suffering from eating disorders, including menstrual problems, gastrointestinal problems, and electrolyte imbalances. Dieting in general can enhance the effects of alcohol and lead a person to become more intoxicated than expected.[52]

Secondhand Binge Effects

Students who binge drink (including HFAs) on college campuses are harming students who are not drinking and threatening others' safety and quality of life. These effects include experiencing sleep disturbances, having property damaged, being insulted or humiliated, being in a serious argument, having to *babysit* a drunken peer, and being a victim of the aforementioned physical and sexual assaults.[53] Many HFAs are often not aware of the harmful effects that their drinking has on others unless confronted by those affected negatively.

COLLEGE ALCOHOL POLICIES

Universities are often afraid to reveal that they have a problem with alcohol, although everyone knows it anyway. But we've seen important benefits from focusing on the problem and taking a tough stand.
—Robert L. Carothers, President, University of Rhode Island[54]

Through the years, an endless number of programs, policies, rules, and education initiatives have attempted to control college drinking. They originate at the college, community, state, and national levels. Most colleges and Greek systems are well aware that alcohol issues exist on campuses across the country, and many have been developing educational programs to try to combat such drinking.

Some of these programs include requiring incoming freshman students to take an online training program, such as AlcoholEdu® for College, intended to increase awareness about alcohol and provide the colleges with research data. Over five hundred colleges around the country have implemented this three-hour course, and even some sororities, such as Chi Omega, have begun using it in various chapters around the country.[55] Many colleges have rules to help minimize alcohol-related problems on their campuses. In 2007, the University of Mississippi, ranked second by the Princeton Review's list of top party schools, decided to punish students for public drunkenness or possession of alcohol by a minor. Their two-strike policy results in a semester suspension.[56] Many HFAs base much of their self-esteem and justification for their drinking on success in college and outside accomplishments. This policy threatens to remove the very thing to which HFAs cling: their outside accomplishments. Without experiencing concrete consequences of their drinking, HFAs are often not able to face their problem. Some colleges are canceling large, alcohol-free campus events because of the unintended consequences of prepartying to excess, which has resulted in alcohol poisoning and other serious injuries. The University of Massachusetts at Amherst banned drinking games in 2006.[57] Around the country, 248 schools have banned print and broadcast ads for alcohol when promoting sporting events.[58] Two years ago, the California state university system banned alcohol promotion on campus of drink specials and even hired a student to remove alcohol flyers. The practice of *in loco parentis*, Latin for "in place of parent," which has been used in the past by colleges and universities,[59] has been implemented by the University of Wisconsin in Madison. Because the university now assumes such duties and responsibilities, if a student is taken to alcohol detox, a dean will call his or her parents. If a student receives an alcohol violation, then the dean has the right to choose if the parents will be called or if the student will be released to the care of abstinent friends.[60] The University of Iowa is ranked twelfth in the Princeton Review's list of top party schools, and so starting in fall of 2008, more classes will be scheduled on Fridays. This decision came after the results of a University of Missouri study showed that students with Friday classes were less likely to drink on Thursday nights.

Three years ago, Harvard University hired a director of alcohol and other drug services. Barreira joked that the fact that they hadn't hired this type of professional in the past "was a statement of either deep denial or chronic inebriation."[61] Travia fills this professional role and believes that "everyone is always looking for the silver bullet to solve the alcohol problem on campus," and that one program will not work for all alcohol issues. He suggests that "casting a wide net" of different well-implemented alcohol programs is more effective. At Harvard, he utilizes a comprehensive approach that includes early intervention for students before they even reach the campus by having them take the AlcoholEdu® for College online course; administration of the Alcohol Use Disorders Test on National Alcohol Screening Day, followed by individual discussions with students about how they scored; Alcohol Communication and Education Skills training for faculty, staff, and athletic departments; the implementation of Drug and Alcohol Peer Advisors; the Brief Alcohol Screening and Intervention for College Students sessions; a social norms marketing campaign;[62] and reduced access to alcohol at large social and athletic events. For example, hard alcohol has been banned at football game tailgates, ID bracelets are mandatory at games for legal-aged drinkers, and rented trucks are prohibited from tailgating.[63] Overall, Travia believes that the best way to prevent HFAs from sliding through the cracks of the mental health and health care systems is increased awareness, dispelling so many of the "preconceived notions out there of the homeless guy on the corner. It's not that, it's your parent, your professor, your roommate."

Some researchers, lawmakers, and educators believe that laws at the state or national level will help to alleviate the alcohol problem on college campuses. John McCardell, former president of Middlebury College in Vermont, launched an organization called Choose Responsibility. This group urges lower drinking ages in addition to heavy regulation of eighteen- to twenty-year-olds. He believes that "prohibition does not work. Those [under 21] who are choosing to drink are drinking much more recklessly, and it's gone behind closed doors and underground and off-campus."[64] Iowa and Nebraska have statewide keg registration requirements, while Oregon, Utah, and West Virginia enacted laws to suspend driver's licenses of underage drinkers for alcohol-related offenses.[65]

The national *Surgeon General's Call to Action to Prevent and Reduce Underage Drinking*, published in 2007, reports statistics and a thorough analysis of this issue, proposes alcohol prevention and reduction strategies for individuals under twenty-one, and addresses ways to prevent the onset of alcohol-use disorders.[66] In addition, the Surgeon General published a *Guide to Action for Families* to help control this problem at the family level.[67] In 2002, the NIAAA put together the Task Force of the National Advisory Council on Alcohol Abuse and Alcoholism in response to alcohol-related deaths and negative consequences of excessive college drinking. The result was a fifty-page document titled *A Call to Action: Changing the Culture of Drinking at U.S. Colleges*. This report specifically targets alcohol policies and education for three main groups: alcohol-dependent drinkers and at-risk drinkers, the student body as a whole, and the college and the surrounding community.[68]

Considering all the research and effort put into these alcohol policies, programs, laws, and rules, the question remains, Are they working? Cohen reports that funding for alcohol prevention is limited. Therefore many colleges are able to target only certain types of drinkers. She has found that Harvard's medical amnesty policy has helped encourage students to take care of each other. She adds that having this type of college policy, in which there are no repercussions for those taken to the hospital for alcohol-related issues as well as for those who take them, has encouraged students to get help. Although Harvard has found an increase in the number of students admitted to hospitals for alcohol poisoning, she speculates that students were previously hiding the problem and not getting help, which could potentially have led to deaths.

Travia observes that most college alcohol prevention programs are targeted toward problem drinkers and alcohol abusers. These populations may be able to be influenced into more responsible drinking behaviors. In contrast, HFAs may find ways around these rules and policies as well as tune out or ignore the educational programs. Several HFAs reported getting into trouble with campus police or being on disciplinary probation but still managed to drink alcoholically and graduate. Mulligan feels that very few college alcohol policies actually work for alcoholic students—those students who benefit are generally not problem drinkers or alcoholic. She adds that those students who come to college with an established history of drinking are hard to reach with preventive strategies because at that point, a focus on treatment is already needed. She believes that for alcohol prevention to be effective, it may need to start in eighth or ninth grade.

"HINDSIGHT" REFLECTIONS OF THE AUTHOR

College was an excuse for me to move to a new place, meet people from all over the country, and, most of all, party the way that I wanted, with no rules. In choosing a college, I considered several characteristics: a lower-pressure academic life, a beautiful campus, a large number of students, and, most important, a wild social life. I applied to six large state universities and was accepted at and decided to attend my first choice—one of the top-rated party schools in the country. My cousins loved their college experience there and had assured me that the Greek system was active and full of social opportunities.

As soon as I arrived, my drinking took off. Most weekends, I would go out with my friends, black out, and then wake up in random places. One particular example of the danger in which I put myself regularly was when my sorority sisters and I traveled to Las Vegas. I woke up hungover, somewhere in the suburbs of Vegas, with a strange man. In a moment of horror, I ran out the door and sat on the curb of a pawn shop for hours waiting for a cab—I had no idea where I was. Suddenly, I had flashes from the evening before of driving his BMW to his condo and even stopping at a drive-through taco place. I was crying and scared from the evening, but I was back drinking two nights later. On another occasion, I woke up in a fraternity member's room lying in urine on top of a feather comforter. He had left, but I panicked and took all the bedding to my sorority house to wash it and then returned it as quickly as possible with a note. Senior year in college, I woke up hungover in my sorority house on the couch in the living room, once again lying in urine. I realized that I didn't live there anymore and that a man had walked me there the night before because I couldn't remember where I lived. Laughing with my friends about these events and my alcoholic ability to forget about negative drinking experiences allowed me to continue drinking this way.

The following journal entry was written after I graduated from college and touches on four years of living for weekly fraternity parties, spring break, football games, and drunken weekend trips. Throughout college, I did not have the desire to keep a journal because I was too preoccupied both with drinking and with completing academic assignments. Drinking had become so commonplace that I didn't feel compelled to reflect on it. I was driven to live that lifestyle.

Past Journal Entry: December 9, 1998, Age 21
Independence: a privilege that I fought for throughout most of my childhood. My battle to do as I pleased, whenever I pleased, was constant throughout my teenage years. I felt that I knew better than my parents about the harmlessness of activities that I wished to engage in. To me, going to an "R" rated movie before I was 17 seemed harmless. I dreamed of a day when I didn't have to lie about what I was doing or where I was going. From my perspective, I didn't care if my parents said "no," that only affected whether or not I told them what I was doing. I do regret that I began to justify lying to my parents. I felt that they were overprotective and that I should be allowed to do the things that other kids my age do.

To me, college was a giant slumber party that I would not have to leave. It was bliss—everything that I hoped it would be. I was in my element, surrounded by like-minded individuals with minimal rules. I pushed it to the limit.

Receiving the "Pledge Class Lush" award, the "Kissing Bandit" award, and the "Academic Excellence" award pretty much summed up my college experience. Having to hide my drinking throughout my high school years meant that college was "pig heaven" for me. No curfew, no parents, no limitations. Just absolute freedom. I had longed for this point in my life for years and it had finally arrived.

In my mind there was no such thing as drinking too much. Blacking out and acting outrageously became commonplace. When older girls in my sorority tried to reprimand me after punching my freshman dorm roommate in the face, I would *not* listen. I was almost not allowed to initiate into my sorority because of my drunken actions, but I cried my way in. These girls were not my parents and I was so set on having my independence that no one was going to take it away. When my best friends tried to help take me from a party after excessive drinking, I would not listen. I was feisty, loud, aggressive and absolutely out of control. How many times did I have to wake up in the morning learning about my evil actions the night before from other people? It was humorous at first, but eventually it became hurtful to all involved.

For the first time in my life, I needed to control myself. My parents were not there punishing me. I was punishing myself in my own way. No one could teach me the lessons that I was learning. I had to go through them myself. I pushed my own safety to the limit and knew subconsciously that it was a rebellion. How many close calls did I have to survive, how many mornings did I need to wake up with fragmented memories of the night before?

I didn't even feel guilt. I blew it off and continued to get good grades. To me having good grades would compensate for anything stupid that I did in my social life. Good grades would keep my parents quiet and make me feel as though my life was in control.

Someone was looking over me during these times of erratic behavior. I survived college and I survived my own rebellion. I have finally come to terms with my weakness. Now as I look back at my college life, I cannot believe the years I could only dream about have come to a close.

Rebellion against my parents is an excuse that the disease of alcoholism led me to use in justifying my drinking, for an alcoholic will drink for any reason or for no reason at all. I used my parents as an excuse to act out, and I would drink "at them." This past journal entry describes a moment of grace from God that gave me insight that I had a problem.

Throughout college, I was able to get around all the rules of the college and my sorority. I avoided the requirement to be a sober person at a party and not having alcohol in the sorority house. I prided myself on being the target of a sorority meeting request that "whoever left the six empty handles of dark Bacardi rum needs to stop having alcohol in the house." I was caught by Boulder police drinking at a party one day for a football game and received a minor in possession charge. As a result, I was mandated to attend an alcohol awareness class through the college, and I laughed and mocked it entirely, bragging about the 180 days a year that I had drank. When college ended, I started to become aware that I needed to be held responsible, but my drinking lifestyle carried on. I continued to get away with my behavior on the surface, but it became clear that this disease was taking a toll on my soul.

4

ADRIFT: HIGH-FUNCTIONING ALCOHOLICS AS EMERGING ADULTS

I suppose I am frightened of adulthood because in many ways it seems to represent the end of fun.... I am not ready to stop having the "young" kind of fun. Sure, I like the symphony and the theater. But I also, frankly, like to drink and smoke. I like to dance all night to techno music. I like to flirt, hook up, fall in love.... When will I have to stop doing all these things?

—Olivia from *Quarterlife Crisis*[1]

Societal shifts throughout the past few decades have let many individuals in their twenties have endless life opportunities. The path to adulthood is no longer linear or predictable. While this period of life can be exhilarating, it can also be uncertain and stressful. This life phase between adolescence and adulthood is being referred to as *emerging adulthood*, a term coined by Dr. Jeffrey Jensen Arnett in his book *Emerging Adulthood: The Winding Road from the Late Teens through the Twenties.*[2] Just three decades ago, twenty-one-year-olds may have already married, had a child, completed their education, and settled into a career. However, today, most young people are not marrying, becoming parents, or finding a long-term job until their late twenties or even thirties.[3] According to Arnett's research, these changes are in part due to the fact that about one-third of all college graduates are going on to graduate school.[4] Occupational shifts in the past few decades have been most dramatic for women, who are now equal in number to men in obtaining law and business degrees and almost equal in completing medical degrees.[5] Other factors in delaying marriage include the ready availability of the birth control pill and changes in sexual morality.

The five main characteristics of emerging adulthood consist of an age of identity exploration, instability, self-focus, feeling in-between, and possibilities.[6] In this age of self, individuals are focused on their own needs. In decades past, young people embraced adulthood responsibilities and perceived families as a source of emotional stability as well as accomplishments in their own right. Today, adulthood obligations are viewed as limiting independence, life opportunities, and spontaneity. Young people see adults who are overworked, divorced, and stressed and view adult responsibilities as life hazards to avoid.[7]

Typically, this period is one of experimentation with alcohol; however, once typical adulthood roles are assumed, research indicates that alcohol usage tapers off. It is also a turning point for many young people in terms of their life direction (i.e., positive or negative) and substance use.[8] High-functioning alcoholics (HFAs) either avoid adult roles to accommodate their drinking or try to hide their drinking while making an effort to hold on to their adult responsibilities.

Some of the personality traits of HFAs and alcoholics at all ages are comparable to those characteristics of the emerging adulthood phase. Alcoholics in general tend to constantly search for ways to make their lives more exciting, and many thrive on freedom, which is often provided by drinking, rather than by obligations. Drinking is their escape from the mundane and often their way to cope with the stress that this period of not knowing often creates. Many individuals in emerging adulthood don't want to settle and have high expectations out of life.[9] Many HFAs and alcoholics in general are always looking for external gratification that they believe will make them feel satisfied, whether it is moving to a new place, dating a new person, or having an exciting night out. A certain restlessness drives many HFAs to drink in this futile search for life fulfillment. Consequently, the combination of the pressures and independence of the emerging adulthood period can lead HFAs to experience significant disease progression and stunted emotional development.

Drinking Patterns and Personality Characteristics

I was always able to keep things running ... There was a lot of "spit, shine, and polish" going on to keep myself appearing as though I was functioning well.
—Justin, HFA

I lived for drinking on the weekends, and I would actually shake before going out because the cravings were so intense. . . . I'd be drunk and hanging over a parking meter, and friends would comment, "You work at a health and fitness club?"
—Jasmine, HFA

For those eight hours of work, I was in hyperactive, overachiever mode.
—Mark, HFA

Research by the National Institute on Alcohol Abuse and Alcoholism (NIAAA) has suggested that increases in drinking during emerging adulthood often occur in Western society as a result of personal, biological, professional, and emotional developmental changes. Social and environmental constraints decrease, and individuals are free to choose their lifestyles.[10] HFAs are able to make their own choices about drinking—choices in usage that may not have been acceptable in adolescence. In the past, HFAs may have used alcohol in social situations but now may be using it to relieve general life stress. In addition, once HFAs reach age twenty-one, they have greater access to alcohol, which in turn increases their opportunities to drink. One study emphasized the danger of problem drinking patterns during emerging adulthood, concluding that heavy drinking after age twenty-eight is less likely to stop in the future.[11]

HFAs report that certain personality characteristics and traits allow them to drink alcoholically while functioning professionally and/or academically in graduate programs. These characteristics include the following:

- Attachment to external success
- Need to prove themselves
- Desire to exceed parental levels of success
- Good communication skills
- Outgoing and gregarious personality
- Ability to function in "survival mode"
- People skills
- People-pleasing tendencies
- Large amounts of physical energy
- Meticulous work ethic
- "Workaholic" characteristics
- Likeability
- Strong physical constitution
- Desire to succeed materially
- Competitive nature
- High professional/academic skill sets
- Ability to compartmentalize professional and/or academic life from drinking life

In addition, many HFAs report that pressure from other family members to succeed is a powerful motivator. A seventy-nine-year-old dentist reflects that his father was "hard on me ... if I got an eighty-eight he would tell me to get a ninety-two." Another male dentist who graduated early from undergraduate and dental school explains that his father was a German immigrant with a strong work ethic. His father instilled the belief that "the way to succeed in this country is to get an education" and that it was important to "do it fast and do it right." A twenty-six-year-old female therapist reports, "I felt a lot of pressure to be perfect, get impeccable grades, be the best athlete, be likeable, etc. If I didn't want to do something that my father wanted me to do, he could never see where I was coming from or be supportive of who I was as a person." One thirty-two-year-old Web engineer felt he had the drive to work hard because "my mother was a shining beacon of what a human being is capable of.... She had a crippling disease, incredibly bad luck, got up every day to go to work and went to school." His single mother instilled in him that "there is no excuse.... You get up every day and go to work and do the best that you can do, and if you don't do that, you are subhuman."

During this time, those who drank heavily in college may drink more normally. Although some research indicates that heavy drinking declines in the general population during the period from age twenty-one to thirty, this period represents a high risk for the onset of alcohol-related problems. Drinking problems begin to progress into both alcohol abuse and alcohol dependence.[12] HFAs may begin to stand out in certain social crowds when drinking, which may lead them either to migrate toward peers who drink like them or to drink alone. A twenty-six-year-old teacher who started her career working at a nonprofit organization observed that during her first year out of college, her friends started drinking less. So she started drinking alone, which she felt would allow her to "drink without hassling others." Then she would hide her phone to avoid calling people while she was drunk, a practice commonly referred to as *drunk dialing*. Because of her isolated drinking, her world became very small. In contrast, a twenty-five-year-old physical trainer reported that she drank about ten times as much after college than during and that she was confused and upset when those in their mid-twenties around her began to settle down and drink less. She believed that "my twenties were for drinking, my thirties were going to be for drinking at my friends' weddings, and my forties would involve a bottle of wine, and all of the stay-at-home mothers would be envious because I would still be partying." A thirty-one-year-old librarian reported that she had tried to control her drinking in college to succeed, and by this time in her life, she found people with whom she could go to bars daily.

At this point, some HFAs may begin to sense that they have a problem with alcohol, but they are not necessarily fully convinced or ready to seek treatment. Loved ones may also start to notice that the HFA's drinking is becoming a problem. The librarian added that because her father is a recovering alcoholic, she had a moment of clarity in which she saw herself drinking like he once did. She began to "investigate" Twelve-Step Recovery meetings but then decided that she could control her drinking on her own. One young professional began to "cut loose those who saw the alcoholic side of me" in an effort to preserve his drinking habits. The physical trainer reported that her roommate expressed concern over her drinking and would "babysit me when I was drinking and make sure that I got home safe in a cab." One doctor admitted that during the year he was a chief resident in medical school, his wife attended Al-Anon[13] and later staged "an intervention of sorts." This prompted him to curtail his drinking for a brief period to prove to her that he could control it.

GRADUATE SCHOOL

Graduate school, for many, is the pursuit of higher education and a professional specialty and is often a necessity for those pursuing careers in law, medicine, education, or psychology. For others, it is an escape from the real world and a way to deny that their college years have ended. Some attend graduate programs directly after college, some several years after, and others later in life. Travia reports that although there are little data on graduate students' drinking, these students have higher rates of alcoholism than undergraduate students, and their drinking habits are more ingrained.

The drinking cultures of graduate programs vary by the type of field students are in and the particular school. Cohen has observed that the number of HFAs tends to be higher in Harvard University Business School and Harvard Law School than in the undergraduate program. She sees this problem as rooted in the cultures of these programs because "alcohol is such a large part of the culture of what they do career-wise." Specifically, the law school culture is such that cohorts (groups of class members) are expected to go to bars for what is ironically called "Bar Review." This is considered an important social networking scene, and if students don't participate, they are at a disadvantage for making professional connections. Cohen adds that this drinking culture is reinforced when partners from prospective law firms give presentations to the best and brightest possible recruits while offering and consuming large amounts of alcohol. This gives the message to the students that being accepted into the culture of the firm means that they, too, must consume large amounts of alcohol and then be able to get up and go to class or work the next day and function. Travia gets referrals from the various Harvard graduate schools and states that the mean age of the law students is twenty-three, which is generally younger than the mean age of students in other graduate programs. He affirms that the law students have a reputation for heavy drinking and that the culture is a virtual pressure cooker of stress.

Alice, an alcoholic featured in *Happy Hours: Alcohol in a Woman's Life*, reported that she was considered a light drinker at her prestigious law school. She confirms that there was overwhelming pressure to drink and that "social and academic responsibilities went hand in hand." It never occurred to her during this time that she had a problem because those around her drank so much more than she did. However, alcohol took its toll, and one year after graduating at the top of her class, Alice sought treatment. When she shared this news with classmates, they "became upset" because it "put them on notice" and forced them to look at their own drinking.[14] One thirty-four-year-old lawyer who attended a prestigious law school directly out of college stated that drinking alcohol was completely acceptable in her program. She added that at the beginning of the week, you were expected to discuss what you did over the weekend and that it was "always about the story." She observed that there were few married people in her class and that it was a "bunch of young twenty-somethings." She found herself living a double life: going out with those who partied hard and then studying with the "brainiacs" before tests. She juggled relationships and drinking and felt that she "couldn't just stay with one life."

Cohen observed that the Harvard Business School culture leads students to feel that they have to be able to socialize with their cohorts, hold their liquor at all social functions, and also get good grades. Because the business culture in general is based on networking and schmoozing, it is necessary to have a high tolerance for alcohol. She stated that this leaves women at a disadvantage both because they are in a male-dominated field and because they metabolize alcohol differently than men. When women try to keep up drink for drink with men, they end up intoxicated, which is viewed as a shortcoming. She has observed that the students do not see their drinking as "we are going out to get loaded," but as "this is business." She adds that these types of graduate school cultures are "breeding high-functioning alcoholics" in that students are expected to drink hard, network, and maintain their academics. Travia adds that the average age of Harvard Business School students is twenty-seven. Some of these students have had amazing experiences making multi-million-dollar deals over drinks on Wall Street.

In contrast, some HFAs report that they tried to isolate themselves during graduate school to excel, that they preferred to hide their drinking, or that their graduate schools did not have a heavy drinking culture. One HFA stated that when she was getting her master's degree, she "got by in graduate school by going to class, going home, and avoiding everything." One therapist explained that when she moved to a new city and enrolled in a mental health counseling master's program, she felt lonely living with roommates whom she didn't know and started drinking on her own. She would drunk dial people on the phone and not remember the conversations; at times, she would even call her parents crying. All the while, she maintained a job and an A average.

Medical school students are no less exempt from having alcohol problems. In one study published in the *Journal of the American Medical Association,* 11% of medical school students met the criteria for excessive drinking, and 18% were identified as alcohol abusers. The students who were problem drinkers had better scores on their first-year board exams and better overall grades than their classmates. The authors noted that "it is ironic that medical students who abused alcohol showed evidence of better academic performance when most studies of high school and college students have reported the opposite relationship." The authors suggested several explanations for these findings, speculating that because medical students are academically capable, they are able to compensate for their "maladaptive drinking patterns." Another theory was that "hardworking and academically successful medical students require, or feel they deserve, a mechanism such as drinking to dispel the pressure and tension associated with their studies." This ironic ability is the crux of the denial of HFAs, their loved ones, and their colleagues. This study emphasizes that academic success can be an obstacle to seeking help; many medical students fear "being stigmatized or penalized in their career progress for admitting to any psychological problems or for using psychotherapy."[15]

A seventy-one-year-old dentist who drank throughout dental school stated that the heavy drinking at his school was considered socially acceptable. Another dentist reported having an alcoholic roommate who was six years older than him, and they both gravitated to the bars throughout dental school. He credits his "decent brain" for not having to study very hard and went on for an additional year of schooling to specialize in pediatric dentistry, despite his drinking. One forty-two-year-old doctor thought that medical school would keep him too busy to drink. However, when he moved to a new city, he avoided any socializing and drank alone each night. He eventually stopped going to some classes and would "binge study" the notes for twenty to thirty hours before an exam. He reported that his grades were above average. He would drink more during the less challenging clinical rotations and went to work tipsy a few times. Another doctor stated that he drank less during his intern year because of the rigorous schedule of thirty-six hours on duty and twelve off. He reflected that the culture of his medical school did not foster drinking. He then entered the military as a flight surgeon for three years, and his drinking accelerated as he was surrounded by heavy drinkers. When he returned, he limited his drinking to weekends and "sailed through residency...and I was chosen as best teaching resident." He graduated from medical school with honors—all the while drinking alcoholically.

YOUNG PROFESSIONALS

For some HFAs, becoming a young professional signals the first time that they struggle to function while drinking alcoholically. Young professionals may or may not have attended college and/or graduate school. Beginning a job often means facing the real world and the many life responsibilities that come along with the world of work. Drinking can become that retreat to the carefree days and allow HFAs to hang on to their past in some way. One young professional found herself going to work most days but then calling in sick at times. She stated that her boss was a recovering alcoholic and "caught on to my habits," which led her eventually to quit her job. Another young professional who was a daily drinker during and after college found it hard to "hold it all together." He would show up for work and not drink during the day, and reported that he had a "knack for being able to say the right thing," which allowed him to continue to function professionally. In contrast, he struggled in his personal life and had several romantic relationships that "were a mess." His circle of friends had dwindled to two roommates who drank, but there was always tension because he didn't help with house duties.

The computer field has attracted many high school graduates. "When the dotcom boom was on, students wouldn't even complete their bachelor's studies," says Joe Merola, senior administrative fellow in charge of restructuring at Virginia Tech in Blacksburg.[16] A successful Web designer who never attended college started out as a *weekend warrior*, a person who abstains from alcohol all week and then binge drinks on the weekends. He was able to keep up this drinking pattern for a while, until he started his own Web- and video-based company. His life was less structured and his drinking "began to take off." Meanwhile, his marriage began to suffer. Once he was legally separated from his wife, he felt "free" and reported having blackouts routinely.

A survey conducted among employees at some of Britain's leading banking, law, television, advertising, consulting, and accounting businesses found that one-third of young professionals are hungover at least two workdays. Most of those surveyed were graduates of prestigious colleges in England, including the researcher himself, who graduated from Oxford University. Ironically, those who claimed to be the most hungover were also the most health conscious. Results of this Web-based survey also found that young professionals feel pressure to consume alcohol, and at large banks and consulting firms in particular, they were expected to keep up with "a macho culture that demanded after-hours drinking sessions." Even though many reported that it was tiring to have to drink so often, "it's considered daring to see how much you can drink and still make it to your desk in the morning."[17] One HFA in her mid-twenties reported that at one point, she worked at a health club in the sales and marketing department; she observed that her colleagues partied and drank together constantly. At another job with a small recruiting firm of young professionals, she reported that the drinking culture was similar and that they all "partied hard together." She struggled to maintain sexual boundaries with her male coworkers and behaved inappropriately in other ways while drinking with coworkers. She reported that she changed jobs about every six months but was consistently employed and always showed up for work, labeling herself a "workaholic."

Some individuals become professionals for the first time after completing their graduate studies. Cohen also counsels professionals required to attend employee assistance programs for alcohol problems. She states that based on some graduate school cultures, "it is no coincidence that students graduate from top-notch schools and go to the work force with expectations that drinking is not only socially acceptable but a necessary part of their life. They do not self-define as alcoholic because they are not drinking alone and their peers do the same."

QUARTERLIFE CRISIS

If happiness is the difference between what you expect out of life and what you actually get, a lot of emerging adults are setting themselves up for unhappiness because they expect so much.
—Dr. Jeffrey Jenson Arnett[18]

The transition to the "real world" has never been tougher.
—Alexandra Robbins, coauthor of *Quarterlife Crisis*[19]

Despite their unlimited life options, a significant number of people in their twenties are having life difficulties. These young adults sometimes feel that they should be enjoying life, while also feeling fulfilled. The media reinforce the idea that study and hard work are a guarantee to having it all. When individuals suddenly realize that their jobs are not the dream careers they thought they would be, they begin to worry and feel alone.[20] This phenomenon has been named a *quarterlife crisis* by the two twenty-something authors of *Quarterlife Crisis: The Unique Challenges of Life in Your Twenties.*[21]

The quarterlife crisis can manifest in many ways, but it is essentially a period of "overwhelming instability, a panicked sense of helplessness and a feeling of chaos" that correlates with the transition to adulthood.[22] Many individuals in their twenties who have been sheltered in school settings for most of their lives, particularly those who go to college, undergo some type of culture shock. Those in their early twenties are no longer expected to know what they want to do with the rest of their lives professionally and personally.[23] Once the honeymoon period of a first job is over, their minds tend to wander about what they truly have a passion for.[24] They knew how to manage in academic settings with grades and clear-cut goals, but then that structure and social community is lost. Maura, a recent college graduate featured in *Quarterlife Crisis*, feels that "college is like an anchor and when you graduate, that's taken away. It's scary not to know how permanent things are anymore."[25] Justin, age 24, reflects, "I was having this postpartum-like depression because college was my life—all of my friends were from there.... I felt safe there because I didn't have to make any life decisions that were going to turn out disastrously."[26] Singer and songwriter John Mayer even refers to this phenomenon in the lyrics of his song "Why Georgia" with the verse, "It might be a quarter life crisis or just the stirring in my soul, either way I wonder sometimes about the outcome of a still verdictless life."[27]

When HFAs or those who tend to drink heavily go through this type of crisis, they naturally turn to alcohol to numb the pain or fill the void. Or they don't experience the full extent of how lost they feel because they are preoccupied with drinking. Alcohol becomes their anchor, and along with it may be a social circle of peers who want to continue the college party. Courtney was featured in a segment of the *Oprah Winfrey Show* that addressed the quarterlife crisis phenomenon. She felt lost in indecision about her future and felt that "the only fun I have is when I am out with my friends drinking, not thinking about the huge questions in life.... I think I drink too much, I go out to get drunk, not to socially drink, doing shots.... It's a 'let's get drunk' mentality...hooking up with people when it was meaningless."[28] Dr. Drew Pinsky is a nationally recognized addiction medicine specialist, author of *Cracked: Putting Broken Lives Together Again,* and the resident medical expert on the reality television show *Celebrity Rehab with Dr. Drew*, which first aired in 2008. Dr. Pinsky was featured on this *Oprah* show and stated that "young adults in crisis are more vulnerable to addiction and depression." He added that Courtney uses alcohol to numb herself and to avoid dealing with how she is feeling. He observes that the media tell this generation that the solutions to how they are feeling are to buy things, drive fast cars, do drugs, and have sex.[29]

A study by the NIAAA found that drinking during emerging adulthood can assist in forming friendships.[30] Samantha, a twenty-five-year-old interviewed in *Quarterlife Crisis*, reported that she "found solace in my roommates, creating a surrogate family that I could focus on so that I could avoid dealing with my insecurity and fear.... Going out every night and planning elaborate activities and trips with my roommates became a constant in my life."[31] Individuals having a quarterlife crisis may also experience unstable social networks once they have left college or moved to unfamiliar places.[32] Alcohol may temporarily fill this loneliness or lead to making temporary "drinking friends." One young professional HFA said she felt lost after college, which led her to continue to party as though she was still an undergraduate. She felt low self-esteem and therefore defined herself based on her professional life and on how much she drank and partied. Many HFAs describe similar feelings of being lost, lonely, and depressed during these years yet find it easy to blame life circumstances and seek solace in drinking.

Research indicates that alcohol-related problems tend to be higher during the early adulthood years than in any other part of the lifespan.[33] Professional or academic difficulties during this time for individuals who are not married or are not parents contribute to problem drinking as well.[34] Research studies have found that the risk of the onset of alcohol-use disorders is higher for those who have remained single or become divorced than for those who are married.[35] Emerging adult HFAs experiencing a quarterlife crisis are vulnerable in terms of both their drinking and their emotional well-being.

"HINDSIGHT" REFLECTIONS OF THE AUTHOR

Young Professional

After graduating from college, I decided to move to Los Angeles with three of my sorority sisters. After four years of constant parties and excitement, moving home would have been anticlimactic. I had majored in broadcast production management and always dreamed of a career in the television industry; moving to Los Angeles was one step closer to this dream. I was so excited to have a plan for life after college, with the added assurance that I could keep the party going.

I was immediately hired by the Disney Channel and lived in a bright and spacious apartment in Manhattan Beach, directly across the street from the ocean. The sun set past the palm trees, and I fell asleep to the sound of the Pacific Coast waves. A new phase of my life had begun, but not without some of the old—alcoholism followed me. As an HFA, I limited my drinking to Thursday, Friday, and/or Saturday nights, and I never allowed it to prevent me from going to work. Although I went to work incredibly hungover on some Fridays, I suffered through the day and deluded myself and others that I was in control of my life. The high pace of the television industry complemented that of my social life.

Within weeks of my arrival, I was involved in a car accident. I had been drinking, and I totaled the car. The next day, when I woke up hungover, I realized that I had drank too much, triggering intense feelings of fear and guilt. Luckily, I was found not responsible for the accident—I repressed the event and moved on.

Past Journal Entry: January 31, 1999, Age 22—Drinking: A Love/Hate Relationship
I left college as a "social alcoholic." I try not to live life with regrets, but everything that I do regret in my life stems from drinking. It scares me that I cannot even count the number of nights that I have blacked out. It scares me that I have said

and done things to my loved ones and not even remembered, it scares me that I am a different person when I am intoxicated, it scares me that my body accepts such large amounts of poison, it scares me that no matter what I have done and regretted while drinking, I have chosen to drink again.

Past Journal Entry: September 3, 1999, Age 23

It is time to separate myself from a force that has been present in my life for 8 years. It has been a source of enjoyment, freedom and escape. It has broken the ice in social situations as well as in physical ones. It has relaxed and numbed my entire body and mind.

In reality this force has led me to have memory lapses, place my life in danger, say hurtful things to loved ones, embarrass myself, feel hungover, eat unhealthily, lack motivation, waste excessive amounts of money, put the lives of others and myself in danger, lie, gain weight and break the law.

Therefore, it is my 23rd birthday gift to myself to take at least a 6-month break from drinking. This phase of drinking heavily every weekend needs to come to an end. I refuse to have a boyfriend, husband, family and then "slip up." I am tired of feeling my mind racing and being fidgety and cloudy from hangovers. I am tired of being more concerned that I am having a drink than noticing the company I am with. I am tired of saying "that is the last time that I will get that drunk," "what did I do last night?," "how did I get home last night?" and "I feel like shit."

And so this week has begun my journey through sobriety. I feel that documenting my observations along the way will give me the strength to continue if I should question my promise to myself. Seeing these thoughts that I have had for so long actually in writing validates and acknowledges the reality and force of them in my life. I have not led a trouble-filled life. I am fortunate that one of the biggest problems in my life is something that I have the choice to control. It is with certainty and determination that I am breaking free into the world of sobriety—a very foreign land to many in my generation.

I was unaware at this point that I did not have the ability to control my drinking and that this addiction was far more powerful than my "choice." The negative effects of alcohol were beginning to impact my life, and this was a moment of grace that granted me a respite. I was convinced that six months of abstinence would allow me to drink normally afterward.

Past Journal Entry: September, 17, 1999—Weekend Drinking Anticipation

As I drove home from a week of work, I wondered how my desire to drink and unwind at the end of the week had suddenly been terminated. Almost every week of work ended with an uncontrollable urge to drink and "let the weekend begin." Some weeks I could barely make it to Friday.... Often, as I was driving home from work, I could taste the margarita. I already anticipated the buzz, the relaxed feeling in my shoulders that told me that this was going to be a great night—a night that would inevitably turn out "forgettable." Some Fridays I would even have a drink while I was getting ready because I couldn't wait until I got to the bar at 9 P.M. I seemed to think that three stiff margaritas, a few Long Island ice teas, and a rum and coke were not going to be enough for the night. My intentions were often to "get a buzz, not to be drunk." I cannot count how many times my buzz led to a blackout.

Waking up in my outfit from the night before and of course the "you won't believe what you did last night" stories were always worth a good laugh for several years. However, they are not funny to me anymore; they scare me.

It boggles my mind that in Manhattan Beach I have been so drunk that I have forgotten where I lived and the cab driver had to look at my license to get my address. I then ran out of the cab without paying...the cab driver chased me and my roommate had to pay the cab fare. Another time I passed out on a bar stool, and three cops were shining flashlights in my face....I slept in my neighbor's apartment because I thought that I was locked out of my apartment, but I really had the key. I didn't ever think that I was drunk if I didn't have a blackout. In my distorted view, if I remembered having any control over my actions, then I was only buzzed.

How many times can one person be lucky? Does a person's luck run out? Well, I don't intend to give my luck a chance to run out in this area of my life because I *can* control it.

When I abstained, I began to glimpse the consequences and danger of my drinking. I saw that there was something wrong with the way in which I had behaved in the past. I was building a case against alcohol, and it appeared that I had convinced myself that I did not really want to drink. My collegelike drunken behavior was not funny anymore, and I started to feel self-conscious.

Past Journal Entry: September 28, 1999—Awareness at Work
Going to work is a battle—I am trapped physically in a way. However, mentally I am free—no one can control my thoughts there. I feel liberated to have my book that I am reading with me—in case I need to escape from the controlled, power-driven, unrealistic, bullshitting, uniformity-driven environment that I somehow have become absorbed in. I am an observer of this—it is all a case study. Corporate America—I don't want a part of it.

This was the beginning of my quarterlife crisis, in which I became disillusioned with my dream career in television production. Drinking had enabled me to remain content at my job because I had that release on the weekends— but now I was stuck in sober reality. I began to see clearly that this career path was not a reflection of my true self, and my rose-colored-glasses view of the entertainment industry was starting to fog up.

Past Journal Entry: March 4, 2000—Celebrating Sobriety (with Alcohol)
It has been 5 months and 3 weeks, my friend was in town and the time was right. I ordered a mandarin Absolut vodka and soda and began to sip it....My stomach began to feel warm and in a few minutes, like a girl who had never drank before, I began to feel giddiness and an innocent happiness come over me. I wanted to feel the onset of a buzz, but that was all. In no way did I desire to enter into the world of being drunk....I openly articulated that I felt buzzed, because for once, I noticed....A feeling of power came over me as I placed half

of my mixed drink down—I didn't need the rest, I was relaxed enough. *I had control,* and I was not chasing my buzz.

I was unwilling to wait that extra week to complete the six months of abstinence. The fact that I could, at times, control my drinking increased my level of denial that I was an alcoholic. I continued to write statements such as "*I had control*" in my journal, almost trying to convince myself that I did. The fact that I was able, at times, to pace myself and not black out served only to increase my delusion.

Graduate School

I chose to leave Los Angeles in the spring of 2000 and move back to the East Coast. To clear my mind and find peace, I moved to the enchanting island of Nantucket, Massachusetts, for the summer. I craved solitude and intended to spend the summer gathering my thoughts and writing a book, while working as a waitress at the Nantucket Golf Club. This was my summer to simplify my life, read the book *Walden,*[36] connect to nature, and soul search. Inevitably, I became distracted by alcohol, and my summer of introspection turned into a three-month drinking binge. I went out to the bars almost every night and drank to excess on countless occasions. As the clarity of my period of abstinence clouded, the guilt and awareness of my drinking slowly left my consciousness as I sank deeper and deeper into the heavy drinking culture of Nantucket.

The following September, I left the island and settled permanently in Boston. I found a beautiful apartment with several friends. After three months of heavy drinking that summer, I decided once again to purify my system and abstained from alcohol for three months. I began to have anxiety and digestive problems. I could not see the connection between the anxiety and the medical issues I was experiencing—and the fact that my medical problems began when I abstained from drinking for several months. I was intrigued by the idea that Eastern medicine may have had something to offer me, and in November 2000, I became a patient at the Mind/Body Medical Institute (M/BMI). During my time at M/BMI, I realized my passion for the field of psychology. I applied to graduate schools and was admitted into a counseling psychology master's program at Northeastern University. During this two-year graduate degree program, I was chosen for a much sought after counseling internship at a college in Boston. I promised myself that I would not have blackouts now that I was in graduate school.

Past Journal Entry: November 25, 2001, Age 25
Well, once again I am writing because I drank too much. No one has commented, I just know that I *really* need a plan of attack, and I am not willing to give drinking up. I am going to count and look at my watch, there has to be a way that I can monitor myself better. I will have some clarity soon about this issue.

I felt guilty and aware that I had passed another line in the sand of not getting drunk in graduate school. I continued to think and write in circles regarding alcohol, and my denial was creeping back.

Past Journal Entry: September 30, 2002, Age 26

In some way I feel alone about my drinking issues. I feel like I've gone over them so many times. Each time I promise myself that I will not get wasted, and inevitably I do. I am *not* in control, even though I try to be. Alcohol is more powerful than me. I know all of the drinking "tips"—but I ignore them all. I feel that I am entitled to drink like everyone else, but I can't. *I black out!* I am anxious and depressed the next day, and I still do it week after week. I spend a lot of money and act carelessly and irresponsibly, but why? It is not me; it is a chemically altered state that shows a side of myself that is not truly me. I don't want to hurt or scare people, but I do. Why? Because I have fun?

Past Journal Entry: December 15, 2002

Being single can be a lost time in your twenties. You see so many paths, but are unsure which to go down. The question of what life will be like in the future is a cloud following us around. I feel a bond with those in my same situation—no anchor, just friends and family that will always be a constant.

Past Journal Entry: December 17, 2002

I have "it" career-wise, now I need "it" personally. Maybe I am in transition—still not having to be an adult but not being a kid either. I feel that so many of us are lost in this sea of options. We need to find a route to navigate and be able to get back into ports if the currents steer us astray.

In May 2003, I graduated with my master's degree. I started to emerge from my quarterlife crisis, but I sensed some type of void that alcohol filled only temporarily. Obtaining this degree was just one more external achievement to compensate for my internal battle with drinking. I knew at this time that I had a problem with alcohol, but I was in the midst of living two lives and could not settle on just one.

5

FALLING UPHILL: PROFESSIONAL, INTELLIGENT, AND ALCOHOLIC

In some professional industries, there can be a normalized tradition of drinking. It can begin while attending college, then progress into a graduate school program that supports a culture of drinking, and then continue into the workplace that uses alcohol as part of the social and sales environment. Alcohol consumption, abuse, and tolerance can develop throughout the corporate life cycle, and it's not always talked about because drinking can be viewed as part of "just doing your job." For example, when a sixty-year-old CEO with a heart attack gets admitted into the hospital and then goes into unexpected alcohol withdrawal, there may be confusion from family members who wouldn't consider him or her to be an alcoholic. To the outside world, this individual may appear highly functional and successful, with drinking regarded as part of an executive lifestyle; however, alcohol dependency can still exist.

—Theresa Bullock Cohen, LICSW

"Work hard, play hard" is often a high-functioning alcoholic (HFA) motto in the professional world for individuals of all ages. Established professionals consciously and subconsciously find ways to present themselves well while hiding their addiction. This holds true for HFAs in various phases of their careers. The image of a successful professional contradicts that of the stereotypical alcoholic, therefore building a wall of denial for loved ones and colleagues of HFAs who are accomplished professionals. Drinking is the balance needed to offset the pressure and routine of their professional and personal lives. As these individuals establish themselves and gain a positive reputation in their community, they begin to have more at stake in keeping their alcohol problems hidden. Therefore the cycle of drinking and either isolating or fitting in becomes necessary for survival. The professional years for HFAs are ripe for creating a double life because it is imperative for them to find a way to factor drinking into their lives, while maintaining a positive image.

Research on professional HFAs does not appear to exist. However, employee assistance programs have acknowledged and provided resources for professionals struggling with alcohol problems (see Chapter 7). The *New York Times* best-selling memoir *Drinking: A Love Story* by Caroline Knapp became a groundbreaking portrait of a female alcoholic and increased awareness about HFAs. Knapp graduated from Brown University and was a successful journalist while drinking alcoholically.[1] One textbook about substance abuse used in a counseling psychology master's program has only a single paragraph focused on HFAs in its alcohol addiction chapter. The reference for this scant information is Knapp, who considered herself an HFA but is neither a researcher nor an expert on this topic. This paragraph states that "a majority of those with alcohol use problems might be best described as 'high-functioning' individuals who have jobs, responsibilities, families, and public images to protect. In many cases the individual's growing dependency on alcohol is hidden from virtually everyone in the alcoholic's world, including the drinker. It is only in secret moments of introspection that the alcohol-dependent person wonders why his or her alcohol use is somehow different from that of the non-alcoholic drinker."[2] Given this statement and its implication that there are a vast number of professional HFAs, the question remains as to why there is still such a lack of attention to and information about this topic.

HEADLINES

Newspaper and magazine articles written about successful and admired professionals involved in alcohol-related incidents catch the public eye. In September 2007, a story reported two cases of launch-day intoxication of NASA astronauts. According to air force doctor Colonel Richard Bachmann Jr., who headed a controversial astronaut health study, the bigger issue was "NASA's apparent disregard of mental health and behavior issues among astronauts and the reluctance among flight surgeons and astronauts to report improper conduct." He went on to state that denying these types of problems exist, "challenging the veracity of the findings, referring to them as unproven allegation or urban legends rather than acknowledging how difficult raising such concerns can be, do[es] not encourage openness and safety, make future reporting even less likely, and increase[s] the risk of future mishaps or incidents."[3] Denial about HFAs in professional positions exists on all levels, and individuals in certain professions are sometimes assumed to be immune from having addiction or personal problems in general. Many believe that not talking about these problems will make them disappear. Instead, this silence allows alcoholism to go unnoticed, feeds the cycle of denial, and puts the lives of HFAs as well as those who depend on them professionally in danger.

In October 2007, a veteran Boston firefighter was killed in a fire. A state medical examiner found him to have a blood alcohol level of 0.27, three times the legal limit. This led to an investigation of substance abuse testing and treatment within the fire agency.[4] In response to the firefighter's death,

Boston mayor Thomas M. Menino stated, "I think there's more call now [for change] on this issue than before. We must do something."[5] Unlike the Boston Police Department, which conducts mandatory random drug tests, the fire department tests firefighters only when there is a reason.[6] In San Francisco, a surprise inspection of a firehouse found four firefighters drinking alcohol. Unfortunately, it may take a tragedy for alcohol issues to be taken seriously among professionals.[7] Many fire departments have "confronted drug and alcohol abuse in their ranks."[8] New York, Chicago, San Francisco, Baltimore, and Houston are among the cities that have implemented random mandatory drug tests, which have been found to be "effective as deterrents."[9]

In July 2007, a special education teacher was found guilty of her fourth driving under the influence (DUI) offense, was sentenced to four and a half years in jail, and lost her license for a decade. She entered a detox facility, which implies that she had been heavily drinking while maintaining her job.[10] The chairman and CEO of Home Box Office, Chris Albrecht, agreed to resign at the company's request after he was arrested and charged with assaulting his girlfriend in a parking lot. In an e-mail message to the network's employees, Albrecht wrote that he had been sober and in an alcohol recovery program for thirteen years and that "two years ago, I decided that I could handle drinking again. Clearly, I was wrong."[11] These professionals lost their jobs not because of failed job performance, but because of dangerous consequences of alcoholism. Ultimately, the law caught up with them, and tangible losses forced them to address their addiction.

Dr. William Talbot nearly lost his job as a surgeon at Lovelace Hospital in Albuquerque, New Mexico, over a decade ago, when administrators learned that he had a drinking problem. A wrongful death suit had been filed against him on behalf of a patient on whom he had operated. His history of alcoholism went under the radar for years before the public found out through the state medical board. Court records indicate that several staff members had smelled alcohol on his breath at work, but he covered up by stating that he had a gum disease and was using a lot of breath fresheners. A nurse reported that he had alcohol on his breath while operating on a patient for a ruptured aneurysm. Although he eventually was sent to a rehab facility, the concern is the length of time it took for Talbot's alcoholism to be addressed by administrators and the medical board. Talbot is not alone as a doctor struggling with alcohol issues. In fact, from 1983 to 2006, about 119 of the estimated 360 doctors or physician's assistants in New Mexico who have faced action by the state medical board habitually abused alcohol or other substances.[12]

These types of articles repeatedly astonish the public because professionals such as astronauts, firefighters, teachers, doctors, and so on are expected to have certain behavior and lifestyles. These stories bring attention to the topic of HFAs and break the stereotype of the skid row alcoholic for a moment—but then the moment passes. These types of headlines may force various professions and professional boards to face the fact that there are undoubtedly others within their field struggling with alcoholism who are going untreated.

WORKPLACE CULTURES

In the American culture, individuals often define themselves based on material possessions. This culture of consumerism and quick fixes is the perfect setting for alcoholics.[13] So many individuals look for something outside themselves to feel happy or to feel content—alcohol can do just that. Successful professionals constantly push themselves to achieve and to get the degree, job, raise, or promotion that will finally make them feel good about themselves. For many HFAs, the drive to achieve and drinking go hand in hand, filling a certain emptiness that may exist within. Research on workplace environments indicates that women who work in male-dominated occupations are more likely to have alcohol problems than those who work in female-dominated occupations. When men establish the office routines, there are more opportunities to drink. "Groups of people who work together, whether in small teams or larger organizations, develop shared beliefs and practices that can influence alcohol use."[14] The blending of employees' work and social lives influences their drinking behaviors both during and after work.[15] When a culture of heavy drinking exists within a company or profession, a certain group-think protection exists. There is strength within the social group, and the power and reinforcement of the group trump any criticism of the group's drinking that members may receive from individuals outside of the group.

Society and the media tend to glorify drinking. However, for an alcoholic, drinking is not a harmless activity—it is a lethal one. Peters has observed that there is heavy drinking at medical and dental conferences. He has done extensive work in educating medical and dental professionals about the "conspiracy of silence" regarding alcoholism among doctors. An article by Peters in the *Journal of the Massachusetts Dental Society* estimates that dentists and other health care professionals have a higher incidence of substance abuse because of a general attitude of acceptance for using drugs to alter one's state of mind, the greater availability of drugs, and the high percentage of health professionals who have parents who abused alcohol and drugs (which led their children to choose one of the caring professions).[16] The article explains that alcoholism escapes early detection in the dental field because of the solitary nature of dental practices, allowing dentists to be isolated from peers; denial of dental organizations of the disease; the absence of substance abuse education in the dental school curriculum; and a lack of research on drug and alcohol dependency among dentists.[17]

One recovering HFA dentist reflects that he did not drink during his medical schooling but began once he joined the navy. Within a year, he was drinking daily, and he continued drinking while he practiced dentistry. Although he did not have to answer to a boss, he tried not to have alcohol on his breath around patients because he felt "extremely conscious of his reputation and image" professionally. He never drank during the workday, but would start "about sixty seconds after getting home," and switched from beer to vodka so that his wife wouldn't be able to smell it. Years into his drinking, he noticed that his hands were shaking in the morning, and when he looked into the mirror, his "eyes were bloodshot, and they had a hollow dead look, nothing . . . empty. . . . I will never forget it." He reported going to at least three psychiatrists, who "never picked up on my drinking" and continued to prescribe antidepressants and sleeping medications for him. Another dentist never considered himself an alcoholic because of the stereotype, was introduced to a recovery program at age thirty, and then relapsed for twelve years. Throughout the relapse, he was "hospitalized over forty times" to detox because he drank in binges. Meanwhile, he managed to succeed at work, and his well-respected dental practice grossed more every year, even during his "worst drinking." His secretary rescheduled all his appointments while he was hospitalized, and when he returned to work, he carried on. He believes that there has been a tremendous lack of attention to doctors who are alcoholic because conventional wisdom is that they are "too well-educated, too moral and too intelligent to be alcoholic." He offered to help a fellow alcoholic dentist, who turned it down, and the following year, at a dental conference, his colleague was found frozen to death in his car after drinking.

According to the Committee on Drug and Alcohol Dependence of the Dentist Health and Wellness Committee, affiliated with the Massachusetts Dental Society, the prevalence of health care professionals with alcohol or drug addiction is between 8% and 13%—a rate higher than that of the general population.[18] This is a concern for many reasons, including the fact that doctors in denial about their own alcoholism are less likely to see it in their patients.[19] A forty-two-year-old family practice doctor reported that once he finished medical school, he told himself, "Now I am a doctor, I have to stop drinking." He then forced himself not to drink for three days at most, but then drank heavier when he resumed. He felt a true battle within himself in that he was doing great things but still drinking—at this point, he realized he was an alcoholic. Another HFA reflects that once he became a doctor, he decided to move to his hometown, where his family was well known. His intention was that this lack of anonymity would force him to drink less for fear of others' opinions. Instead, he began to go to the local city bar to drink on his days off. He was being groomed to become the chief of staff at a very young age and had received numerous professional awards. He reported that he lived in a "three-thousand-square-foot house, had three cars, was dying on the inside—but I looked great on the outside." No one with whom he worked would have guessed that he was alcoholic. In fact, his professional partner casually stated at the year-end review, "One thing that I want you to watch is that if you are on call and you have had a few drinks, take some breath mints." This doctor went on to state that *MD* stands for "malignant denial" and that it is pervasive throughout the medical community. Doctors subconsciously realize that if a colleague is an alcoholic, then he or she is susceptible to alcoholism. However, because doctors know about illness and disease, they feel that knowledge is protective and that they can take care of themselves. This contributes to their own denial and to denial about those with whom they work. Sanchez has observed that doctors are "generally very smart, have high IQs and are obsessive and control-ling," which are good qualities for their profession but can become detrimental if they "get too much out of whack." He adds that doctors are groomed to think of themselves as a "breed apart," to deal with job-related stress and to compartmentalize and objectify dealing with patient illness and death. He feels that this work stress elevates to a level of distress as a result of addi-tional personal problems—doctors are not trained to talk about them or to deal with conflict. Therefore they may turn to alcohol and drugs to cope and may have genetic vulnerability leading them to develop alcohol and substance use disorders.

According to a report by the federal Substance Abuse and Mental Health Services Administration, alcohol is the substance most typically abused by public safety officials. A 2007 report indicated that 9.1% of a group that included law enforcement officials and firefighters drank heavily during the previous month.[20] One female HFA lawyer reported that when she used to go out drinking with colleagues in a major metropolitan city, she would be surrounded by heavy drinking district attorneys and cops, including those who were married and cheating. She added that she was surrounded by a lot of "disgusting" behavior. She has found that alcoholism is prevalent among attorneys, and it was common for her colleagues to go out for drinks at lunch or dinner. However, now that she is in recovery, she has felt "you were almost put under cross-examination by these attorneys if you didn't drink.... You almost thought because you didn't drink that they didn't have as much respect for you ... that you're not one of the 'boys.'" Charlie, a New York attorney, drank about a fifth of Johnnie Walker every night. His hangovers led him to take until noon to feel "human," and he would come to work late and "try to do eight hours of work in four hours." He believes that "alcoholics can be high achievers in the short run, because they're driven and compulsive."[21] The legal profession has developed a reputation as having many heavy drinkers. One study in the *International Journal of Law and Psychiatry* found that problem drinking had developed in 18% of lawyers who had practiced for two to twenty years and in 25% of lawyers who had practiced for twenty years or longer.[22] Another statistic indicated that 30% of lawyers have been found to abuse alcohol.[23] The American Bar Association has found that lawyers and judges are overachievers who tend to take on excessive amounts of work. Therefore they tend to escape from these stressors through alcohol and drugs.[24]

Throughout history, the military has had a reputation of fostering heavy drinking. A research article by the National Institute on Alcohol Abuse and Alcoholism confirms that 27% of young adults in the military aged eighteen to twenty-five years reported heavy binge drinking, and these numbers dropped significantly to 8.9% for twenty-six- to fifty-five-year-olds. The Marine Corps was found to have the highest binge drinking rate at 38% among young adults, and the air force has the lowest rate, at 24%. Men in the military were found to have a significantly higher rate of heavy drinking than women. Most alcohol-related problems, such as missing duty or decreased productivity, were found among the youngest personnel, who did not attend college. This research study points to several factors within the military that promote binge drinking. There are cultural traditions, particularly within the navy, that involve binge drinking and drinking to points of intoxication when on shore leave, after work, and particularly when on "liberty" during deployment. Another factor that may influence excessive drinking is the availability of alcohol in foreign and national bases and ports. In the 1980s, the military implemented strict policies aimed at reducing alcohol and drug usage, which included increasing alcohol prices on bases,[25] removing alcohol from traditional ceremonies, and implementing programs such as the Personal Responsibilities and Values: Education and Training program and health promotion programs. Research data indicate that these policies were more effective in reducing substance usage than alcohol usage.[26]

One fifty-three-year-old retired air force lieutenant colonel reports that he drank alcoholically throughout his entire military career, which began after college. He notes that his drinking habits correspond with the culture of the bases at which he was stationed. In the 1970s, on his first few assignments, he recalls that everyone could "get away with being blasted" and that he and his colleagues would socialize at the officer's clubs and play ball games on base with beers in their hands. The military culture promoted drinking, social events revolved around alcohol, drinking and driving was common, and colleagues covered up alcohol-related problems for one another. He reported that halfway through his career, changes occurred in air force alcohol policies that dramatically changed the drinking culture. Consequences for DUIs became harsher, and all keg parties needed to be approved by senior officials. He and his colleagues took these restrictions seriously because if convicted of a DUI, on or off the base, they would receive an "article 15." Considered the kiss of death, this mark on their record would prevent them from future rank promotions. These changes in the drinking culture led him to start isolating when he was drinking. About every other night, he would drink in his basement while doing work, away from his wife and children. The proudest day of his life was when he was promoted to lieutenant colonel—his career was the most important thing in his life and he would do anything to protect it. He reports that alcohol rarely prevented him from performing his professional duties: he hardly called in sick, only drank on the job at social functions, and never drank at lunch. He became paranoid of others "thinking that I was a drunk." Therefore, if there was a social event, he would methodically drink two to three drinks before going out, he would restrict himself to having three drinks in public, and finally, he would rush to get home so he could drink as much as he wanted. In addition, he began to rotate the liquor stores from which he would buy alcohol and only used cash so that there was no way to trace his purchases.

A sixty-eight-year-old CEO drank two fifths of alcohol a day for forty years and started to have memory lapses and disturbing behavior. That led to his being removed from his job. A chairman of the board collapsed before an important meeting and began to vomit blood from ulcers that he had developed after thirty-five years of drinking. One senior vice president who is a recovering alcoholic himself stated, "The number of active alcoholics in the senior management ranks in this company is astounding, yet only one in ten is willing to get help."[27] In one study of women with graduate and professional degrees, the high-ranking female executives may have been more likely to drink than those of comparable age and education in lower-level jobs.[28] The assumption that people in positions of power have it all together is common. However, the truth is that executives are just as vulnerable to addiction as are the rest of the population. In fact, these types of alcoholic professionals are the hardest to detect (and help) because of the following reasons:

- They are generally not closely supervised at work
- Connecting a developing addiction with deterioration in work quality is difficult
- These professionals are assumed to have "learned to deal successfully with the tensions and pressures of corporate life"[29]
- Those in lower management positions tend to cover up for their bosses
- High pay allows professionals to avoid financial problems from their addiction
- Professionals often believe that their excessive drinking is a reward for their years of hard work
- Few colleagues are aware of what is wrong with the senior executive or are willing to confront him or her
- Because of the societal stereotypes about alcoholism, many view asking for help as a sign of weakness and fear being judged by colleagues[30]

Some HFAs are attracted to extreme lifestyles and high-pressured professions such as media-based jobs. That is not to say that certain professions create HFAs, but that individuals who are predisposed toward alcoholism or have a history of heavy drinking are at higher risk of alcoholism in heavy-drinking settings. Drinking after work or on the weekends becomes the reward for their hard work. Pete Hamill, in his memoir, *A Drinking Life,* writes about using his success as a journalist to justify his drinking, stating, "Through all this time, I managed to do a lot of work: newspaper columns, magazine articles, a first novel. . . . If I was able to function, to get the work done, there was no reason to worry about drinking. It was part of living, one of the rewards."[31] Hamill found himself caught up in the drinking culture of his career—meeting colleagues and networking at the bar while blowing off steam. He surrounded himself with other heavy-drinking professionals, which increased his denial about his alcoholism in that "I never thought of myself as a drunk; I was, I thought, like many others—a *drinker.* I certainly didn't think I was an alcoholic. But I was already having trouble remembering the details of the night before. It didn't seem to matter; everybody was doing the same thing. We make little jokes about having a great time last night."[32] Augusten Burroughs, author of the *New York Times* best seller *Dry: A Memoir,*[33] is an HFA who managed to drink alcoholically while maintaining his six-figure job at a Manhattan advertising firm. He downed a liter of Dewar's a night and sprayed cologne on his tongue in the morning to hide the smell at work.[34] His creativity and talent allowed him to compensate for his drinking. Like Hamill, Burroughs blended into the fast-moving and social media-based field. One fifty-eight-year-old HFA who is a radio talk show host and television personality reported that he was an active alcoholic throughout his career but that he fit into the culture of that industry. He stated that one radio contract entitled him unlimited food and drink at several local restaurants. He and his alcoholic boss would take so-called liquid lunches and put their drinks on their company tab. Then he and others would go out to bars between the 6:00 P.M. and 11:00 P.M. news, drink heavily, and return to work. This behavior was normalized because it was done within the group context and was part of the "insanity" of their workplace culture. The quality of his work performance was negatively affected by his drinking at times. This included when he spoke live on television after heavy drinking and announced "in the shitty" instead of "in the city." He was subsequently fired, but because of his "gift of gab" and talent, he was immediately able to find another desirable job.

In contrast, some HFAs who work in environments in which the culture does not promote drinking still find themselves drinking alcoholically. One woman reported that she drank heavily in college and drank even more when she started working at a bank. She does not blame her drinking on the work culture; she believes, "[I] was seeking my own level, and I managed to find the frat house in a conservative industry."[35]

DRINKING PATTERNS AND PERSONALITY CHARACTERISTICS

My general health could go—sleeping regularly, eating well—all could go when I drank, but I would always make work a priority.... How could I be an alcoholic? I am doing so well professionally.

—Joseph, HFA, Web engineer

I thought that I would be classier if I drank expensive whiskey—but it is all the same when it comes up and you fall off the bar stool.

—Susan, HFA, teacher

People with my education, my class, my standing in the community, my successful husband could not be alcoholic.

—Elizabeth, HFA, professor

When it came time to think about my drinking, if I was alcoholic or as bad as "them," it was easy to point to the fact that I kept working, I didn't beat my kids, we have enough money to have a decent home, two cars and we go on vacation. It was easy to deny that I have a problem.

—Chris, HFA, dentist

The drinking of HFAs follows general patterns and characteristics at various phases of their lives. However, alcoholics eventually find any reason to drink, including having a wonderful job, a fulfilling marriage, and loving children.

The truth is that there is no "guarantee against alcoholism."[36] One female flight attendant stated, "There was a period where good things happened all the time, and I was very happy. So, I drank because I was so happy. But when bad things happened, such as a breakup, I drank over those, too. Finally, I drank in response to everything."[37] HFAs who drink to celebrate in social settings when they are feeling happy often believe that this exempts them from being alcoholic. In their minds, alcoholics are miserable, lonely, and isolated drinkers. As some friends of HFAs start to drink normally in their late twenties and early thirties, HFAs may seek a circle of friends who drink regularly and heavily. Often, they find this group through associates at work or through a heavy drinker with whom they live. They no longer know what it is like to wake up without a hangover, particularly on weekends.[38]

Alcohol complements those who are intense and structured when not drinking. This "double life" for many HFAs starts when they begin to drink and peaks in their professional lives, when drinking alcoholically isn't always as socially acceptable as it was previously. Knapp reports that she had always been obsessively neat and organized; this trait carried over to her work, and adhering to rituals throughout her workday and keeping a rigid routine were comforting to her. She adds that both she and her father were "hard-working, obsessive, creative people who got stuff done and then checked out at the end of the day."[39] Scorzelli notes that many HFAs are respected and admired professionally until "the dark time," when they come home and drink. Knapp eloquently writes that "alcoholics compartmentalize: this was classic behavior, although I wouldn't have known that back then. I've heard the story in A.A. meetings time after time: alcoholics who end up leading double lives—and sometimes triple and quadruple lives—because they never learned how to lead a single one, a single honest one that's based on a clearcut sense of who they are and what they really need."[40] One thirty-two-year-old Web engineer was rehired at a job with a significant increase in salary and good benefits. He appeared "put together" during the day, but he described going home and drinking warm whiskey from the bottle on work nights and then returning to work hungover. He stated that from the time he was seventeen until the present, the longest time that he had been unemployed was thirty days and that it was "the most frightening time in my life." Work can provide a feeling of security and control for HFAs—something they can hold on to when their drinking becomes unmanageable.

Not all HFAs start drinking when they are in high school or college, but may begin as professionals. One sixty-three-year-old college professor reports drinking for the first time when she was twenty-one years old. After about a decade, her alcoholism began to progress, and she was drinking each night. She felt that she was able to function well and maintain her drinking because she was conscious of appearances and she "really knew how to set the stage." She describes herself as a private person who "loved sneaking something...my own little pleasure" so that she wouldn't be caught and judged.

Mulligan has observed that the disease of alcoholism progresses as the years pass for HFAs. Greater demands begin to be placed on them at work and home, and they are "able to compensate less." Some HFAs are no longer able to hold it together, and signs that their alcoholism is negatively impacting their lives begin to show. One thirty-year-old HFA reflects on a time when she was a substitute teacher and child care worker. She describes that on the outside, she looked good, but over time, alcoholism led her to isolate; she didn't answer the phone or open her mail. A seventy-nine-year-old dentist remembers when his drinking began to affect the quality of his work. He received an anonymous letter from a patient that stated, "Whatever happened to that nice guy who was my dentist?" He showed the letter to his wife, and she responded, "They are right." Soon after, he consulted with a colleague on a patient who had her teeth knocked out. He experienced extreme guilt and shame about his hangover when he noticed how shaky his hands were.

Recognizing clear-cut signs of alcoholism among professionals is often difficult. Personality traits and the drive to succeed often overcompensate and allow these professionals to hide their addiction. Cohen's work on the addiction psychiatry team at Boston's Brigham and Women's Hospital has given her firsthand experience with professional HFAs who come to the hospital for other medical problems such as heart attacks. Sometimes an alcohol assessment can be done before the procedure, but in emergencies, the hospital must rely on the family's often inaccurate account of the patient's drinking patterns. The HFAs may then experience alcohol-related complications, which can force them to stay in the hospital for fourteen to twenty-one days. The HFAs have essentially been "outed" because of a medical issue, and Cohen's team may be called in to do an intervention. The addiction psychiatry team often faces barriers such as personal and family denial, shame, cultural barriers, and the unwillingness of the patient to deal with his or her alcoholism. She often sees company executives, bar owners, teachers, construction workers, school bus drivers, and others whose jobs involve the safety of others.

The longer an HFA drinks, the further the disease of alcoholism progresses. The following are red flags for professionals in general and for alcoholic progression:

- Inappropriate attitudes about alcohol, including viewing drinking large amounts of alcohol as a necessary part of a job
- Unusual patterns of alcohol usage, including reaching for a drink as relief from stress
- Quickly gulping three or four drinks at social and work functions to "loosen up"
- Having the compulsion to drink more than others socially
- Being critical and disapproving of nondrinkers
- Becoming irritable and defensive about excessive drinking
- Personality changes such as a typically quiet person becoming extremely extroverted or a typically outgoing person becoming withdrawn
- Changes in work routines or productivity
- A decline in the usual quality and quantity of work, including missed deadlines, chronic lateness, sloppy work, and poor presentations

- Displaying poor professional judgment
- Calling in sick or not coming in to work (if able to work from home), specifically on Mondays and/or Fridays
- Being unaccounted for in the middle of the day
- Taking frequent medical leaves of absence
- Having the smell of alcohol on the breath, especially early in the morning
- Shakiness and trembling hands
- Changes in facial skin, including an increasingly ruddy complexion and visible small blood vessels on the nose and face and red eyes in the morning
- Gradual increase in weight, mostly in the abdominal area
- Appearing run down or fatigued in the morning
- Complaining of little energy and having trouble concentrating
- Being hyperactive and unable to sit still
- Having repeated random injuries, such as broken ribs or arms, that are reportedly due to "accidental falls"
- Drinking excessive amounts of caffeine before being able to start functioning[41]

RELATIONSHIP DYNAMICS

Treadway has observed that HFAs can drink without necessarily any overt negative consequences, but their personal lives, their souls, and their deepest relationships "slowly can begin to atrophy in a way that can contribute to the deadening of a marriage over the period of 20 years without alcohol ever being identified as the problem." He gives the example of a married HFA who deals with his or her emotional needs through alcohol. This individual has a seemingly functional marriage because difficulties are medicated with alcohol. Treadway adds that alcohol can actually help HFAs to function, do their jobs, handle their children, and put up with lives that they couldn't manage if they didn't drink. One seventy-two-year-old dentist reflects that his drinking negatively affected his marriage and that is "the insidious part of the disease." His wife eventually started drinking with him because she decided to "join you instead of fighting you." He admits that his values were compromised; he was not being kind and loving, and his marriage became "on the edge."

Renaud has observed that female HFAs tend to drink more because of relationship issues and to cope with stressors. She finds that women hide their drinking more than men do, especially if they have a family. Knapp agrees that women have different drinking patterns than men, and that is part of what motivated her to write *Drinking: A Love Story*. She was moved by Hamill's memoir *A Drinking Life*, in which he depicts himself as a "boisterous hard-drinking reporter, out covering wars," and she felt that women wrestle with different issues than Hamill did when he was drinking. She feels that women drink to deaden "conflicted" feelings, including wanting intimacy, while also fearing it.[42] One thirty-year-old woman recalls that she had a boyfriend with whom she had chosen not to have sex because she was "saving herself." The first time she drank, she left a party, drove to his house, and lost her virginity. Alcohol can lead women to behave more aggressively, act out sexually, present themselves as tougher than they really are, and make unwanted sexual choices.[43] Situations at work can become troubling when a woman's drinking leads her to use sex to gain power and physical intimacy. Kelly, featured in *Happy Hours: Alcohol in a Women's Life*, is an alcoholic businesswoman at an insurance company in New York. She was frequently invited to entertain clients because she was young and personable. She often drank too much on these occasions and blacked out, wondering—with shame and guilt—about what had occurred the night before. When she began to test the limits of her "power over men" and crossed the line at a business dinner by whispering suggestive comments to her boss about his friend, she was subsequently fired.[44] Drinking and sexuality can begin to coexist in an addictive cycle of anticipation and a high, followed by a crash that includes emptiness and shame. The urge to find relief and fill the void is temporarily satisfied by pursuing another sexual encounter.[45]

Alcoholism penetrates every aspect of romantic relationships, marriages, and families. One thirty-four-year-old reported that she became engaged during her fifth year as a prosecuting attorney. When she got married, her drinking patterns changed, and she started going to more dinners with her husband and other couples, as opposed to frequenting bars and parties. Her behavior at the end of the night was still "not adultlike," and she would get so drunk that she would black out, curse at her husband, and then pass out on the couch. Eventually, her husband stopped carrying her up to bed and started leaving her passed out on the couch. A few years later, she took a high-powered job at a law firm, where she worked long hours and made good money. She truly hated the type of work that she was doing and started to hide her nightly drinking from her husband by sneaking drinks out of the refrigerator. She drank wine from her glass, returned to the fridge to refill the glass, and then gulped the wine back to the level it was when her husband had last seen it. In some ways, she realized that there was an issue, but she justified her drinking because of her belief that "I am an attorney, I am successful at what I do, I am entitled to a few glasses of wine; it loosens me up and it is the reason that I am able to continue . . . and as long as I am able to go to my job, then there is no problem."

Soon after a seventy-nine-year-old dentist and his wife of fifty-four years were married, his wife began complaining that their marriage was not what she thought it should be and she asked if they could go to counseling. He agreed to go, and after two years of individual therapy, he suspected that the problem could be his drinking, although they both drank. His wife would comment on his drinking; finally, she decided to go to Al-Anon, and eventually, she entered into a Twelve-Step Recovery Program. Although he felt "the heat was on," he continued drinking for many more years. He never harmed his children physically when he drank, but on reflection, he now realizes that his alcoholism led him to emotionally abandon them.

Cohen has observed HFAs as parents and has found that they are not much different from low-bottom alcoholic parents in terms of the emotional effect on the children. In fact, sometimes dealing with low-bottom alcoholic parents is easier because the children live with the truth that their parent is alcoholic, which clearly explains why "Mom lost her job." In contrast, when an HFA parent appears financially and professionally successful, but negative things are happening, such as infidelity, fighting, or car accidents, children are often confused as to what is wrong. HFA parents often treat their children inconsistently in that one day they may respond calmly to a question and another day react harshly. The child doesn't know why this is happening, and the alcoholism remains hidden within the family dynamic. Cohen sees the children of HFAs grow in one of two ways: (1) they identify with the parent's alcoholism and struggle with addiction, fail, and get in trouble with the law, or (2) they are hypervigilant overachievers while walking on eggshells, hoping that if they are perfect, their alcoholic parents will treat them well.

"HINDSIGHT" REFLECTIONS OF THE AUTHOR

Immediately after graduating with my master's degree, I was hired for a much sought after counseling job at a prestigious psychiatric hospital. I felt fortunate to have this professional opportunity, and I was determined not to drink excessively because I was now a "professional." The job involved working every other weekend, and on several occasions, I arrived at work hungover—yet another broken drinking promise to myself. One time, I went out to the bars for the yearly high school reunion-like evening that took place the night before Thanksgiving in my hometown, even though I had to work at 3:00 P.M. the next day. The morning after going out, I woke up in a strange place and struggled to get to work. I remember sitting in the hospital parking lot doing deep breathing because my anxiety was so intense, and I felt almost unable to function. However, instead of calling in sick, I pushed myself through the workday, proving to myself that my drinking was not interfering with my career. I felt deeply hypocritical about leading therapy groups and acting as a role model for young women who were trying to overcome food addictions. My life was becoming more compartmentalized as I made sure to keep my work and drinking life separated. When I drank, mainly on weekends, I repressed my desire to be a role model professionally.

My living situation became increasingly social as more friends began to rent apartments in the same brownstone complex, which affectionately earned the names "Melrose Place" and "The Courtyard." I had succeeded in creating a family of friends, so there was always someone willing to go out to drink, although these friends were "normal" drinkers. In some ways, I began to feel that I was living back in my sorority house in college, while maintaining a professional career. We would go out to the bars together and exchange humorous stories the next morning from the night before. However, as the years passed, I seemed to be continually drinking more than those with whom I was going out.

I began to feel shameful about my drinking. I would neurotically call my friends the next day or talk to my roommates the day after blacking out for reassurance that they were not upset with me. Sometimes, to further alleviate the guilt of drinking too much, I would obsessively clean my room. Waking up to the stale smell of smoke on my clothes and the messy bedroom from the night before added to my shame. These cleaning episodes became compulsive, and I was unable to sit still until every inch of my body and room were clean. This was one more attempt to create the illusion that if things looked orderly on the surface, then my drinking was manageable.

I started therapy during graduate school under the guise that I wanted to learn what it was like to be a client in therapy. The topic of my drinking came up frequently, and my therapist and I would set up plans to replace drinking with other activities I liked such as outdoor sports, yoga, and other spiritual practices. However, these quick fixes lasted only for a brief time, and then I was back to my old drinking ways.

Past Journal Entry: January 6, 2004, Age 27
Sometimes I feel like telling those who I may have disappointed or upset that I am fucked up and I don't know where my love life is going, so I act impulsively. There may be only physical drive and not a true sense of feelings.

We try so hard to find themes in life. Maybe sometimes life is random and I *don't make sense.* I guess that for every action there is a reaction. I just need to decide if it is worth it. When I feel happy, I drink. . . . it takes me higher to a place of numbness and pleasure. I feel manic sometimes. . . . All of this energy, where to put it. I keep thinking about getting a tattoo, why? To express an internal part of myself. . . . There is something surfacing. A discontent, restlessness, and a search for a higher plane of existence.

"Restless, irritable, and discontented" describe the alcoholic, according to the *Big Book.*[46] I am searching for something, but finding nothing, as I begin to let alcohol back into my life. I behaved in ways that I regretted on New Year's Eve, and several of my friends were upset with me. The guilt lingered, and I began to feel horrible about myself. The highs were ending, and I was left feeling low. Years of drinking were beginning to create a void in my life—I sensed it, but didn't attribute it to my alcoholism.

Past Journal Entry: January 13, 2004
Tonight at dinner a friend made a valid point. I am battling myself a lot. . . . The different parts of me are battling. It is hard for me to balance because one side takes over and then the other does.

I feel like the stress in my life right now is due to things that I have done drunk once again. When will this get old for me already? I am like a broken record. Why can't there be a conclusion to this? My guilt about my friends being upset with me is rooted in alcohol. Maybe I need to lose a friend to wake the fuck up. I *need* to slow down and regroup.

I was getting sick and tired of my drinking and the self-destructive cycle in which I was stuck. Alcohol led me to behave in ways that were not truly reflective of me.

Past Journal Entry: January 17, 2004

So, I am on the *Candida* diet per doctor's orders. I have been asked by my doctor to cleanse my system of sugar (including alcohol) for 3 months. My digestive issues have been acting up again and I had testing done.

I had such a hard time tonight with my urges to drink. It literally haunted me for hours.... My friend's phone call at 4:00 P.M. to go out early to the bars, until midway through my night at the bar. My nondrinking muscle is weak.... I felt temptation in my face and the promise of a good night. I am less excited to go out when I know that I am not drinking, and I become a bit more reserved. I feel like I have this demon that keeps haunting me in so many different ways: anxiety, friends, and intimacy. All of my regrets have been due to my drinking, yet I crave it—why?

I want to make a vow that I will use this angst in my life to do something productive. So that when I feel this torn feeling, I will make the right choice and do some good or an action to better about myself. Tonight I lifted weights; writing could work as well.

I am seduced by all that alcohol brings with it: the comfortable haze and knowledge in the morning that I had an amazing night even though the details are not clear; the thrill of not knowing where the night will take you. It is my comfort zone, it is part of me and I am struggling to cut it out of the quilt that is me.

I continued to have digestive problems, and another doctor concluded that I had an overabundance of *Candida albicans*, a yeast, in my digestive tract. The treatment was to cut out sugar and alcohol from my diet. It was not a coincidence that yeast feeds off sugar and that heavy drinking had potentially caused this problem; I had not been honest with this doctor about how much I was drinking.

I wondered why I craved alcohol despite the negative consequences, and the answer was simple—I was an alcoholic. I was convinced that something else will save me: writing, helping others, lifting weights. To an outsider, the answer was so clear, but it was so difficult for me to see the truth.

Past Journal Entry: January 22, 2004

I have never been so happy to be alone as I am now. I truly find it empowering. I have been focusing on a project to "purify" my life mentally, physically and spiritually. For the first time in over a year, I really don't care what boy calls. I am not depending on a man right now. I regret that a man is pursuing me, because I am so content on my own.

Interestingly enough, this change occurred exactly when I began my diet and abstained from drinking. I feel in control of my life and I am taking charge of my health as well. Each day I realize the sense of discipline that I have but this exists only when I am sober.

My sense of inner strength and feelings of control over my life began again when my drinking stopped briefly for the *Candida* diet. I had an excuse to temporarily stop drinking, and this led me to feel a sense of empowerment in my life and to have a clear conscience. My mood was more stable, and I felt a sense of clarity.

When I cheated on the diet and started drinking heavily again, I felt an overwhelming wave of failure and a sense of regression. My moods fluctuated based on the role that alcohol played in my life, and it had the power to penetrate every aspect of my existence—soul and consciousness. Even though my career and social life were thriving, I was suffering internally. This dissonance created a battle that I could not outthink.

6

ATTEMPTS TO CURE THE PROBLEM: OUT OF CONTROL AND HITTING BOTTOM

That hope that the next time I will get my drinking under control kept me in bondage. But once I learned the truth of there being no hope—I got the most hope.

—recovering alcoholic

To high-functioning alcoholics (HFAs), controlled drinking appears to be a solution to the problems they experience when they drink too much. If they could drink moderately, then they could have alcohol in their lives without suffering the consequences of excessive drinking. Control is the glimmer of hope that enables their infatuation with alcohol to continue. HFAs often watch their friends and colleagues who drink normally, envying how effortlessly others can manage their intake. In fact, those who drink with an HFA often question what is wrong with their heavy-drinking friend or loved one. HFAs report hearing many suggestions from those who witness their heavy drinking: "Why can't you just drink less?" "Just try harder!" "Figure out how many drinks it takes for you to blackout and drink two fewer." For normal and even problem drinkers, the alcoholic's drinking appears to be a mystery—especially when smart and accomplished HFAs are able to complete tasks, achieve goals, and solve problems in other areas of their lives.

Often, through failed attempts at controlling drinking, HFAs are led to their bottom, which can be defined as "the place an alcoholic must reach before he or she finally is ready to admit that he or she has a problem and reaches out for help."[1] It often takes repeated defeat in controlling drinking for an individual to chip away at his or her denial enough to see that he or she is alcoholic.

EFFORTS TO CONTROL DRINKING

If you have to control something, then it is out of control.

—recovering alcoholic

I wasn't interested in controlling my drinking, I was interested in controlling the negative consequences of my drinking.

—recovering alcoholic

When I controlled my drinking I couldn't enjoy it, and when I enjoyed my drinking I couldn't control it.

—recovering alcoholic

Control is defined as follows: "to exercise restraining or directing influence over, to have power over, to reduce the incidence or severity of especially to innocuous levels."[2] The definition of the word *control* implies that there is a force that needs to be contained and that a person with control has power over something. Controlling drinking becomes the mental obsession of so many alcoholics. At one point in their drinking, HFAs may have been able to drink moderately and then "at some stage of his drinking career he begins to lose all control of his liquor consumption, once he starts to drink."[3] Many HFAs who are trying to control their drinking begin to convince themselves that the next time they drink, they will do so moderately. However, even when they continually fail at this goal, they believe over and over again that their new control tactic will finally work. The *Big Book* poses questions for the alcoholic: "If hundreds of experiences have shown him that one drink means another debacle with all its attendant suffering and humiliation, why is it he takes that one drink? Why can't he stay on the water wagon? What has become of the common sense and will power that he still sometimes displays with respect to other matters?"[4] The answer is because alcoholic individuals experience a mental obsession about taking a drink; when they take that first drink, a physical craving is set off and control of intake is lost.

All of the HFAs interviewed reported trying to control their drinking at some point, by using a wide variety of methods:

- Having a friend monitor how much the HFA drinks
- Abstaining from alcohol for various lengths of time
- Volunteering to be the designated driver
- Attempting to drink moderately throughout some, most, or all of their drinking
- Trying to control intake to please or appease others
- Strictly adhering to the two-drink test of drinking two drinks each day for thirty days
- Abstaining from alcohol but substituting other addictions or vices (e.g., illegal or prescription drugs, sex, food)
- Limiting the number of drinks in public and then having more drinks privately
- Eating a big meal before drinking
- Drinking water in between alcoholic drinks

- Limiting the amount of money taken to bars, or not bringing a credit card
- Predetermining the number of drinks to have that day or night
- Reading spiritual books
- Isolating and avoiding social drinking occasions
- Sticking to drinking one type of alcohol
- Having only one day's worth of alcohol in the house
- Making promises with God not to get drunk
- Deciding to stop drinking alcohol for a period of time
- Drinking substitutions, such as cough medicine and mouthwash, because these "don't count"
- Trying to stop drinking "just before blacking out"

Although HFAs have come up with many creative ways to control their drinking, they all report that these techniques ultimately do not work and eventually lead them to realize that their drinking is "out of control." One seventy-two-year-old diabetic HFA reports that at times, he used insulin to control his drinking because it allowed him to metabolize alcohol better. He also knew in the back of his mind that because of his medical condition, he should be "a little more careful" about his drinking—however, he still drank alcoholically. A twenty-eight-year-old recalls using religion, prayer, and Bible study to control and stop his drinking. These techniques would work for a few days, and then he was back drinking, "like a walking reflex." The *Big Book* states that "by every form of self-deception and experimentation, they [alcoholics] will try to prove themselves exceptions to the rule, therefore nonalcoholic." The *Big Book* then confirms that some of these strategies to control drinking are commonly used and adds that "some of the methods we have tried" include "drinking beer only, limiting the number of drinks, never drinking alone, never drinking in the morning, drinking only at home, never having it in the house, never drinking during business hours, drinking only at parties, switching from scotch to brandy, drinking only natural wines, agreeing to resign if ever drunk on the job, taking a trip, not taking a trip, swearing off forever (with and without a solemn oath), taking more physical exercise, reading inspirational books . . . we could increase the list ad infinitum."[5]

Therapists like Mulligan have engaged problem drinkers in controlled drinking strategies, such as contract setting, to limit alcohol consumption. She asks them to create concrete and measurable goals, such as drinking no more than three drinks in an evening or no more than two times per week. An inability of the problem drinker to adhere to these contracts is an indication that he or she may be an alcohol abuser or alcohol-dependent.

THE MODERATION CONTROVERSY

The American Psychiatric Association reports that one of the biggest controversies of the 1990s in the U.S. alcohol treatment field involved the Moderation Management (MM) movement, founded by Audrey Kishline in the late

1990s. MM is a mutual-help organization with the goal of helping its members to achieve "moderate" drinking. The crux of the controversy was that MM supporters believed that this program would attract problem drinkers who were not alcohol-dependent and who did not want to join abstinence-only organizations such as Alcoholics Anonymous (A.A.) or professionally run twelve-step treatment programs. In contrast, treatment and research communities feared that MM was "a dangerous temptation to alcoholics" and would feed into their denial that they could control their drinking without abstaining.[6] The controversy reached a head when Kishline was charged with two counts of vehicular homicide in a car accident when driving the wrong way on an interstate road. Her blood alcohol content was reported to be 0.26%, more than three times the legal limit in Washington. She encountered tension with followers after she made a post on the MM Web site that included the following statement: "I have made the decision recently to change my recovery goal to abstinence rather than moderation.... I am now following a different path, and to strengthen my sobriety I am attending Alcoholics Anonymous, but will also attend Women for Sobriety and SMART Recovery."[7] She also stepped down from her position as MM spokeswoman. Her lawyer stated that she had realized several months before the accident that she needed to abstain from alcohol but was struggling to do so.[8]

A study published in *Psychiatric Services: A Journal of the American Psychiatric Association* found that there are similarities in beliefs in the primary text of MM, *Moderate Drinking: The Moderation Management Guide for People Who Want to Reduce Their Drinking*,[9] and in the *Big Book*. Both state that there is a difference between a problem drinker, who is able to return to controlled drinking, and the chronic drinker, who is unable to moderate his or her drinking and should abstain from alcohol. One significant difference is that the MM text denies that alcoholism is a disease, viewing it instead as a habit or learned behavior. The text adds that "it does not make sense to take every conceivable bad habit, tack on an 'ism,' and call it a disease."[10] Another major difference is that some twelve-step program advocates believe that MM may intend to help only non-alcohol-dependent problem drinkers, but that these members are actually alcoholics in denial who think that they can learn to drink moderately.[11] The *Big Book* states that "most of us have been unwilling to admit we were real alcoholics. No person likes to think he is bodily and mentally different from his fellows. Therefore, it is not surprising that our drinking careers have been characterized by countless vain attempts to prove we could drink like other people. The idea that somehow, someday he will control and enjoy his drinking is the great obsession of every abnormal drinker. The persistence of this illusion is astonishing. Many pursue it into the gates of insanity or death."[12]

Dr. Ana Kosok is the executive director of MM and was previously the program director from 2000 until 2006. In addition, she is an MM member and has been open about her own drinking problem, which she was forced to address when she was diagnosed with hepatitis. She stated that she did not want to stop drinking and that she had none of the typical "sign posts," such as hangovers, to motivate her to quit. It took about two years to assimilate MM's behavior change techniques to get to the point where Kosok now drinks, at most, five drinks per week. She describes the MM objective as "harm reduction" that encourages any improvement in drinking. She explains that MM expects members to assume personal responsibility for their actions, and that about 85% of the program consists of behavioral techniques and tools that can be tailored to fit individual needs. Instead of using a spiritual approach, MM helps problem drinkers to manage their drinking by a nine-step program based on cognitive-behavioral principles and social support. This includes providing information about alcohol, moderate drinking guidelines, drink-monitoring exercises, goal-setting techniques, and self-management strategies.[13]

In speaking with Kosok, she does not use the term *alcoholic* and reports that most members of MM would not qualify as alcohol-dependent. She reports that about 25% of MM members join—knowing that they have an alcohol problem—with the goal of finding out if they are able to control their drinking or if they need to join an abstinence-only recovery group. In fact, one of the "Assumptions of MM" is that "moderation is a natural part of the process from harmful drinking, whether moderation or abstinence becomes the final goal. Most individuals who are able to maintain total abstinence first attempted to reduce their drinking, unsuccessfully. Moderation programs shorten the process of 'discovering' if moderation is a workable solution by providing concrete guidelines about the limits of moderate alcohol consumption."[14] Members have the option of choosing goals of either moderation or abstinence, but Kosok states that people rarely join MM to abstain. MM offers about twenty face-to-face meeting groups nationally and three internationally as well as, since 1996, a variety of online groups on a Listserv, via the organization's Web site (http://www.moderation.org).

Kosok conducted research on MM, which was published in the *International Journal of Drug Policy* and focused on what types of drinkers seek out the MM program. Her results indicate that members are extremely high functioning and have a mean age of forty-four years; 94% are college educated, 80% are employed, and 77% have an annual income of over fifty thousand dollars. Findings indicate that 66% of MM members are women, while only 33% of A.A. members are women.[15] Before joining MM, about 32% of members had sought help from A.A. and 25% from counseling. Kosok stated that members coming from abstinence-only recovery groups such as A.A. are encouraged to maintain their abstinence until they have read the MM text, spent time in the group (there is a Listserv specific to members coming from A.A.), and set up structure, and then it is recommended that they are to "be careful." She acknowledged that the MM success rate is extremely difficult to measure because of the short-term nature of the program, which is not designed for long-term participation. Therefore the group has not been able to track members' moderation adherence once they leave the program. Kosok's research concluded, in terms of the Short-Form Alcohol Dependence Data questionnaire, that 28%

of members were in the low range for alcohol dependence, 62% were in the medium range, and 10% were in the high range. These figures are higher than those in the past and imply that MM is attracting more alcohol-dependent members than before—but is not necessarily tailored for them.[16]

The MM program includes suggested drinking limits: for women, no more than three drinks per day or more than nine drinks per week, and for men, no more than four drinks per day or more than fourteen drinks per week. In addition, for both men and women, MM recommends that individuals have three to four nondrinking days per week, not to drink and drive, and not to drink in situations that "would endanger yourself or others."[17] MM also provides suggested guidelines in describing a "moderate" drinker:

- Considers an occasional drink to be a small, though enjoyable, part of life
- Has hobbies, interests, and other ways to relax and enjoy life that do not involve alcohol
- Usually has friends who are moderate drinkers or nondrinkers
- Generally has something to eat before, during, or soon after drinking
- Usually does not drink for longer than an hour or two on any particular occasion
- Usually does not drink faster than one drink per half hour
- Usually does not exceed the 0.055% blood alcohol content moderate drinking limit
- Feels comfortable with his or her use of alcohol (never drinks secretly and does not spend a lot of time thinking about drinking or planning to drink)[18]

Research has been conducted about whether or not it is possible for alcoholics to be taught to control or moderate their drinking. Dr. George Vaillant is a professor at Harvard Medical School and a researcher and psychiatrist at Brigham and Women's Hospital in Boston. In his book, *The Natural History of Alcoholism Revisited,* he summarizes past research on this subject. One longitudinal study by Helzer and colleagues studied 1,289 men and women who were alcohol-dependent and found that only 2% were able to return to moderate drinking (not exceeding six or more drinks in a sitting four times a month and having no alcohol-related problems) for one or two years.[19] There have been efforts to induce controlled drinking in alcoholics. The Sobells designed a behavioral therapy program that is often referenced by advocates of controlled drinking.[20] At first it appeared that the program was successful in a two-year follow-up. However, in recent interviews with the original twenty alcoholics who had been taught controlled drinking, the Sobells found that four had died from alcohol-related causes, eight were currently drinking alcoholically, one was missing and believed to be drinking heavily, six were able to remain abstinent from two to ten years, and only one was reportedly controlling his drinking.[21] Vaillant ascertained that it is rare that alcohol-dependent individuals would return to moderate or normalized drinking. He believes that laboratories have reported success in returning alcoholics to normal drinking with only a very few patients.[22] Therefore he feels that abstinence is "practical and a statistically more useful therapeutic focus."[23]

Caron believes that MM for alcoholics is "like trying to be half pregnant—you either are or you are not." He feels that there may be a percentage of people who can use moderation to help them "collect themselves," but "to me it sends the wrong message." Caron adds that moderation is modern society's attempt to work with people where they are at and a social way of saying "I can't be direct with that person." Scorzelli believes that MM is geared toward alcohol abusers and that it provides a "menu" that alcoholics cannot follow or maintain.

Levy, author of *Take Control of Your Drinking... and You May Not Need to Quit,* believes that it is possible for some, but certainly not all, alcoholics to control their drinking. A study published in the journal *Alcohol Research and Health* concluded that about 30% of individuals who were diagnosed as alcohol-dependent two years prior were able to evolve into "low-risk drinkers" or "abstainers" consistently for one year. However, there are several factors in this study that the authors acknowledge may have inflated this percentage, including individuals who may have naturally matured out of their drinking problem.[24] Levy has observed that therapists may find the process of working with clients to formally moderate their drinking useful in terms of diagnosing their alcohol problem. He feels that the moderation process can also be helpful for clients in that "people need to discover for themselves whether or not drinking moderately is possible.... If they find that it is not, they will then be willing to go for abstinence.... So it can be a great way to engage people in looking at their drinking and to come to terms with what they need to do to resolve the problem." Some alcoholics believe that this failure at moderation is what led them to realize that they were alcoholic. Proof of this is that the MM movement admits that about 30% of their members go on to abstinence-based programs.[25] Levy believes that 100% of individuals with drinking problems first realize that they cannot control their drinking before they make the decision to abstain. He reports that when clients struggle to moderate their drinking to the point when drinking is not even being enjoyed, then they generally decide to abstain. For those who have difficulty moderating but still insist on drinking, he may raise this as an issue and explore why they continue to drink instead of abstaining. However, Levy believes that ultimately, "it is really up to the client to come to the conclusion that they need to abstain in order for a recovery to occur." Kosok has found that her individual psychotherapy clients are mainly middle-aged and need about three to four sessions until they feel that they can moderate their drinking on their own. She has observed that some of her male clients are heavy drinkers and have been unable to moderate. She tells them that "the MM techniques are not working for you," and if they are opposed to attending A.A., she recommends that they take Antabuse (a drug used to treat alcohol-use disorders). When taken regularly, this medication causes individuals to experience adverse physical symptoms, such as nausea, when they drink alcohol.

Clearly individuals in MM and those trying to control their drinking outside of a structured program or therapeutic setting have experienced negative consequences of their drinking, or they would not be attempting to control it. Therefore, if they did not already have some type of preoccupation with, unhealthy relationship with, or addiction to alcohol, then they would simply stop drinking, given the negative consequences that they have already experienced: "Moderate drinkers have little trouble in giving up liquor entirely if they have good reason for it. They can take it or leave it alone."[26] For some, the determination to find ways to keep alcohol in their lives, instead of abstaining, may in and of itself be a symptom of their alcoholism.

HITTING BOTTOM

I have come to the conclusion that there is in truth only one bottom for all of us and that is the depth to which an individual's conscience and physical being can sink without the death of both body and soul. That is our real bottom, and it must come irrespective of material or social status.

—recovering alcoholic[27]

You know you've hit bottom...when your behavior spirals downward faster than you can lower your standards.

—Charlie, recovering HFA[28]

The alcoholic elevator goes in one direction—straight down. The good news is you can get off at any time you want: after you've truly accepted that you're a member of the crowd, after you've gotten scared or desperate enough to see what direction you've headed, it's a choice you make. Get off or keep going until you end up six feet under.

—Caroline Knapp, *Drinking: A Love Story*[29]

Some alcoholics have to lose everything they have, including their job, family, housing, money, and integrity, before they are willing to give up drinking alcohol and/or to be open to receiving help. In contrast, others are able to stop drinking before their lives become completely ravaged; they may still have their job or family.[30] Each alcoholic has a unique bottom, and some alcoholics report having several bottoms along the way that they have ignored. Generally, HFAs experience bottoms that are emotional and internal, including feelings of shame, remorse, loneliness, and/or hopelessness. Some don't have a home or family to lose, which limits the type of bottom they may have. In contrast, lower-functioning alcoholics often have bottoms that involve losing their jobs, family, and housing in addition to going through emotional suffering. These alcoholics go on for years denying that their lives are on a downward spiral, despite these losses. Some HFAs are lacking the "gift of desperation" that may motivate low-bottom alcoholics to get help. For others, high functioning only lasts until the disease progresses and the person cannot function anymore.

For many HFAs, their failed efforts to control their drinking are the concrete proof they need to discover the depth of their addiction. Certain drinking experiences may then allow this reality to sink in and lead them to admit that they need help. One thirty-one-year-old considers that her final bottom was her relapse after months of sobriety, which was "my first deliberate attempt at controlling drinking.... I consciously attempted to drink a single shot of whiskey, honestly thinking that I would be able to leave it alone because I found that particular type of alcohol distasteful. This first shot led to me drinking nearly the whole bottle in a very short time. I felt as if I was at the mercy of something compelling me to drink when I didn't want to." A forty-six-year-old recalls that during his senior year in college, he started to control his drinking to convince his ex-girlfriend to get back together with him. "Up until then I drank deliberately, now I was trying to just have two drinks and go to the library.... Then when I had two drinks, I had to have more." He was at the "jumping off point," and couldn't imagine his life with or without drinking—so he reached out for help.

Many HFAs report that their bottoms are primarily emotional. They may look well on the surface but are struggling internally as a result of their drinking. Knapp writes that "hitting bottom is usually something that happens internally, where no one else can see it."[31] A thirty-three-year-old man adds that his bottom was "almost purely emotional in nature. I had built up a life which depended completely on fragile outside factors to maintain my sense of emotional well-being. This included a girlfriend, drinking buddies, and my job. Several factors at once converged to pull this structure down." One twenty-four-year-old recalls that she was stuck in a cycle of drinking to avoid anxiety and low self-esteem—her view of the world became completely negative. She stated, "I was twenty-one years old and when I looked in the mirror I saw an eighty-five-year-old woman. I felt completely dead on the inside, and any zest for life that I once possessed was completely snuffed out." She feels that her true bottom was "the complete inability to connect with other human beings, feeling totally desperate and alone, wanting to stop drinking but not being able to and hating myself." A twenty-six-year-old remembers that she was sad about quitting her job, she was single, and she felt that she had an unhappy and miserable life. She describes, "I didn't want to live—not to kill myself—just not to live." She drank for two days straight and woke up knowing that she "couldn't drink anymore," and reached out for help. She has remained in recovery ever since.

For some HFAs who are accustomed to success and are perfectionists by nature, their bottom may be subtle, but enough to prompt change. One student began to notice his straight As slip to Bs, and this was an indication of the beginning of his bottom. A doctor who woke up hungover with hand tremors realized that his patient that day was getting "shortchanged" because of his drinking. This was unacceptable to him professionally and ethically and eventually led him to get help. He has been in a Twelve-Step Recovery Program for twelve years.

Being an HFA and hitting a low bottom are not mutually exclusive. In fact, some HFAs hit low bottoms and continue to relapse afterward. One fifty-two-year-old had always drank secretly and did not let his family know when he was having a hard time. He felt that he was doing great things professionally as a physician, but he knew that he was an alcoholic. He anticipated a hard month at work and knew that he could not drink and continue working. However, he could not stop drinking and felt therefore that he did not have any options—he planned to kill himself. A female friend gave him the advice to e-mail an organization of physicians who are in recovery. He immediately received a return e-mail from a recovering alcoholic physician that literally saved his life. He has been in recovery for over three years since his first Twelve-Step Recovery Program meeting. A twenty-six-year-old believed that a bottom had to be an experience "so bad and painful that you would know you couldn't drink again." She proved to herself that a low bottom does not guarantee sobriety. After three days of binging on alcohol, this graduate student attempted suicide. She woke up three days later to the cries of her parents as she lay in the intensive care unit of a hospital with tubes in her nose, arms, and throat. However, "like a true alcoholic... I drank within three days of leaving the hospital and went to rehab for the following twenty-two days." She has since relapsed five times in three years but has now been in recovery for over a year. A seventy-nine-year-old recalls concluding that he was miserable, his wife was mad at him, and his children were upset with him. He would wake up and think, "Oh shit, another day; I wish I wouldn't wake up." He became suicidal and had thoughts of driving off a local bridge. At his wife's suggestion, he contacted her cousin, who was in a Twelve-Step Recovery Program, and he started going to meetings out of obligation. He stayed sober for three weeks and thought that he could control his drinking. Soon after, he was back to his regular drinking habits and once again became depressed and suicidal. He finally noticed a decline in work performance and fell off a bike drunk; he began attending meetings again and has been in recovery ever since.

Some HFAs, through a moment of grace and spirituality, are inspired to reach out for help. A thirty-four-year-old saw many aspects of her life "come to a head." She disliked her job, she was thinking about having children, and she landed in the hospital for a physical illness. While in the hospital, she was not able to consume food or liquids and she had spiritual moments of clarity, and she felt that "we have one life to live, one body—if I continued on this road then what's the point?" In a "moment of weakness," she called her stepbrother, who was in a Twelve-Step Recovery Program, began going to meetings, and has been in recovery for three years. A thirty-year-old describes her bottom as a spiritual awakening. Her drinking had led her to become emotionally numb, to feel like she was going crazy, and her roommate was about to call her father because she was not paying her bills. For the first time in her life, she went "to the foot of my bed, on my knees—cried like I hadn't cried in years and prayed, 'God, please help me.'" She adds that her prayers were answered and she has received all of the help she has needed to stay in recovery for over three years in a Twelve-Step Recovery Program. A sixty-three-year-old shared that her bottom was "slow in coming... it was like I was swimming in the dirty ocean floor of alcohol's wasteland for several months." She was facing devastating financial problems in her life that were not directly related to her alcoholism. "It was the typical way a high-functioning alcoholic suffers—the slow deterioration of personal values and quality of life structures—until the lightbulb goes off." Her lifelong spiritual practices "kicked in" when she was reading a spiritual book that led her to conclude that "my drinking was a lie and my pride was keeping it in place and I could no longer live this way." She called her therapist and told her that she was going to a Twelve-Step Recovery Program meeting that evening.

Some HFAs report having an obvious bottom but then relapsing and hitting an even lower bottom. One dentist reported that he knew something was wrong with his drinking even though his career was flourishing. He asked a lawyer friend who was in a recovery program for help, and although he joined the program, he did not put much effort into his recovery. He was in recovery for ten years and then relapsed for twelve years, stating that his disease had progressed even while he was not drinking. His next bottom was when he received two citations for driving under the influence (DUI) in three days (by the same policeman). His lawyer convinced the judge to release him to a treatment facility, where he received thirty-five days of intensive treatment. He has remained in recovery for twenty-nine years since.

Other HFAs report that their bottoms were neither something that they noticed at the time nor anything that would have motivated them to get help. These individuals were forced to address their alcoholism by their loved ones or by the law. One twenty-five-year-old stated that her best friend gave her an ultimatum to get help for her drinking. She complied because she was extremely dependent on her friend's opinion of her. However, she feels that she truly hit her emotional bottom when she was in sobriety. She stopped drinking while it was still fun and benefited her in many ways. Once the alcohol was removed, she began to experience painful emotions; she has remained in recovery for over two years in a Twelve-Step Recovery Program. Although a thirty-three-year-old man reported hitting an emotional bottom, the law also played a part in leading him to get help. He was arrested for a DUI when he was twenty-one years old and lost his license. He went to a "DUI retreat" and was assessed as needing to attend Twelve-Step Recovery Program meetings for two months to have his license returned. He completed this mandate and decided that he identified with people in the meetings and has remained in recovery for eight years since. One fifty-eight-year-old man confirmed that the only reason he agreed to a thirty-day stay at an alcohol rehabilitation center was because of pressure from his wife. He had no intention of permanently staying in recovery and viewed the stay as a way to "save my ass." Looking back, he can see that he had previously hit bottoms that he had ignored and his wife had forced him to confront what would become his last bottom.

HFAs often define themselves based on their careers, and thus the threat of losing a career can be enough to bring them to their bottoms. A fifty-three-year-old describes how the last time he drank, he became violent and started to hit lamps and furniture in his house with a tennis racket. When his distraught wife approached him, he pushed her, and then both his son and wife called the police. When four cop cruisers arrived, he went into his backyard and wished "that the tennis racket was a gun so I could shoot myself." He was terrified that he would be kicked out of the military—which was his entire identity. He spent the night in jail and the next day was brought for a psychological assessment. For the first time, he was able to admit that he was an alcoholic and was willing to do anything to save his family and career. Therefore he willingly entered rehab and has been in recovery ever since. He was able to keep his military rank and job (but would never be able to be promoted) under the conditions that he did not drink again, went to counseling, and continued attending a Twelve-Step Recovery Program.

Some HFAs report that their bottoms lasted for a long time and may also have involved relapses. A thirty-two-year-old describes his bottom as beginning with the dissolution of his marriage and ending two years later, after he landed in a local emergency room four times, including two times during Thanksgiving week. He told his roommate that he wanted to die and had thought of suicide often. After this, he blacked out and was again taken to the hospital and told that his mental and physical condition was life-threatening. Even this did not scare him enough—he left the hospital and went drinking, which landed him back in the emergency room with tachycardia and numbness in the left side of his body. Soon after his hospital release, he entered a Twelve-Step Recovery Program and relapsed about four times in the beginning. After eleven months of sobriety but not putting effort into his recovery, he relapsed; he immediately returned to the program and has now been in recovery for over a year.

Individuals do not have to hit a low bottom to stop drinking. A former treatment counselor states that "the conventional wisdom held that alcoholics had to hit bottom before they could get better. We'd like to raise that bottom so that people don't have to fall as far before they get help."[32]

"HINDSIGHT" REFLECTIONS OF THE AUTHOR

Controlling Drinking

I spent four years trying to control my drinking. This began when I abstained at age twenty-three for six months with the intention that this would turn me into a so-called normal drinker. Throughout the years, I tried endless strategies to help control my drinking, including ideas such as exercising before I went out to bars to release stress so that I would then drink less. Ironically, the treadmills in my California gym faced the bars, and I would visualize what type of margarita I was going to have that night. I tried to drink only beer because I didn't like the taste and it had a lower alcohol content than hard alcohol. However, once I was buzzed, I would start drinking shots of hard alcohol because I felt like I was not getting drunk enough. At times, I would drink water in between drinks and ordered drinks made with extra soda and less alcohol. When I began to explore Eastern philosophies, I tried to apply the principles of meditation to my drinking. At one point, I listened to a meditation tape before going out to bars to keep myself "connected to God" so that I would not black out.

Past Journal Entry: September 3, 1999, Age 23
Is this force in my life—this toxin called alcohol—worth consuming after evaluating the pros and cons? Maybe for those who can naturally moderate their intake. However, I do not have that ability. There are techniques that have been recommended to help one drink responsibly: eat a large dinner, drink one drink then water, drink beer, drink slowly, work out before going out, etc. These techniques work sometimes, but not all of the time. This is not acceptable for me.

This journal entry marked the beginning of my attempts to control my drinking, and three years later, I was still struggling to gain this control. Therefore I decided to see an MM therapist to help me to learn to drink normally. I felt that my current therapist did not specialize in this area. I refused to completely abstain at this point because I did not believe that my alcohol problem was bad enough to take such an extreme measure, and I was willing to do anything to keep alcohol in my life. After I filled out an intake questionnaire, the therapist stated that my profile was not one of a person who could easily moderate. She warned me that "asking a heavy drinker to moderate their drinking is like asking someone to eat just five potato chips—it is easier not to have any at all."

However, she was willing to work with me. My mother came with me to one appointment and also questioned whether I would be able to moderate my drinking. I was completely convinced that if I put my mind to this process and had the appropriate outside help, I could accomplish this goal. My first assignment was to abstain from drinking for one month. I was also instructed to keep a log of my feelings, cravings, and struggles throughout the month in a brief format. The following entries are from that log:

Abstinence Log: June 19, 2003, Age 26
Out at bar with friend from school. I was only tempted when a cute boy offered me a drink. I had thoughts that I don't want to be dating someone who drinks a lot.

Abstinence Log: June 25, 2003—Sober Date
A glass of wine could have enhanced this date. However, the knowledge that I had to work the next day decreased the urge.

Abstinence Log: June 28, 2003—Friend's Birthday
I was nagged to drink by a lot of people. I engaged in some debate with people about sobriety. Observing drunk and arguing people made being drunk much less desirable. I felt that my emotions and anger were in better control because I was sober.

Abstinence Log: June 29, 2003
I got up and went running—it was so nice not to be hungover!

Abstinence Log: July 1, 2003—One Abstinent Month!
I did not have the desire to drink just because my one month was up! I stayed home but almost went out.

After my successful completion of one month of abstinence, I began the second phase of treatment. I was instructed to keep track of the number of drinks that I had each week. I was told not to have more than seven drinks per week, and I could not have more than one drink per hour or a maximum of three drinks per night. I felt ready to make these changes in my life and to make moderate drinking a part of my lifestyle and nature.

Moderation Drinking Log: July 10, 2003—Rock Concert
One hard alcohol drink and then stopped and was watching guy that I had been on a date with play in a band. It felt hard to stop.

Moderation Drinking Log: July 11, 2003—New York City
One large drink, 1 shot.

Moderation Drinking Log: July 12, 2003
I had a psychic reading at friend's house and had 1 margarita.

I had planned a trip to Nantucket with my friends as a yearly tradition since the summer I had lived there. My therapist had specific instructions for me during this vacation. I was given a "bonus" drink that week because it was a special vacation, so I was not to have more than eight drinks per week, no more than three drinks in one sitting, and no more than one drink per hour. After my month of abstinence and the support of this therapist, I was ready to apply all that I had learned to a trip that would have a lot of drinking temptations.

Moderation Drinking Log: July 18, 2003
I went out at 11:30 P.M. and had 2 drinks and stopped without a problem knowing that the bars closed at 1:00 A.M.

Moderation Drinking Log: July 19, 2003
Went to dinner with friends and no one drank at dinner. I had half a drink, 1 tall drink at Bamboo Supper Club bar. I felt good but stopped drinking again.

Moderation Drinking Log: July 20, 2003
I had 3 drinks at the Muse dance club. I did not have a desire to have more.

Moderation Drinking Log: July 21, 2003
I had a glass of wine at dinner and felt a bit buzzed. Then I drank half a drink at the Lobster Trap bar and 1.5 drinks at Schooner's bar. This was the hardest night to stop, but counting kept me from having more.

Moderation Drinking Log: July 22, 2003
Stayed in and did not drink.

Moderation Drinking Log: July 23, 2003
I drank 1 glass of wine at dinner. Then I drank 2 big drinks and 1 normal size drink at the Rose & Crown bar.

Moderation Drinking Log: July 24, 2003
I felt the urge to drink and had a lot of energy to go out. I drank a mudslide drink, 1 big drink (slowly) and another big drink. I wanted another drink and felt buzzed, but realized that it was late. I felt in control but realized that I was bending the "rules" a bit.

Moderation Drinking Log: July 25, 2003
I knew that I was not going to follow the "rules" because we went out at 9:00 P.M. and were going on a "pub crawl." I drank a half a drink at Fairgrounds Restaurant, 1 mixed drink shot, 1 strong "Elbow Bender" drink, half an espresso martini, half a vodka tonic, and 1 mixed drink at the Chicken Box dance club. I never felt more than a buzz, and I stopped drinking at the last bar. There were too many drinks being pushed at me all night and it was hard to keep turning them down.

Moderation Drinking Log: July 26, 2003
I was more lenient tonight about the "rules" because I had so obviously broken them the night before. I drank 1 drink quickly at Kitty's bar, 1.5 drinks at the Bamboo Supper Club bar, 1 drink at Chicken Box, and I had 2 beers. I felt a subtle buzz and was hanging out with a boy.

Moderation Drinking Log: July 27, 2003
I had 2 drinks and 1 Jell-O shot.

I reluctantly handed my vacation drinking log over to my therapist after returning from my trip. Needless to say, she was not pleased with my drinking pattern this vacation week. She stated that I went above the week total of eight drinks in just a night. I truly felt that I had done well because I never blacked out. I also felt like she had no idea of how disciplined I had been compared to those around me on the island. However, I had excused the rules about the speed at which I was to drink as well as the quantity of drinks altogether.

Moderation involved a lot of time and energy directed toward thinking about drinking and/or not drinking. I was starting to feel like I was wearing a leash and going to drinking confession each week. I then began to bend the rules even when I was not on vacation such as not counting the shots of hard alcohol that I was drinking in between my three allowed drinks. I would make pint-glass-sized drinks at house parties that consisted mostly of vodka and a splash of tonic water. I was told by friends that I would walk around in a blackout telling people that I was not drunk because I had only had "three drinks." Overall, I felt that moderation therapy helped me to decrease the number of times that I blacked out, which then led me to justify terminating therapy.

My final attempt at controlling my drinking was designating three occasions per year in which I could drink all that I wanted in a safe environment. Within two months, I had drunk to the point of blacking out over ten times.

Hitting Bottom

Past Journal Entry: February 3, 2004, Age 27—Rock Bottom
I am really at a low point with my drinking. I have realized that my drunken actions are affecting my friends in negative ways. One of my friends was crying to me about the fear she experienced last night when I left the bar in a cab with a boy she had never seen before. She said that she had tried calling my cell phone repeatedly and that I didn't answer it. She went on to explain that the fact that I never came home until the following morning led her to worry all night long about my safety. I am dancing with the devil and this needs to end.

I have looked into recovery programs. I have proven that in some situations I cannot moderate, and I continue to black out and put myself into danger. I cannot fathom complete abstinence but I will see how one of these programs will work for me.

I had gone out to a bar for the Superbowl and I remember that I called my mother and told her that I was going to have only three drinks. I then coerced a friend into sneaking drinks with me so that others who were concerned about my drinking wouldn't notice. Eventually, I blacked out and left the bar with a male stranger. None of my friends knew where I was that night, and I didn't answer my cell phone all night because of my drunken state.

I distinctly remember waking up that morning hungover, staring at a strange ceiling, not knowing what city I was in, and I thought, "I can't do this anymore." I shamefully walked to the subway with my outfit on from the night before, loathing each moment of being in public. When I arrived home, several of my friends sat me down to talk about my drinking. They told me that they were concerned and scared for me as well as tired of trying to keep an eye on me when I was drunk. They explained that when I was drunk, I wouldn't listen to them and that I did only what I wanted, leaving them worried and frustrated.

I did not want to behave this way any longer, and I realized that continuing this way would be a downhill journey—I would destroy my life eventually. I was truly out of control when I drank, and I now knew that I would continue to behave this way as long as I drank.

In a depressive state, I called my mother and told her about the night. I subconsciously knew that I needed to admit the events of the night before to her while I was still hungover and vulnerable. I also knew that once any amount of emotional strength returned, I would forget about my remorse and would drink again.

Past Journal Entry: February 5, 2004

I have hit my own personal rock-bottom. Not like you see in the movies, but my own version of that. I am an alcoholic, there is no denying it. I have so much potential, but I am back to square one.

Past Journal Entry: February 6, 2004

I went to the doctor today and I confessed my sins. I am certain that my behavior is self-destructive, but I am not convinced that I need to quit altogether. I know that I need to abstain now—the future is uncertain—I am giving up a part of myself and I am not sure how it will be replaced. I have a lot to give to the world. Now I need to figure out how—with a clear mind and focus.

A few friends think that I am being hard on myself—although most think that I need help. It is that doubt in my mind that gets magnified when others challenge my disgust at my behavior. The counselor may have some advice. I am truly confused and deeply sad. I am consumed by thoughts about this issue all day long.

This journal entry shows that my denial had returned when I stated, "I am not convinced that I need to quit altogether," after concluding in a prior entry that "I am an alcoholic." It is as though I had another scheme to keep alcohol in my life even when it was clear that I had exhausted all moderation options. My hangover began to wear off, and I had gained some distance from the shame of the Superbowl night. The fact that I began to consider drinking again made it apparent that I needed outside help—this disease had a hold on me.

PART II
RECOVERY

7

A NEW START: THE PATHS TO SOBRIETY

Another glass of whisky but it still don't kill the pain
So he stumbles to the sink and pours it down the drain
He said, it's time to be a man and stop living for yesterday
Gotta face it

Cause' I don't wanna' spend my life jaded, waitin'
To wake up one day and find
That I let all these years go by
Wasted

Oh I don't wanna' keep on wishin,' missin'
The still of the morning, the color of the night
I ain't spendin' no more time
Wasted[1]

—*Wasted*, sung by recording artist Carrie Underwood

Researchers, addiction experts, sober alcoholics, medical professionals, religious believers, and spiritual pursuers all have differing opinions of what an alcoholic needs to recover from alcoholism. After examining varying perspectives, it is clear that there are many paths to recovery and that those alcoholics who seek help can find a program that leads them to maintain long-term recovery.

Being sober and being in recovery are not the same. An individual who is sober, without a recovery program, is simply abstaining from alcohol. These individuals are commonly referred to as *dry drunks* suffering from untreated alcoholism because the void that alcohol fills is still present. Sober alcoholics may start to act out by engaging in addictive behaviors such as shopping binges, excessive gambling, disordered eating, acting out sexually, and/or overexercising. Many sober alcoholics tend to become jealous of others who are able to drink normally, feel depressed and/or anxious, isolate to avoid being around alcohol, develop negative attitudes, and risk relapse. They are attempting to live the same life that they led while drinking and have neither changed themselves nor grown emotionally or spiritually—necessary elements for true recovery.

RECOVERY PROGRAMS

> Two long-festering sores came to the surface at Hazelden [rehab]. It was there I was made to face the fact that I was an alcohol addict. I did not believe it. I had a battery of defenses. Jews were not drunks. Drunks were the kind of people we passed in the gutters, the kind I had tried to help through years of work with the homeless. Not my kind.
> —Kitty Dukakis, *Shock: The Healing Power of Electroconvulsive Therapy*[2]

Various types of care are available for those beginning the recovery process. It is important for individuals to consult with a medical professional and/or addiction specialist to find out the most appropriate form of treatment. For alcoholics who are physiologically dependent on alcohol, a detoxification (detox) facility is generally needed to safely withdraw from alcohol. Unfortunately, it is estimated that only 10% of alcohol-dependent individuals are hospitalized for detox. Some alcoholics may be advised to enter into a residential or inpatient alcohol rehab facility to remove those triggers present in their everyday surroundings—allowing them to focus solely on sobriety. Alcoholics leaving a detox or rehab program have the option of living in a halfway house with other recovering alcoholics—offering a highly structured, sober living environment.[3] Others return home and transition to day treatment or start outpatient therapy while attending recovery program support group meetings such as Alcoholics Anonymous (A.A.) or SMART Recovery. For some individuals, it is best to begin recovery with day treatment (a lower level of care than rehab), where therapy groups meet five days a week, returning home in the evenings. Most alcohol rehab, day treatment, and halfway house programs in the United States are based on the disease model of alcoholism. They follow the Twelve Steps of recovery and integrate A.A. meetings into their treatment plans.[4] However, several treatment programs offer other support group options such as the Secular Organization for Sobriety (SOS), SMART Recovery, or Women for Sobriety (WFS; see Appendix D).

The U.S. Department of Health and Human Services' 2005 National Survey on Drug Use and Health indicates that of the 3.9 million people aged twelve or older receiving treatment for alcohol and/or drug use, 2.1 million attend self-help groups, over 2.6 million enter inpatient and outpatient rehab, 1 million receive therapy through an outpatient mental health center, 773,000 are in a hospital detox, 460,000 receive treatment through a private doctor's office, 399,000 go to a local emergency room, and 344,000 receive treatment while in prison or jail.[5]

Many high-functioning alcoholics (HFAs) never attend the aforementioned types of treatment. Most addiction experts recommend that these individuals attend some type of recovery program support group. Renault believes that alcoholics should utilize these programs because "you cannot do it alone, you need support and you need skills." All of the addiction experts interviewed recommended A.A. for HFAs, but they did not believe it was the only option. The Hazelden Foundation published a research update that reviewed a variety of studies, all concluding that A.A. participation increased the length of both sobriety and overall psychological health. Susan E. Foster, MSW, vice president of the National Center on Addiction and Substance Abuse (CASA), reports that CASA's research indicates that alcoholics who take part in spiritually based programs (such as twelve-step programs) in combination with science-based treatment (such as behavioral therapy) are more likely to remain sober. She also emphasized that alcoholics should be treated for any concurrent mental health problems that could lead to relapse.[6] Specifically, research indicates that A.A. membership along with professional treatment had two times the efficacy than just treatment alone.[7] Vaillant, in his book *The Natural History of Alcoholism Revisited*, estimates that 40% of all recovery from alcoholism has occurred through A.A.[8] Sanchez is amazed by how A.A. works and feels that when it doesn't work for an individual, then "they haven't come to grips with themselves." He does not believe that this program is for everyone but "the fact that it is spiritually based—I've seen people learn to take the religion out of it and just make it work." Duda stated that A.A. is "the way to go.... I have high regard, although I know there are some people who have difficulty finding the right meeting." She recommends that if individuals don't like a particular meeting group, they should try another until they find one in which they feel comfortable. Travia stated that "to my knowledge the Twelve Steps are the most successful treatment program," and he also recommends that his students attend New Directions, a college-age therapy group, for additional support. One clinical psychology doctoral student and recovering HFA believes that twelve-step programs are "unquestionably the best method of treatment." Scorzelli feels that A.A. and SMART Recovery are the best options for recovery programs. Mulligan has observed that A.A. can be "fantastic for people... but I don't think it is for everyone." She feels that "for some people it doesn't work and there is a big stigma for them to overcome—because society says A.A. is the way to go... and people then assume that they are not interested in treatment." Levy confirms that there is not just one path to recovery and recommends that individuals try two to three A.A. meetings for one or two months, and "if it is not for you, then it is not for you"; he then recommends trying SMART Recovery or WFS. Cohen believes it is important to offer clients an "array" of treatment options that include all recovery program support groups, group therapy (which differs from recovery program support groups), and/or individual therapy with a provider who has addiction experience as well as medication options through a board-certified addiction psychiatrist to treat concurrent conditions such as depression. In addition, she feels that bibliotherapy, or reading books about alcoholism and recovery, can help to provide insight and healing.

A.A. is a self-supporting recovery program based on the disease model of alcoholism. The program was founded in 1935 by Bill Wilson, a New York stockbroker, and Dr. Bob Smith, a physician. Wilson had been "relieved of his drink obsession by a sudden spiritual experience" and, as a result, determined that to recover, alcoholics must help other alcoholics.[9] The program describes itself as "a fellowship of men and women who share their experience, strength and hope with each other that they may solve their common problem and help others to recover from alcoholism."[10] Members are encouraged to attend meetings for a lifetime.[11] A.A. considers alcoholics to be powerless over alcohol and therefore in need of finding a "power greater than themselves," of their own conception, which will allow them to recover from alcoholism. The basis of the program are the Twelve Steps (see Appendix E), which were created by A.A.'s founders and intended to create a spiritual awakening for those who work them. A.A. does not consider itself a religious organization; instead, the program is based on spiritual principles. Members are free to interpret the spiritual concepts however they choose, or not at all.[12] A.A. is the most commonly sought form of help for alcoholism,[13] with over 2 million reported members[14] in 150 countries,[15] 105,000 groups worldwide,[16] and online meetings. "Young people" meetings were started in 1946 so that younger alcoholics would be able to transition better into the program.[17] The *Big Book* states that there is a 50% recovery rate for A.A. members, that 25% become sober after some relapses, and that two out of three alcoholics who stop coming to meetings eventually return.[18] According to the A.A. 2007 Membership Survey, 33% of members have been sober for more than ten years, 12% for between five and ten years, 24% for between one and five years, and 31% for less than one year, and the average length of sobriety of members is over eight years. This survey also indicates that 65% of members are men and 35% are women. In terms of professional members, 10% are managers/administrators, 10% are professional/technical, 11% are self-employed, 5% are health professionals, 3% are educators, and 4% are students.[19]

The Secular Organization for Sobriety, also known as Save Our Selves (SOS), is a nonprofit recovery program "dedicated to providing a path to sobriety, an alternative to those paths depending upon supernatural or religious beliefs."[20] This program was started in 1985 by James Christopher, a sober alcoholic, after he attended A.A. and struggled with the program's approach to recovery. He realized that there was a need for another program after receiving many responses to his article "Sobriety without Superstition," written about maintaining sobriety separate from spiritual or religious beliefs.[21] Today, SOS claims to be the largest non-twelve-step recovery program, with over twenty thousand members[22] and meetings held in every state and in twenty-one countries internationally. SOS claims that it is not against twelve-step programs but that its members found that such programs did not work for them.[23] This program believes that moderate drinking is impossible for alcoholics and views sobriety as a first priority. They use a "self-empowerment approach" to recovery that credits individuals for achieving their sobriety and encourages the "use of the scientific method to understand alcoholism." Some of the SOS's suggested guidelines for sobriety include first acknowledging being an alcoholic, reaffirming this truth daily, and making the "Sobriety Priority" a lifelong commitment. SOS believes that "the good life" can be obtained, but no matter what uncertainties life brings, members should not drink and are encouraged to share their thoughts and feelings in confidence with other members.[24]

SMART Recovery is a nonprofit organization that offers free support groups for individuals who want to become free of any type of addictive behavior. SMART Recovery was originally affiliated with Rational Recovery Systems, a for-profit company owned by Jack Trimpey. In 1994, as a result of differences, the nonprofit changed its name to SMART Recovery. Rational Recovery is based on the Addictive Voice Recognition Technique and does not provide recovery support groups.[25] However, SMART Recovery offers over three hundred weekly groups, ninety thousand meetings worldwide,[26] and over sixteen online weekly meetings—allowing some members to participate even if live meetings are not nearby.[27] SMART Recovery offers a scientific foundation, instead of a spiritual one. In addition, addictive behavior is viewed as a "maladaptive habit," rather than a disease, and the term *alcoholic* is not used.[28] SMART Recovery offers a 4-Point Program that includes the following: "Point 1: Enhancing and Maintaining Motivation to Abstain, Point 2: Coping with Urges, Point 3: Problem Solving (managing thoughts, feelings and behaviors), and Point 4: Lifestyle Balance (balancing momentary and enduring satisfaction)."[29] Membership is often for months to years, but generally not for a lifetime, as with other recovery programs.[30]

WFS is the first national self-help program for female alcoholics. It was started in 1975 by Dr. Jean Kirkpatrick, who believed that female alcoholics require a different type of recovery program than men. There are over one hundred support groups nationally and fifteen internationally.[31] Kirkpatrick was once a member of A.A. and then had a relapse that lasted thirteen years. As a result, she realized that she wanted to learn more about herself, and in 1973, she created the New Life Program. In 1975, this program's name was changed to Women for Sobriety Inc., and the New Life Program was incorporated into the Thirteen Statements of Acceptance[32] (see Appendix F). WFS maintains that it can be used alone or with other recovery programs simultaneously, and it promotes change through positive reinforcement, cognitive strategies, "letting the body help" (relaxation techniques, meditation, diet, exercise), and group involvement. The WFS program incorporates a spiritual and meditation component emphasized by Statement 8, which says, "The fundamental object of life is emotional and spiritual growth."[33]

PROFESSIONAL ASSISTANCE PROGRAMS

If it were a matter of knowing better or of intelligence, then we would not be in an alcohol recovery program meeting. This is a room full of smart, well-educated people—but we are all here.

—Chris, HFA, physician

Another path to recovery may be through the workplace. HFAs may willingly seek help and be referred or mandated to receive help through an employee assistance program (EAP) for alcohol-related problems at work. Most HFAs place great importance on their careers; therefore when their drinking begins to interfere with their job performance, they may be more motivated to seek treatment. Most EAPs began in the 1940s as a result of employer concerns about alcoholism among white-collar workers.[34] Around this time, A.A. was a new organization gaining attention, and alcohol-related issues were beginning to be perceived as workplace problems. EAPs once were staffed by recovering alcoholics who trained supervisors to spot alcoholics by looking for visible symptoms such as shaking hands and bloodshot eyes.[35] These programs experienced growth in the early 1970s and became more comprehensive—treating psychological and financial problems in addition to alcohol and drug issues.[36] The National Institute on Alcohol Abuse and Alcoholism (NIAAA) began in 1970 with the goal of mainstreaming alcoholism treatment in the United States. Therefore they started to focus on "the majority of American alcoholics who had intact families and jobs, and who were difficult to identify and motivate toward treatment." This led to workplaces offering resources for "hidden" alcoholics whose behavior was losing money for the company[37]— further confirming the prevalence of HFAs. Companies either develop their own programs (internal EAP) or hire an outside EAP as a resource for their employees. However, research indicates that employees are often embarrassed to be seen using these services internally and that there is often a lack of long-term follow-up in EAP programs for alcoholics—leading to an increase in relapse rates.[38] In Cohen's experience as a therapist contracted for EAPs, she has observed that professionals rarely seek help specifically for alcoholism. These professionals most often come to therapy to report interpersonal conflicts, loss in job functioning, being passed over for a promotion, or having lost a job or a relationship; through assessment, it becomes apparent that alcohol is contributing to these issues. Some employees are mandated to treatment because of a positive random drug test or the finding that alcohol is the underlying problem in an interpersonal work conflict.

HFAs may also enter into recovery after receiving professional disciplinary action for alcohol-related incidents. This type of work issue may be considered the ultimate failure for HFAs, and they may wonder what colleagues may be thinking of them or if their careers are in jeopardy. In addition, it may be the first time they are able to face the truth of their alcoholism because an HFA's career is a strong motivation for him or her to get sober. Fortunately, in the past few decades, specific professions have created assistance programs that provide help for alcohol and drug problems. Some professions have developed their own specialized programs, which include, but are not limited to, lawyer assistance programs (LAP) and physician health programs (PHPs), which vary from state to state but essentially have the same function. Much like EAPs, these programs deal with myriad issues in addition to alcohol and drug problems. Some professional assistance programs are targeted specifically to address drug and alcohol problems. The Committee of Drug and Alcohol Dependence (CDAD)–Dentist Health and Wellness Committee, affiliated with the Massachusetts Dental Society, is one such program and exists solely at the state level.

PHPs began after the American Medical Association Council on Mental Health prepared a landmark policy paper titled "The Sick Physician: Impairment by Psychiatric Disorders, Including Alcoholism and Drug Dependence." In 1974, therapeutic alternatives to discipline were developed, and alcoholism and other drug addictions were recognized as illnesses. By 1980, after increased education and awareness about these issues, almost every state had implemented these programs.[39] The Federation of State Physician Health Programs Inc. is a nonprofit corporation that assists state PHPs but does not oversee them. The purpose of PHPs is to diagnose alcohol and substance abuse issues, mental health conditions, and physical illnesses in physicians. In addition, these programs offer varying levels of treatment or referrals to treatment programs and professional monitoring.[40] Some programs provide educational outreach to doctors and medical students—a ripe audience of potential HFAs. For example, Sanchez speaks at medical schools about substances and the role of PHPs and then does a live interview with a patient with a substance problem, often alcohol, to help increase the ability of medical students to identify and address alcohol-use disorders in their patients. He believes that many medical students and doctors focus more on patient care than taking care of themselves. For those doctors mandated to receive treatment for alcohol and drug problems, there are strict requirements that generally include a contract (three to five years), random weekly urine screening, and weekly attendance at either A.A. or Narcotics Anonymous meetings, in addition to a weekly twelve-step-based physician support group, individual therapy, and work monitoring by the PHP and chief of service where the physician is working.[41] Noncompliance with the contract results in an investigation by the medical licensing board, and the physician faces the chance of losing his or her medical license—depending on the severity of the case and if patient harm was involved. PHPs that are well funded and well staffed are able to monitor physicians closely and have a physician recovery rate of 85% to 90%.[42] Once doctors have the freedom to choose recovery meetings, it is recommended that they attend open twelve-step meetings in addition to their physician support group meetings because there is a higher relapse rate for those attending only physician support groups.

In 1988, the American Bar Association created the Commission on Impaired Attorneys and then changed the organization's name in 1996 to the Commission on Lawyers Assistance Programs (CoLAP). Fifty states have developed LAPs, which are staffed with lawyers (many in recovery) and/or trained professionals. Typically, they provide peer counseling, lawyer-specific recovery meetings, and referrals to twelve-step programs. Those with professional staffs also provide evaluations and, in some cases, interventions, not only for alcohol/drug problems, but also for an expanding array of other personal difficulties. CoLAP also offers a Web-based Listserv, providing a confidential vehicle for law students who want to become sober or maintain recovery.[43] Alternative disciplinary programs offer the possibility of reduced disciplinary measures for lawyers found to have engaged in professional misconduct who make a binding commitment to take part in a regimen of treatment, self-help groups, drug/alcohol testing, and so on, and are overseen by the LAP. The specifics of these programs vary from state to state, however, they are all intended not only to support lawyers' recovery, but also to protect the public and "the integrity of the profession."[44]

CDAD was formed in 1980 as an autonomous committee affiliated with the Massachusetts Dental Society. The main goals of this committee are to help alcohol- or drug-dependent dentists get into recovery before their professional performance is affected and to increase awareness of alcoholism and drug addiction by educating dentists, dental educators, dental students, and licensing boards. About 75% of disciplinary actions taken toward dentists are "a direct or indirect result of alcohol or other drug misuse."[45] In Massachusetts, this figure is about 50% due to CDAD's early identification efforts. CDAD assists dentists in each stage of recovery by providing services such as interventions, treatment referrals, aftercare monitoring, and retraining into their profession. CDAD recommends twelve-step programs and offers about twenty peer support group meetings (twelve-step based) per month in three areas of Massachusetts that are open only to physicians and dentists.[46] According to Peters, who developed CDAD, these peer support meetings are meant to be a "shoehorn" to integrate these professionals into twelve-step programs but are not meant to be a substitute. He has found that those who maintain long-term recovery are generally involved in a twelve-step program in addition to the peer support meetings. Another HFA dentist initially relapsed several times in a Twelve-Step Recovery Program and found that he compared himself to the worst drinking stories, leading him to believe, "I am not that bad." Therefore, once he started attending the peer support meetings, he was better able to identify with other dentists' and doctors' stories and then acclimate back into a Twelve-Step Recovery Program.

EARLY SOBRIETY

I enjoyed the way I felt sober. I enjoyed discovering a new way of life. I enjoyed the process of recovery. I wasn't just not drinking, I was discovering myself.
—recovering alcoholic

Early sobriety is a bitch.
—recovering alcoholic, seven months sober

It is hard to remain teachable, especially when you've been a success.
—Dr. Daniel Gatlan, Executive Director of Renaissance Rehab[47]

Just as there are different paths to recovery, there are different experiences for individuals in early sobriety. Alcoholism penetrates so many aspects of an alcoholic's life and is "like the cup of water on your desk that spills and goes everywhere. You didn't think there was much water in that cup, but it ruins so much." Ironically, alcohol can also be the glue that holds HFAs' lives together, and when getting sober, HFAs are often surprised at how many aspects of their lives begin to fall apart. This pattern is the opposite of that for some low-bottom alcoholics who, after getting sober, often regain employment, housing, material possessions, friends, and family. Low-bottom alcoholics often report feeling better about themselves and begin to associate sobriety with feeling healthy and improved self-esteem. In contrast, HFAs may already be employed and have the possessions that low-bottom alcoholics have lost. Throughout early sobriety, many HFAs report being unable to handle the stress of their high-pressured careers and feel less capable when sober than they did when they were drinking—the opposite of what they expected. They feel that because they are now sober and doing the right thing, that they should be rewarded. Instead, what lies ahead is a difficult road to recovery for which they will have to work. Early sobriety challenges individuals to stay abstinent and fill the void once filled by alcohol with recovery program meetings, program material, spirituality, and sober peers. It signifies the beginning of changing old beliefs, behaviors, and lifestyle—leading individuals to embark on the process of finding their true selves.[48]

Throughout early sobriety, HFAs may experience common symptoms of untreated alcoholism, including the following:

- Cravings to drink alcohol daily, even if previous drinking was sporadic
- "Drunk dreams" of relapse that may even lead to hangover sensations upon waking up as well as feelings of shame and guilt lasting into the day
- Random mood swings, irritability, anxiety, sadness, and edginess that may be alleviated by going to recovery program meetings or talking to another sober alcoholic
- Cravings for sweet foods
- Difficulty sleeping
- Urges to act out sexually, have shopping binges, gamble, have workaholic tendencies, overeat, overexercise, and other compulsive behaviors
- Clinging to people, places, and things to feel better
- Thoughts that they are not alcoholic after previously concluding that they are
- Romanticizing drinking by remembering only the good times and forgetting the problems
- Feelings of emptiness and loneliness
- Fear of being around people or going places

HFAs are used to projecting an image of perfection on the outside. Therefore, when they get sober and begin to struggle, it is often difficult for them to be completely honest with group members, therapists, and loved ones about having a hard time. One HFA in early sobriety projected an image of being "happy, friendly, smiling and people pleasing," when on the inside, she was "dying." She found that people in her recovery program did not reach out to her because they were more apt to help those who were visibly sick and suffering. She found everything about early sobriety "really hard" and felt she lost her "best friend" (i.e., alcohol) in addition to close friends. During her first year of sobriety, she was not ready to stop drinking, and throughout her second year, she was "feeling my feelings...and fears were coming true." She felt herself growing and likened it to the "terrible twos."

Other HFAs experience what is commonly referred to as a *pink cloud* in early sobriety. A pink cloud is a point of overconfidence in which an individual notices positive changes in his or her life that indicate he or she is "succeeding" at staying sober.[49] Some alcoholics begin to feel better physically and are able to function better without hangovers—suddenly they feel a sober "high." However, pink clouds are temporary and can lead people to become complacent in terms of their recovery and in helping others because the lack of discomfort reduces the motivation to work toward recovery. One HFA recalled, "I felt extremely euphoric in early sobriety and physically cleansed." Another HFA stated that she had a pink cloud for about the first year of her sobriety, and then recovery became more challenging for her as she began to work the Twelve Steps and struggle emotionally.

Because HFAs have generally been successful in their lives, they sometimes feel that this will exempt them from having to expend much effort on their recovery. One HFA recalls that he went to recovery program meetings for about eight to nine months and did nothing else. He experienced emotional pain when his roommates moved out and his girlfriend broke up with him, and this motivated him to reach out for help from others in recovery. He also discovered Twelve-Step Recovery Program "young people" meetings, which allowed him to connect to other recovering alcoholics his age. Individuals who don't put effort into their recovery may experience a *sober bottom*, in which they realize that they need to listen to suggestions and make changes in their lives—or they will suffer.

Some HFAs transition well into early sobriety and become immediately active in their recovery program. One woman recalled that she was "pretty happy to be sober. I felt that I had finally figured out what was wrong with me. I had been so unhappy for so long....I really embraced the work in my recovery program—stepwork, service, and going to a lot of meetings. For the first time, I felt that I had real friends and I truly felt like I was somewhere I belonged." Another HFA attended her first meeting with her mother, who was also in recovery and warned her daughter that "you're probably going to be the youngest and you may not have done what they have done...but you need to identify and not compare." This mind-set allowed her to relate to the feelings that were shared in the meetings, instead of comparing her story to everyone else's. She was able to listen to stories of "men putting needles in their arms and Ivy League professors because we all feel the same....I'm just an alcoholic—I don't preface it with high-bottom." A man who became sober at a young age recalls that "from the beginning I identified with the emotions and not the losses...regardless of the losses, the things that bind us together are our emotions." Another HFA who got sober later in life recalls that "emotionally, I felt exuberant and very safe that I had come amongst people and principles that made sense and would not fail me.... Physically, I felt good after a few days and I had no harsh symptoms whatsoever. It took me about a week to learn how to fall asleep without passing out, or how to adjust to evenings without blackouts."

Many HFAs report that they compare their drinking "stories" to those of low-bottom alcoholics in Twelve-Step Recovery Programs. HFAs feed their alcoholism by focusing on how they are different or better than other alcoholics. Renault has commonly observed HFAs who believe the stereotype that all alcoholics are homeless and then become stuck thinking, "I'm not as bad as . . . " and "I didn't drink like them"—instead of focusing on their own sobriety. One HFA doctor admits that he had "professional arrogance" and didn't see himself as being "quite that bad" as the stories that he heard. However, he realized that he "wanted what they had" in terms of recovery. Another woman, who got sober at a young age, admits that "it was extremely difficult in the beginning, because I truly thought I was different. It took me at least one year of continuous sobriety to admit to my innermost self that I was alcoholic and like other members of my recovery program." One male HFA felt that he was different from other alcoholics in that "I am not selfish.... I care more about others than most alcoholics." Once he was able to ask for help, his outlook changed, and he began to make changes in his life and gain true self-awareness. A woman recalls that it took a long time to accept that she was alcoholic, feeling that is the "hard part about being an HFA—we haven't lost a lot." Another woman recalls that she cried in the back row her entire first meeting. She was in a room of forty people and most were working-class men. She came from "an upper-middle-class family and felt like this wasn't where I was supposed to be—I separated myself a great deal." She eventually found "young people" meetings and a sponsor who was also an HFA; this allowed her to see that "there were people like me, who were my age, who were trying to work on this disease." A sponsor is a sober alcoholic who leads another sober alcoholic through the Twelve Steps of recovery and also serves as a guide for navigating life in sobriety.

For some HFAs, their first days of consistent sobriety occur when they are in a rehab facility. Their early sobriety differs from those not in rehab in that there is less freedom and choice in participating in recovery. For these HFAs, the challenge begins when they have to apply the recovery skills learned in rehab to their real lives. One HFA, who had experienced chronic relapses, recalls that rehab led him to be "faced with myself," and he experienced many emotions that alcohol had numbed out. His belief that "real men don't cry" was challenged as he cried uncontrollably for the first time. Rehab for another HFA allowed him to begin the process of working on his issues, and he felt layers of himself being "peeled like an onion.... I wondered, how deep does this thing go?"

Some HFAs who would benefit from going to a detox facility choose not to; they typically experience extreme physical and psychological problems in early sobriety. One man described, "For approximately sixty days of early sobriety, I was physically overrun with acute anxiety attacks and physical pain from withdrawal and stress. My emotional status cycled between apathetic and suicidal, and I was practically incapable of communicating." He then became immersed in his recovery program and experienced "marked improvement in mood and hope . . . and then at five months I entered into a two-month angry phase."

For some individuals, the discomfort and angst of early sobriety can also lead them to relapse. Recovery is not a linear process, and some HFAs gain more confidence in themselves after staying sober for some time—and then their disease deludes them into thinking they can drink normally. After relapsing, some report that they are able to surrender to the idea that they are alcoholic and become more involved in their recovery program. One HFA recalls that after he relapsed, he returned to his recovery program feeling more stable, willing to talk about things that were bothering him, and more motivated to make the changes necessary to maintain recovery. Another HFA recalls that her relapse confirmed her inability to control her drinking, and she returned to her recovery program with renewed dedication.

BARRIERS TO TREATMENT

In our society, when you get cancer, people feel bad for you, and when you are an alcoholic, people get mad at you.

—recovering alcoholic

Most HFAs are out in the world suffering.

—Jim, recovering alcoholic

The fact that HFAs have a job, friends, and family who don't believe that they need treatment is a real challenge.

—Julie, recovering HFA

Only a small percentage of individuals who need treatment for alcohol-use disorders actually receive it. The U.S. Department of Health and Human Services National Survey on Drug Use and Health determined that 23.2 million people, or 9.5% of the population, aged twelve or older needed treatment for alcohol and/or drug use problems. However, of these, only 3.9 million received treatment—leaving 19.3 million individuals untreated. Of those who received treatment, about 2.5 million had alcohol-use disorders. In 2007, an NIAAA study concluded that 24% of alcoholics have received some type of treatment, a slightly lower rate than a decade ago. Those who receive treatment are, on average, thirty years old, which is an average of eight years after they developed their true dependence. The NIAAA's Division of Treatment and Recovery Research reports that alcohol and drug abuse treatment, when used, is more effective than treatment for many medical disorders.[50]

So, why are so few alcoholics receiving any form of treatment? The answer lies in understanding the barriers to receiving treatment. For HFAs, the level of their own denial is heightened by the denial of society, their loved ones, and their colleagues. One HFA believes that societal ignorance and denial about alcoholism filters down to the individuals with alcohol-use disorders, preventing them from getting treatment. He stated, "We tend to think that if the outside facade is what society defines as success, then I surely couldn't have any inside problems."

Most HFAs report that their families were in denial of their alcoholism. Renaud observes that some alcoholic's families have a negative image of alcoholism and they "don't want that issue in their family system"—leading them to ignore the problem. For other HFAs with family members who are low-bottom alcoholics, it becomes easy to be "compared" out of having a problem. One HFA with an alcoholic father recalls telling his brother, "I think that I might have a drinking problem," and his brother replied, "No, you're not like Dad." Another HFA felt that her alcoholic mother "set the bar low" for the family—leading her father to be in denial of his daughter's alcoholism. Other HFAs report that their family members may be aware of their alcoholism. However, these family members may have what one HFA doctor labels *secondary denial*, or being aware that someone is alcoholic but thinking that his or her alcoholism isn't that serious. He observed that his wife knew he was an alcoholic, but she believed that he was "not that bad of an alcoholic" because he was still functioning. Secondary denial often prevents loved ones from addressing this issue with HFAs, preventing them from getting treatment. Another trend for HFAs is that family members may not succeed in a treatment intervention because of their financial dependence on the alcoholic. This financial "leverage" may allow the HFA to continue drinking, despite the efforts of his or her family. After a family therapist staged an intervention for an HFA dentist with a lucrative career, a wife, and eight children, the dentist told his family, "If you don't like it, then you can leave." He concluded that they had "no leverage," and continued to drink.

Most HFAs are able to maintain their jobs while drinking alcoholically—contributing to their belief that they are "functioning" and not in need of help. One HFA reports that no one in the military had ever said he was an alcoholic. He reflects that the military culture in the early days of his career was such that colleagues would look out for each other, and "unless you crossed that line and screwed up, had a DUI, had domestic disputes, were drunk and disorderly, were picked up by the cops—anything that would flag you—then the attention would come down.... Up until that point, if people thought that I had a problem, they were not telling me."

Doctors have powerful influence over the beliefs of their patients. Therefore, when they are not properly trained, are in denial, or enable a patient's alcohol-use disorder, they are standing in the way of proper treatment. HFAs, in particular, may go undetected by their doctors, especially if they are not showing typical signs of alcoholism such as liver damage or physical withdrawal. However, doctors are not being adequately trained to recognize more subtle symptoms of alcoholism such as increased blood pressure, increased triglyceride levels, insomnia, and mood swings. The American Medical Association prepared a report that described the poor record of doctors in diagnosing alcohol-related problems in their patients, particularly in women. In addition, a study by CASA indicates that only one in seventeen doctors asked patients to complete an alcohol assessment. Without an alcohol usage screening, patients may be diagnosed with other conditions, and unnecessary medication may be prescribed—further masking the problem. Foster emphasized that doctors need better training in screening for, diagnosing, treating, and referring those with alcohol-use disorders to addiction specialists. She also feels that doctors need to understand that spiritually based recovery groups can be effective and that they should also have information about other support groups available for patients.[51] One HFA doctor has noticed that new doctors are recognizing alcoholism as a disease and are better at diagnosing it. However, they have difficulty persuading their patients to seek specialized help. Research has also shown that doctors may have stereotyped ideas of the alcoholic profile. A study conducted at the Johns Hopkins University Hospital concluded that doctors were less apt to consider that female patients may have a problem with alcohol if they had private insurance, a higher income, and education.[52]

Even mental health professionals may have preconceived images of alcoholic clients. Treadway has observed that therapists have "historically been huge enablers of people with substance abuse problems." He described a case of an active alcoholic who drank daily for fifteen years and reported that the subject of drinking "never came up" in sessions with his psychiatrist through the years. Cohen has observed that the training for addiction specialists is "spectacular," but addiction training is not a licensure requirement for psychologists, counselors, and social workers. One HFA recalls that soon after getting sober and attending a Twelve-Step Recovery Program, she said to her therapist, "Maybe I'm not an alcoholic." Her therapist agreed and replied, "You don't have an addictive personality," going on to speculate that this HFA was sober because she was "a Catholic who deprived herself." These statements led the HFA to relapse for about fourteen years—during which her alcoholism progressed dramatically. In another circumstance, an HFA dentist reported seeing three mental health professionals who did not address his alcoholism. He recalls going to a marital counselor through his church and stated several times that "I think my drinking may be a problem." However, his comments were ignored, and his drinking was never addressed. He then saw a psychiatrist for depression, was not honest about his drinking, and was prescribed medication. Finally, he saw another psychiatrist and admitted that his drinking was "an issue"; the topic was dismissed when the psychiatrist stated, "If I thought you had a problem, I would have an obligation to deal with it." The HFA believes that this minimization of his alcoholism by mental health professionals allowed his alcoholism to go untreated.

One study specifically examined barriers to alcoholism treatment, acknowledging that most people—both men and women—with alcohol-use disorders do not enter treatment. The reasons most frequently cited were "thought it was something you should be strong enough to handle" (28.9%), "didn't think their drinking problem was serious enough" (23.4%), "thought the problem would get better by itself" (20.1%), and "couldn't afford to pay the bill, were too embarrassed to discuss it with anyone, wanted to keep drinking or get drunk, didn't think anyone could help and were afraid of what their boss, friends, family or others would think" (8% to 12%).[53] This study also cites past literature that indicates denial is the most common reason that alcoholics do not seek treatment because "alcoholism nearly always refuses to see itself."[54] Several of the reasons listed previously are variations of denial, leading the researchers to suggest that "denial may serve not only to impede the treatment seeking process, but also to impede perception of a problem altogether."[55] In addition, women were found to hold the belief that their drinking is not the problem, but rather a symptom of another issue, crisis, or social situation. A study funded by an NIAAA grant further explored the concept of denial by asking "high-functioning middle-aged men" to label their own drinking pattern. The results overwhelmingly showed that none of the respondents who abused alcohol and only 12.5% with alcohol dependence identified themselves as even having a drinking problem. The researchers went on to conclude that patients may claim to be moderate to heavy "social drinkers" to clinicians, but may in fact be alcoholic.[56] HFAs often display impenetrable denial that is tightly woven into the idea that their day-to-day functioning at work, their overall success in life, their maintenance of friendships, and/or their family exempts them from being alcoholic. It is the idea that alcoholism and being high functioning are mutually exclusive that must be dispelled through education, the media, and health care professionals to challenge HFA denial.

Some HFAs may transcend their denial and admit that they are alcoholic but may not be ready to get sober. According to the Transtheoretical Model, developed by Dr. Carlo C. DiClemente and Dr. James Prochaska, there are five addiction "stages of change" that can be applied to recovery from alcoholism:

- *Precontemplation stage.* Little or no consideration of changing the current drinking patterns or behaviors in the foreseeable future
- *Contemplation stage.* Examining current drinking patterns or behaviors and the potential for change, possibly in a pro-con analysis
- *Preparation stage.* Making a commitment to take action to change drinking behaviors and develop a plan and strategy for that change
- *Action stage.* Executing the plan, changing drinking behaviors, and beginning to create a new way of living sober
- *Maintenance.* Sobriety is sustained for a lengthy period of time and becomes integrated into the individual's lifestyle

If an HFA is in a Precontemplation or Contemplation stage and others are expecting the HFA to be in the Preparation or Action stage for getting treatment, there will be resistance. It is important for loved ones and treatment professionals to be aware of the stage of change the HFA is in so they may meet the HFA. To move from the Contemplation to the Preparation stage of entering treatment, HFAs must establish significant reasons to motivate themselves toward treatment. Taking action toward treatment requires an incredible amount of motivation and energy and is virtually impossible when the person is completely unwilling to make changes.[57]

Many HFAs are not aware of what various types of treatment may entail. Through movies, books, myths, and word of mouth, they start to form negative images of the treatment environment and worry that they may not fit in. One HFA recalls that he was reluctant to attend a recovery program support group because "I didn't have the homeless person picture of a Twelve-Step Recovery Program, but I had the Stuart Smally self-help book image." It is important that the public is properly informed about what various forms of treatment programs are like. It is common for HFAs to admit that their original ideas about recovery program support groups were negative, but after attending, they realized that their preconceptions were wrong.

The research study on barriers to treatment also concluded that several reasons for failing to seek treatment were related to the stigma associated with having alcohol-use disorders. National findings of the U.S. Department of Health and Human Services have documented "stigma" as the reason for about 20% of individuals with alcohol and/or substance abuse issues failing to pursue treatment.[58] The acceptance of the disease concept of alcoholism is thought to minimize the stigma associated with alcoholism—instead, it may lead individuals to avoid taking responsibility for their alcoholism. This study recommends public education about the need to take responsibility to overcome alcoholism, even though the cause may be beyond an individual's control.[59] The fear of being labeled an alcoholic often propels HFAs to cling to the skid row image of the alcoholic. This allows them to subconsciously compare themselves to the worst case scenario—leading them to feel better than those they define as real alcoholics. Although there may be shame for HFAs in acknowledging that they are alcoholic, once they learn the truth about the disease and connect with other sober HFAs, the stigma may be lifted. Ultimately, addiction experts and the medical community influence people negatively by not addressing or defining characteristics of HFAs—for this allows both the alcoholic stereotype and the stigma to live on.

"HINDSIGHT" REFLECTIONS OF THE AUTHOR

Past Journal Entry: February 10, 2004, Age 27—Early Sobriety
God, let me never forget the evils of alcoholism and the realization that I made the right choice. I chose the right path—somehow—through all of the chaos and highs, I managed to let the pain seep through enough to get sober—but for the grace of God. For you don't realize the pain until you stop—you almost don't realize the misery unless you are separated from it. The lure mystifies me and the simplicity of removing alcohol from one's life is so complicated at the same time.

Early Sobriety

I received an alcohol assessment by an addiction specialist at a local hospital at the recommendation of my doctor. The conclusion was that I needed to get abstinence-based treatment, considering that I had already tried Moderation Management therapy and various other means to control my drinking. The addiction specialist suggested I try a recovery program support group in addition to individual therapy. She added that if I was then unable to stay sober, I would need to attend a day treatment program at a rehab center. This conversation was an eye-opener.

I researched several alcohol recovery programs and decided that I wanted to go to one that was spiritually based. When I had abstained from alcohol in the past, I had sensed a spiritual void. Therefore I was drawn to a program that was designed to heal that part of me and decided to attend a Twelve-Step Recovery Program meeting about a week later.

Past Journal Entry: February 15, 2004, Age 27—My First Meeting

I went to the recovery meeting on Saturday night and was completely amazed at the number of young people that continued to pour into the room.... Some of the speakers' words stuck with me. One girl stated, "Every day I have to convince myself that I am an alcoholic." I feel that way, too, because sometimes I think that I can drink normally, but then I am back at square one. The topic was "one day at a time"—I understand it and it does make the task of sobriety seem more feasible.... I really like the idea of a Saturday or Friday night meeting because those nights are my hardest times. I plan on attending other meetings, but I felt at home at this one.

I felt so many emotions at my first meeting, including the underlying fear that I might see someone to whom I was connected professionally. I also had the urge to justify being at the meeting and explain to others that my life was not falling apart—that I was not like "them"—that I was a "successful professional." I felt pure amazement that there were so many young people in the Boston area sober on a Saturday night! I had luckily been informed about "young people" meetings from the addiction specialist—being around other sober alcoholics my age on Friday and Saturday nights allowed me not to feel so alone.

At this point in my recovery, I believed that I was going to need recovery meetings only on the weekends because that was when I drank most often. I had no idea how much effort true recovery would entail or that I would need meetings during the week. Meetings allowed me to see the truth about my addiction and bring moments of peace into my day. Once I began attending, I was gradually able to see through the fog of my alcoholism and distorted thinking. Alcoholism was a voice within my mind that told me to act and think in a particular way to keep it alive. This Twelve-Step Recovery Program helped me become aware of this internal dialogue and separate the truth from the lies. As I attended more meetings, I began to let go of my own ideas and realized that I needed to surrender "to the winning team." The battle was over, and I could finally acknowledge that alcohol was more powerful than any of my thoughts or self-will.

Past Journal Entry: February 23, 2004
I feel like I am in a bit of shock from the last few weeks. I am making a commitment to abstain from my favorite activity—drinking. I have tried everything and it has come to this. Have I been in denial? Me—who tries to admit everything, all of the time. But I did a good job of repressing things this time—wow.

Is an era of my life over? Am I really consenting to not drink? What the fuck?!? It is my escape, my rebellion, my "I don't care place," my friend, my enemy, my guaranteed good time and I am saying good-bye at age 27. It's been a great run, a fucking blast, the best and worst times of my life—gone. The crap shoot is over, and it is time to find another Nirvana.

After several meetings, I was flooded by memories of my past and fearful about my future sober life. I began to absorb the fact that this was the last stop for me regarding my drinking. I wanted this recovery program to work so that I didn't have to get more intensive treatment, but part of me was in shock that my drinking life was over.

Past Journal Entry: February 29, 2004
Humility—I am an alcoholic. I pray every day that I remember how awful I have felt, the danger that I put myself in, the frustration and sense of failure that a relapse brings me, the urgency of staying sober—that *I am an alcoholic.*

I spoke last night at the meeting for the first time. The topic was humility. I stated for the first time out loud that "I am an alcoholic." Humility is that I am speaking at a Twelve-Step Recovery Program meeting. I fear a loss of humility because that is what one speaker attributed his relapses to. Alcoholism is humbling because everything in your life can be in order, but this one factor can take you down. I actually had needed my mother to tell me that I was an alcoholic, because it helped to humble me.

How have I repressed all of these things for so long, then get sad and down on myself and then do it again? One girl told me that your brain forgets the suffering and only remembers the pleasure—that the bad memories slide off your brain like Teflon. Another girl told me that each day she prays for humility, and to remember all that she has done under the influence of alcohol—never to forget. She said that is why you have to keep going to meetings—so that you see what newcomers have done because of their drinking as a reminder of your past.

Humility was a concept that I had never thought about before getting sober. I realized that my successes in the outside world were not going to guarantee my sobriety. I also feared becoming overconfident in my recovery and thinking that I didn't need to do the work required to recover. At times, I believed that because I hadn't lost things on the outside, I needed to do only half the work that low-bottom alcoholics had to do. Slowly, I began to see that I had the same disease as everyone else in those meetings, although it may not have progressed as theirs had. I imagined what people in the meeting were thinking about me, and I was convinced that I had the highest bottom out of everyone there. At times, I did not feel that my drinking story was bad enough for me to be there. However, I listened to speakers explain in metaphors that "if you are on a train that you know is going to crash, you might as well get off early" and "the alcoholism elevator only goes one direction—downward, and you can get off at any floor." These ideas began to sink in and I was able to accept that if I did not deal with my alcoholism now, it would eventually ruin my life.

Past Journal Entry: March 16, 2004

I was really cranky last week—I am not sure why. I did *not* want to be at the bar—low tolerance for the belligerence there. I felt rather disturbed at the excessive drinking around me because it was a reminder of what I'd done and how so many others engaged in this behavior because of ignorance, denial, addiction, and the search for a good time. It felt like I was being assaulted over and over again, and I wanted it to stop.

During this night out at a bar with my friends, I felt like I was standing still in the midst of complete chaos. People were binge drinking the way that I had wanted to in the past. Men were drunk and staggering into me as others pushed through to get to the bar. The stale stench of beer filled my sinuses and I just wanted to be home. I felt that I was in a toxic environment of people harming themselves with alcohol. For about the first year of my sobriety, I dressed up in my "club clothes," attended my Friday and Saturday night recovery meetings, and then went out with friends to the bars (without drinking). I could not fully let go of my drinking life and didn't want to feel left out of my social circle. I experienced different phases of tolerance for bars and for being around people who were drinking—some nights I felt better than others. The longer I remained sober, the less I wanted to be at a bar. In general, I have found it more triggering to be around people who are binge drinking and taking shots than to be around those casually sipping on a drink. I always drank for effect, and I envied those who still drank the way that I wanted to— excessively.

My mood and physical health also fluctuated as I remained sober. I would look for explanations—the answer was that I was in the midst of early sobriety. I felt like I should be feeling healthy and being rewarded for not drinking—for doing the right thing. I had days when I was in a rage—blaring music as I drove past bars that I knew I could never drink at again. I was angry that my toy was taken away from me and thought life would now be dull and full of suffering—that I was now paying the price for my years of drinking.

Past Journal Entry: April 30, 2004

The thing about alcoholism is that it becomes enmeshed in a person—deceptive and clever. I knew that I drank too much, but I couldn't see the whole picture and some around me couldn't either. I think about drinking every day now that I don't drink.

Throughout the first three to four months of my sobriety, I was shocked at how often I thought about drinking. I had not been a daily drinker, yet I now obsessed about drinking alcohol every single day. Unlike my periods of abstinence in the past, when I knew that I would be able to resume drinking, entering into a recovery program cast finality over my drinking. Reality was setting in—a lifetime without drinking ever again? I began to believe that sobriety would be possible only through the support of this Twelve-Step Recovery Program, one day at a time.

Others' Perceptions

Past Journal Entry: February 29, 2004
Suggestions and thoughts that several friends and acquaintances not in recovery have said to me:
   "You don't start drinking at noon; you can't really be an alcoholic."
   "I drink like an alcoholic, too, I just drink less . . . you should just try to drink less."
   "You should figure out the number of drinks that it takes for you to black out and drink a few less than that."

Soon after getting sober, I admitted to friends and family that I was an alcoholic and needed to be in a Twelve-Step Recovery Program. Some friends admitted they thought I had an alcohol problem, but that I was overreacting and didn't need to be in an abstinence-based recovery program. Others fully supported me and agreed that I needed to get sober. My mother had labeled me an alcoholic before I could admit it to myself. However, my father was unaware of the extent of my drinking, and I decided to open up to him to convince him that I was an alcoholic. At this time, I needed reassurance from my parents that I was alcoholic—fearing that any denial on their part would trigger me to relapse. Even later in my recovery, I have received a variety of responses when people realize that I am an alcoholic, including from a therapist who met me at a professional conference, and commented, "You don't look like an alcoholic; you look so put together." In time, I learned that the way people reacted to my being alcoholic and getting sober had to do with their own relationship to alcohol, their image of alcoholics, and what part of my drinking life they had been aware of.

Past Journal Entry: April 29, 2004
I feel tonight like it all makes sense. My friend summed it up—that part of me that she couldn't relate to was my drunken behavior that she tried to rationalize.... She began to cry as she realized the depth of the problem and all that she did not see. I didn't realize that she wasn't privy to so many years of my drinking—in fact I demonstrated self-control at times in front of her. She felt blind—like she should

have seen it—but I was a master at beating myself up the day after I drank so others didn't have to. It was instinctual, not premeditated. I feel like the pieces of this puzzle are all coming together. The behaviors that my friend couldn't relate to were a result of being alcoholic.

For the first eleven months of my sobriety, 90% of myself was convinced I was alcoholic and 10% was still in denial. When friends or family expressed doubt that I was alcoholic, it would feed into that powerful 10% of my mind that wanted to deny my alcoholism and continue drinking. Therefore I had to be careful about the conversations I had about this issue with people outside my recovery program because I was so vulnerable.

Early sobriety was a roller coaster of emotions and moods. I gradually learned that my reliance on outside things to make me feel complete was slowly letting me down. Removing alcohol from my life had disrupted my equilibrium—I was being forced to find a new sense of balance. It was clear that I needed to grow spiritually and learn to rely on God to recover fully.

8

FILLING THE VOID: SPIRITUALITY, RELIGION, AND THE BOTTLE

Alcoholics are really spiritual seekers who end up at the wrong address.

—anonymous

Spirituality and religion are powerful forces in the lives of most Americans and can provide a sense of meaning, purpose, and structure to an individual's life. In fact, 95% of Americans believe in God, 92% associate themselves with a specific religion,[1] 76% pray regularly,[2] and 26% practice meditation or relaxation techniques.[3] The true power of these beliefs has been demonstrated as individuals have claimed that spirituality and/or religion have saved their lives, transformed them, and healed them mentally and physically. Ironically, throughout history, people have been oppressed and wars have been fought over such beliefs.

Although the terms *spirituality* and *religion* are associated with each other, it is important to distinguish the differences. Religion can be characterized by "a set of particular beliefs about God or a Higher Power shared by a group of individuals, and the practices, rituals and forms of governance that define how those beliefs are expressed."[4] Spirituality is a hard to define construct, for it is experienced differently from person to person. For many, it is a deeply personal response and practice to connect with an outside force or something sacred. This outside force may be called any number of terms, including God, Allah, Jesus Christ, Shiva, Higher Power, the Universe, or it may not be labeled at all. The spiritual can often be understood better in metaphor than in the literal sense: "Although the wind is very powerful and you can feel its presence, in and of itself it cannot be seen. You know it is there by its effect on others. The great trees, the grasses and waves on the sea bend with its force. If you are aware of your surroundings, you know it is there long before you feel it. So it is with the ineffable."[5]

Religion can be a forum to develop a spiritual connection with whatever an individual considers to be his or her God(s). In contrast, some individuals may be religious in terms of their practices and family traditions but may not be spiritually connected to the God(s) of their understanding. Conversely, individuals may identify as spiritual but not be affiliated with a religion. Spirituality generally involves less structure than organized religion, and individuals may integrate it into their lives in their own unique ways. Despite their differences, spirituality and religion may offer individuals an unparalleled source of fulfillment, healing, and serenity.

Spirituality, Religion, and Healing

"The spiritual" is what makes us wholly human. It holds our experiences together, shapes them into a whole, gives them meaning, allows them—and us—to be whole. Without the spiritual, however physically brave or healthy or strong we may be, however mentally smart or clever or brilliant we may be, however emotionally integrated or mature we may be, we are somehow not "all there."

—Ernest Kurtz and Katherine Ketcham, *The Spirituality of Imperfection*[6]

Addiction keeps a person in touch with the god. . . . At the very point of the vulnerability is where the surrender takes place—that is where the god enters. The god comes through the wound.

—Marion Woodman[7]

Modern medicine continues each year to advance, and treatment and cures for diseases never thought possible are now a reality. This technology and knowledge may lead individuals to put extreme trust in their doctors and, at times, to expect the impossible. Dr. Herbert Benson is an associate professor of medicine at Harvard Medical School and the founding president of the Mind/Body Medical Institute (M/BMI), now known as the Benson-Henry Institute for Mind/Body Medicine, affiliated with Massachusetts General Hospital. He has pioneered extensive research studies linking spiritual practices, such as meditation, to improved health and healing from medical conditions such as chronic pain, stress-related illnesses, and cardiac issues. He was one of the first Western physicians to bring spirituality and healing into medicine. A separate analysis of forty-two studies found that religious involvement increased life expectancy by 29%[8] and decreased the incidence of high blood pressure and depression. Supporting Benson's work, this research found that religious and spiritual meditation have been linked to a plethora of health benefits, including decreased chronic pain, cholesterol levels, and pain and anxiety in cancer patients.[9]

The foundation of Benson's work is the Relaxation Response (RR), a physiological state brought on by meditation that is popular with the general public. Research indicates that the RR is highly effective in counteracting the effects of the fight or flight stress response, which triggers the secretion of adrenaline, noradrenaline, and cortisol. Over time, the release of these stress hormones can lead to anxiety, mild to moderate depression, premenstrual syndrome, heart attacks, insomnia, infertility, and many more conditions. Benson reports that there are no effective treatments for the stress response—but that "we all have within us" the opposite reaction—the RR. He adds that to evoke the RR, it is crucial that individuals break the train of everyday thoughts. There are two steps to eliciting the RR: first, repeating a word, prayer, secular phrase, or muscular activity, and second, disregarding everyday thoughts that come to mind and returning to the repetition.

Benson's original work showed that the most common way the RR was evoked was through the repetition of prayers in the traditions of Christianity, Judaism, Islam, Hinduism, Buddhism, and other religions. In his book *Beyond the Relaxation Response,* Benson presented the concept of the *faith factor,* which combines the RR with an individual's personal set of beliefs to create inner peace that leads to "enhanced well-being."[10] Faith, in contrast to religion and spirituality, is "trust in and loyalty to images and realities of power" and may or may not be related to religion.[11] Benson firmly believes that "when you let yourself focus, and get your harried mind out of the way of your body's natural healing ability, calling on beliefs that mean the most to you in life, a peace that defies description may be possible."[12] Benson speculates that the use of prayer in recovery program meetings such as Alcoholics Anonymous (A.A.) may evoke the RR, lower cortical activity in the brain, and allow individuals to listen and better absorb recovery program strategies.

In addition to individual spiritual and religious practices, faith-based communities also contribute to overall well-being. Benson reports that the fellowship offered in spiritual or religious communities and support groups can be "restorative" for the mind and the body. A review of studies indicates that "the social support, sense of belonging, and convivial fellowship engendered by religion 'serve to buffer the adverse effects of stress and anger... [and] may trigger a multifactorial sequence of biological processes leading to better health.'" Research findings have shown that high levels of social connection from family or friends can lead to decreased mortality. A study conducted at Stanford University School of Medicine and the University of California, Berkeley, proved that ten years after breast cancer treatment, women who had been involved in a support group lived eighteen months longer than those who did not.[13] A Dartmouth College Medical School study found that patients undergoing heart surgery who participated in community and social groups were three times more likely to survive. Benson recommends that religious and spiritual institutions help their members to get "ample doses" of social interaction in addition to faith. In fact, research indicates that social isolation can actually lead to serious health problems.[14]

The National Center on Addiction and Substance Abuse (CASA) at Columbia University's research findings indicate that participating in spiritual or religious social networks decreases alcohol and drug usage. The religious values and belief systems of a family have been found to have a protective effect on youth. Specifically, a father's belief in God has a substantial effect on the alcohol and drug use of adolescent girls. Parents' church attendance is linked to having children with a less frequent alcohol usage rate and a more negative view of using alcohol. In addition, children are more likely to attend religious services when their parents do, and teens who consider religion important are less likely to use drugs. CASA's teen survey found that those who reported that none of their friends attended religious services had four times the risk of alcohol and drug use than those who reported that most or all of their friends attended services. Youth who decide to use drugs are more likely to distance themselves from their religion. Adults also benefit from religious and social groups in that they can serve as a "protective factor in both prevention and recovery."[15] These social networks create a sense of belonging and being part of something beyond oneself. CASA found that the effects of Twelve-Step Recovery Programs stretch beyond the spiritual component in that participants may be healed and supported by the group dynamics and group process as well.[16]

ALCOHOL: THE QUICK FIX

Addiction represents the ultimate effort to control, the definitive demand for magic... and the final failure of spirituality. Turning to the "magic" of chemicals signifies the desperate (and doomed) attempt to fill a spiritual void with a material reality—to make "magic" a substitute for miracle.
—Ernest Kurtz and Katherine Ketcham, *The Spirituality of Imperfection*[17]

Alcohol is a powerful force in the life of an alcoholic. So omnipotent is the effect of this substance that the alcoholic chooses it over his or her friends, loved ones, and children—it trumps any earthly entity. In general, most alcoholics believe that if something is wrong within them, it can be "fixed" by something outside of them. Because drinking becomes a way to avoid dealing with problems, it can stunt emotional and spiritual growth. Dr. Elvin Morton Jellinek, an expert in alcoholism theory and treatment, and the developer of the disease concept of alcoholism, believes that "drunkenness can be a kind of shortcut to the higher life, the [attempt to] achieve a higher state without an emotional and intellectual effort."[18] In fact, many alcoholics explain that "right from the start, the feeling they got from alcohol was 'magic'—instant, fabulous, incredible. With no work and little time invested, a drink brought them face to face and heart to heart with divinity."[19] Psychologist William James describes the mystical qualities of alcohol in that "the sway of alcohol over mankind is unquestionably due to its power to stimulate the mystical faculties of human nature, usually crushed to earth by the cold facts and dry criticism of the sober hour. Sobriety diminishes, discriminates, and says no; drunkenness expands, unites, and says yes. It is in fact the great exciter of the *Yes* function in man."[20] It is as though alcohol has the ability to take individuals into an alternative consciousness where there are no limits, and being sober is the letdown that brings one back to reality.

Alcohol typically has a biphasic or twofold effect on normal drinkers in that they feel pleasant effects, such as sociability, increased energy, relaxation, and/or a sense of well-being, up until their blood alcohol level is 0.055 (on average, several drinks paced slowly). After this level, the second phase begins, in which the drinker may begin to feel sluggish, nauseous, dizzy, and/or uncoordinated.[21] Conversely, binge drinking alcoholics report that they tend not to experience or remember the negative feelings and symptoms of the second phase—instead, with each additional drink, they may continue to feel euphoric and then either black out or pass out.

For a while, alcoholics believe they have found the magic "cure"—alcohol allows them to feel comfortable in social situations, brings excitement into their lives, and creates a false sense of nirvana. Gradually, alcohol becomes more and more important in the lives of alcoholics, and they view it as the solution to any and all problems as well as an escape from the mundane. The *Big Book* describes the alcoholic experience of drinking in the following way: "The sensation is so elusive that, while they admit it is injurious, they cannot after a time differentiate the true from the false. To them, their alcoholic life seems the only normal one. They are restless, irritable and discontented, unless they can again experience the sense of ease and comfort which comes at once by taking a few drinks."[22] It is as though they are trying to force a temporary and artificial state of mind to become permanent and real. Active alcoholics may use alcohol as their life map and drinking as their way of relieving pain and finding a sense of wholeness—but it is the wrong map. One alcoholic observed, "The drinking alcoholic is trying to find his way around on Earth with this beautifully detailed map of Venus."[23]

In many ways, alcoholics begin to worship alcohol. However, it is a dead end, and many high-functioning alcoholics (HFAs) report feeling hollow inside and empty. Eventually, they are left with shame and guilt from their drunken actions. Many alcoholics report that they had a hole in their soul that they tried to fill with alcohol and other external vices—but they discovered that the hole is "God-sized" and that it can only be filled spiritually. One HFA reports that "it was spiritual emptiness that got me sober." Dr. Carl Jung, an innovator of psychoanalytic thought and a colleague of Sigmund Freud, describes an alcoholic client: "His craving for alcohol was the equivalent, on a low level, of the spiritual thirst of our being for wholeness, expressed in medieval language: the union with God."[24] This cycle of turning to alcohol to fill a void actually exacerbates feelings of emptiness within the alcoholic: "The search for 'the quick fix,' inevitably unfulfilled by drugs and unsated by material things, leaps next to spiritual realities and the search for 'instant spirituality'—some sort of quick 'spiritual fix.' It is no wonder, then, that 'locating the divinity in drugs' becomes a kind of spiritual death."[25]

SPIRITUALITY, RELIGION, AND ALCOHOL USAGE: THE CONNECTION

Too often clergy and physicians, religion and science, are ships passing in the night. When we separate the worlds of medicine and spirituality, we deny a host of individuals help that may aid their recovery and ease their pain. . . . If ever the sum were greater than the parts it is in combining the power of God, religion and spirituality with the power of science and professional medicine to prevent and treat substance abuse and addiction.

—Joseph Califano Jr., chairman and president of CASA[26]

Addiction experts generally agree that spirituality and religion are important in recovery from alcoholism. Vaillant, in his book *The Natural History of Alcoholism,* writes, "In the treatment of alcoholism, Karl Marx's aphorism, 'religion is the opiate of the masses' masks an enormously important therapeutic principle. Religion may actually provide relief that drug abuse only promises... alcoholics and victims of other seemingly incurable habits feel defeated, bad and helpless.... If they are to recover, powerful new sources of self-esteem and hope must be discovered. Religion is one such source."[27] Mulligan feels that spirituality and religion are "important for those who have that belief system," and she encourages clients in religious communities to use those supports. However, for those alcoholics who are not spiritual, she finds that it is important that they believe in "something outside of them" to recover. Cohen emphasizes that spirituality and religion can be a resource and a support system—a "place where people can gather more strength." She has found that the religious practices around forgiveness and rebirth have been healing for alcoholics because of the negative consequences associated with alcoholism. Duda expressed, "I don't know how people do it without this energy or a force greater than themselves," and added that this force does not have to be called "God." Scorzelli feels that it is an advantage for recovery when alcoholics believe in some type of Higher Power. Caron believes that it is "paramount," and he has observed that "for many people the rediscovery or birth of their faith in God through the Twelve Steps helped them to heal." Levy places less emphasis on spirituality and religion in recovery and believes that "for some it may be useful and not as relevant for others," adding that it is important for alcoholics to find "some meaning in life."

Most of the research on spiritually based recovery programs has been conducted on twelve-step programs. The research findings of CASA further validate the connection between spirituality, religion, and alcohol usage, concluding the following:

- Adults who do not find religious beliefs important are over one and a half times more likely to use alcohol and three times more likely to binge drink
- Adults who have never attended religious services are two times as likely to drink and seven times more likely to binge drink
- Teens who do not have religious beliefs are about three times more likely to binge drink
- Teens who have never attended a religious service are two times as likely to drink and three times more likely to binge drink
- College students who are not religious report higher levels of drinking and binge drinking than those of either Catholic or Protestant religious affiliation
- Individuals who attend spiritually based support groups, such as Twelve-Step Recovery Programs, in addition to treatment are more likely to maintain sobriety
- Alcoholics doing well in recovery often display stronger degrees of faith and spirituality than those who relapse[28]

In general, CASA found that participation in a religious or spiritual practice can create a feeling of belonging, decreasing the need for individuals to turn to alcohol or drugs and providing support in resisting them. Another explanation for some of these research findings is that religions such as Judaism and Christianity expect the use of alcohol to be moderate, while Islam forbids the use of alcohol altogether. Therefore individuals affiliated with these religions may choose to abstain or drink minimally to adhere to these expectations. Additionally, CASA found that "individuals may be less likely to use substances because their personal connection with a Higher Power fills the need that makes substance use unnecessary or provides hope for the future and strength to resist the opportunity to use substances."[29] Another scholarly synthesis reviewed a variety of studies and combined their results, concluding that religious factors led to a decrease in alcohol use in sixteen of eighteen studies and in 89% of subjects.[30] In addition, research by the M/BMI has indicated that regular practice of meditation is associated with decreased drug abuse.[31]

Almost all of the HFAs interviewed were brought up in religious families, mainly denominations of Christianity. However, most stated that they never truly believed the religion of their upbringing, and others stopped believing in their religion before entering high school. Specifically, one HFA reported having a "falling out with the church," and another started to "hate God." Two HFAs recall losing their faith while in college; one became "disillusioned in college and angry at God," and another began to feel "too intellectual for God." Several maintained religious affiliation throughout their lives, two male HFAs reported almost entering the priesthood when younger, and a female HFA considered being a nun but ruled that option out after she lost her virginity when drunk. A few HFAs considered themselves purely spiritual. Those who felt religion was forced on them when they were younger did express initial hesitation about involving themselves in a spiritually based recovery program. In addition, HFAs tend to have an exaggerated sense of their own ability to fix things and to be in control. Spirituality connotes an element of surrender to which they may react. Despite the relationship, or lack thereof, with organized religion, spirituality, and/or a belief in a Higher Power of their own conception, these HFAs have been able to immerse themselves in a Twelve-Step Recovery Program and stay sober.

One research study focused on how individuals' belief in spirituality and religion affects their twelve-step program involvement and found that these beliefs indirectly promote longer-term involvement in twelve-step groups as well as "enhanced awareness during moments of temptation, allowing individuals to learn and practice adaptive coping responses."[32] Another study concluded that individuals with no religious preference may be more likely to attend twelve-step meetings, indicating that strong religious beliefs may actually be a barrier to this type of treatment.[33] A research study published in the *Journal of Studies on Alcohol* found that "an incompatible match between the patient's level of spirituality and the spiritual orientation of the program did not result in premature termination of treatment" and did not affect abstinence rates.[34]

Patients in nonspiritual programs who had low levels of spirituality had poor treatment outcomes. Therefore the researchers concluded that regardless of specific belief systems, individuals will benefit from involvement in a spiritually based recovery program.[35] In fact, newcomers to twelve-step programs may misinterpret the spiritual nature of the programs as being religious or holy. For alcoholics who are feeling shame and guilt about their pasts, this stereotype may turn them off initially from the program because they don't want to feel like a sinner or less than others. However, they soon may learn the truth of the program—that spirituality does not lie in being perfect, but instead in accepting one's imperfections.[36]

SPIRITUAL AND RELIGIOUS EXPERIENCES

I drank to find something outside of myself that was exciting—that made life less mundane. I thought alcohol could take me there . . . a spiritual experience for me is to be content with showing up and not always looking for some transcendental moment.

—recovering alcoholic

What is the key component of both spirituality and religion that allows alcoholics to recover and leads others to desire alcohol less? People generally turn to both in times of pain, in search for meaning, in attempts to grow and change, and in yearning for peace. Many report that spiritual and religious experiences are the core phenomena that have changed their lives in a multitude of ways. There are many documented descriptions, types, and results of such experiences, although science has not been able to pinpoint their source.

For individuals to recover from addictions, they need to change their thinking so that they do not repeat old behaviors. All recovery programs for alcoholism intend to create changes within an individual from the cognitive and behavioral level to the spiritual level. Many researchers and experts in the field of addiction believe that alcoholics cannot think their way out of alcoholism and are powerless over alcohol. Therefore change, and even hope, need to come from a force outside of them. Twelve-step programs, specifically the Twelve Steps, are designed to help individuals connect to a power greater than themselves that can lead to permanent change and recovery. Ultimately, it is through spiritual experiences and, eventually, a spiritual awakening that many individuals either begin to sense this connection or gradually change in ways not possible through their own will.

Spiritual and religious experiences have been defined and described in different ways by various people throughout history. The *Big Book* categorizes these experiences into two types. The first type is what many may imagine and expect when they hear the terms *spiritual* and *religious experience* and may manifest "in the nature of sudden and spectacular upheavals" that are "followed at once by a vast change in feeling and outlook." However, the second type is what most members of twelve-step programs experience and what James has labeled the "educational variety" because "they develop slowly over a period of time.... He finally realizes that he has undergone a profound alteration in his reaction to life; that such a change could hardly have been brought about by himself alone...they have tapped an unsuspected inner resource which they presently identify with their own conception of a Power greater than themselves." It is believed that the awareness of this power is the "essence" of a spiritual experience.[37]

Spiritual and religious experiences have also been explored in contexts other than addiction. Benson has found that most everyone can have these types of experience, and he conceptualizes them as "extraordinary and magical events...the converging of time and circumstance so logic-defiant that one cannot help but feel these events were divinely directed...a life change that comes at precisely the time you need it, or an image you see in a cloud formation." Benson has observed that 25% of those who practice the RR have had spiritual experiences that include "an overwhelming sense of a power, a force, an energy, God if you will," and report having fewer medical symptoms. Elizabeth Gilbert, journalist and author of the *New York Times* best seller *Eat, Pray, Love*, eloquently describes a spiritual experience that took place while meditating at an ashram in India, stating,

> I suddenly understood the workings of the universe completely, I left my body, I left the room, I left the planet, I stepped through time and I entered the void.... The void was a place of limitless peace and wisdom. The void was conscious and intelligent. The void was God, which means that I was inside God.... I was both a tiny piece of the universe and exactly the same size as the universe.... It wasn't hallucinogenic, what I was feeling. It was the most basic of events. It was heaven, yes. It was the deepest love I'd ever experienced, beyond anything I could have previously imagined, but it wasn't euphoric. It wasn't exciting.... It was just obvious. Like when you've been looking at an optical illusion for a long time, straining your eyes to decode the trick, and suddenly your cognizance shifts and there—now you can clearly see it!—the two vases are actually two faces. And once you've seen through the optical illusion, you can never not see it again.[38]

Benson describes an experience that athletes refer to as being in the "zone," which sports psychologists have observed when athletes "experience great happiness, a sense of timelessness, effortlessness and positive thinking."[39] One tennis player describes the zone as "so complete and intense that it evokes a state of almost semiconscious euphoria—one that many believe bears a resemblance to hypnosis, and enables a top player to achieve his or her peak performance."[40] In addition, Benson distinguishes more intense and sudden spiritual experiences by labeling them as *peak experiences*. Dr. Stanley R. Dean, professor of psychiatry at the University of Miami, Florida, stated that these peak experiences "produce a superhuman transmutation of consciousness that defies description. The mind, divinely intoxicated, literally reels and trips over itself, groping and struggling for words of sufficient exultation and grandeur to portray the transcendental vision. As yet we have no adequate words."[41]

Benson discourages patients from striving for these rare peak experiences because he feels that these expectations interfere with the focus necessary to induce the RR. He has found that patients have had a wide variety of peaceful and invigorating sensations through the RR. He has also noted that sacred experiences are also reachable in people's lives and that a past *Newsweek* survey reported 45% of Americans sensed the sacred during meditation, 68% at the birth of a child, and 26% during sex.[42]

Spiritual experiences can have a powerful impact on an individual but may not have a lasting effect. One HFA had a "lightning bolt spiritual experience" in rehab. However, when he returned home, he was still in emotional pain, which motivated him to work the Twelve Steps that are intended to lead to a spiritual awakening—a more permanent change state. Other terms have been used to describe a spiritual awakening, including *psychic change, conversion, transformation,* and *rebirth.* Some terms have more of a religious connotation, but these experiences can be universal and not unique to those with religious affiliations. The Twelve Steps are designed to create this type of awakening, which leads to recovery from alcoholism. The *Big Book* describes a spiritual awakening as "a personality change sufficient to bring about recovery from alcoholism."[43] The book *Twelve Steps and Twelve Traditions,* commonly known as the *Twelve and Twelve,* summarizes that "Maybe there are as many definitions of spiritual awakenings as there are people who have them. But certainly each genuine one has something in common with all the others... When a man or a woman has a spiritual awakening, the most important meaning of it is that he has now become able to do, feel, and believe that which he could not do before on his unaided strength and resources alone... He finds himself in possession of a degree of honesty, tolerance, unselfishness, peace of mind, and love of which he thought himself quite incapable."[44]

Another type of long-lasting spiritual awakening is described in Benson's book *The Breakout Principle,* which aims to guide readers to activate a mind-body impulse that can break past mental patterns. Benson describes a *Breakout* as an "*ongoing* state of improved health, self-awareness, and more productive relationships."[45] He adds that many individuals have experienced a Breakout after prayer or "an encounter with a divine presence."[46] In addition, he reports that many individuals have begun their journey to overcoming problems with alcohol or drugs from a Breakout event. There are four stages of a Breakout: (1) a hard mental or physical struggle; (2) pulling the breakout trigger or letting go and releasing; (3) breakout proper, coupled with a peak experience; and (4) returning to a "new normal" state, including ongoing improved performance and mind-body patterns.[47] Benson has found that a breakout can lead to *peak transcendence,* or a more permanent awakening, based on common features described in scientific and historical literature as well as in interviews with those who report such experiences, including the following:

- *A sense of unity.* Barriers may dissipate and individuals may feel strong feelings of oneness with nature, other people, or God; in addition, there may be a sense of the mind, body, and soul integrating

- *A sense of mystery.* Conviction that there is something beyond
- *A new motivation.* Strong spiritual insight stimulates a drive to change one's life significantly in a permanent way
- *An expanded or fluid sense of time.* Time may seem to stand still, move in slow motion, or speed up
- *A deep, lasting impression about the cosmos, about the overall meaning of life, about God, or about oneself.* Individuals see their place in the universe, leading them to humility as well as to a sense of purpose[48]

James, in his book *Varieties of Religious Experience*, spends several chapters describing conversion experiences. He acknowledges that it is difficult for either an observer or an individual who goes through a conversion to explain how the experience changes his or her entire constitution. One of his conceptions of this transformation is that "we have a thought, or we perform an act, repeatedly [such as drinking alcohol], but on a certain day the real meaning of the thought peals through us for the first time, or the act has suddenly turned into a moral impossibility. All we know is that there are dead feelings, dead ideas, and cold beliefs, and there are hot and live ones and then one grows hot and alive within us, everything has to re-crystallize about it."[49]

Any type of spiritual or religious awakening cannot help a person to recover from alcoholism if he or she continues to drink and refuses to surrender. James tells the story of an alcoholic who admitted that the deep pain he felt after heavy drinking episodes was remorse. He stated that he had never desired to have a religious reformation, but one day, he "felt God's love so powerfully" and had a conversion experience. He never made a promise to himself or to the God of his understanding that he was not going to drink, nor did he surrender, and "I took too much and came home drunk. . . . I felt ashamed of myself and got to my bedroom at once . . . weeping copiously."[50] Drinking blocks individuals from their connection to their source of spirituality. This story illustrates that even alcoholics who affiliate with a religion, consider themselves spiritual, or have had spiritual experiences may not maintain recovery without willingness and, for most, some form of a recovery program.

"HINDSIGHT" REFLECTIONS OF THE AUTHOR

Spirituality, Religion, and Healing

Spirituality was part of my life years before I entered a Twelve-Step Recovery Program. I was brought up in a family with a Roman Catholic mother and a Jewish father, neither of whom actively practiced their religions. They always conveyed to me that I had the freedom to choose my own religion or source of spirituality. As a young child, I had a sense that there was a "God," and I used to pray before I went to bed, especially if I was scared or wanted something. Throughout my twelve years of drinking, I felt more and more disconnected from any sense of spirituality. However, during the periods when I abstained for several months, this spiritual connection would return. In addition, my time as a patient and employee at the M/BMI allowed seeds of spirituality to be planted more deeply. I ended up at the clinic because I was suffering physically and psychologically and therefore was open to spiritual practices such as meditation and prayer. In fact, I experienced great healing when I was there as well as peace of mind. However, at the same time, I was drinking alcoholically. I experienced a true battle between drinking alcohol and spirituality. Sobriety has nourished my spiritual life, and the growth is continual. What began as an immature relationship with spirituality and God has grown and blossomed.

Past Journal Entry: January 16, 2001, Age 24

What is it about suffering that prompts creativity and a deep need for spirituality? Could it be the need for answers or the hope that the pain will end? Or the cruel realization that life is fleeting. Nothing is guaranteed and it takes losing something to realize that there are no guarantees that anything is forever. However frightening these realizations have been for me, they have changed my views about life so drastically.

I tended to be most deeply connected spiritually when I was in emotional or physical pain. I recall waking up alone in the middle of the night riddled with anxiety, but in the stillness, dark, and silence, I sensed that a comforting force was with me—which I chose to call "God."

Past Journal Entry: January 31, 2001

I also want to feel closer to God either through more meditation, temple, or other philosophical and/or psychological pursuits. I made this decision yesterday, and it was as though a cloud lifted—it could have been a coincidence... or maybe not.

Throughout the later years of my drinking, I found myself on a spiritual quest. I longed to work on this aspect of my being and sensed that relying on God would lead me to peace. However, I was not yet able to see that alcohol needed to be removed from my life to allow me to grow in that dimension.

Past Journal Entry: May 23, 2001

This world of peace within me has been possible because of the Mind/Body Medical Institute. This feeling of peace and clarity is accessible any time through yoga, running, and breathing. It is this peaceful place that makes the world of alcohol not so desirable. This world is fulfilling. Eventually, I hope to shift my cravings more and more toward the peaceful world within me... it will come.

The M/BMI was teaching me spiritual practices that were helping to heal physical conditions. However, I was blocked from the full benefits because I was still actively drinking. There was one part of me that yearned for the peace of spiritual practices, such as yoga and meditation, but the alcoholic part of me craved the artificial high of alcohol.

Past Journal Entry: November 28, 2001
Spirituality—God—I feel the sense of both in silence and at work, when I am truly working toward connecting and touching people's lives. That is how I know that I am on the right path in life professionally. Although I have distanced lately from God because of socializing (drinking), I know that He is still there—a source of strength for me to rely on when anxiety overwhelms me. In yoga, the stillness is a comfort and a stable sense of being.

I felt blessed in my career to be able to help others who were going through difficult times in their lives. I knew becoming a therapist was my calling, and I sensed a spiritual element present during each interaction with a client. I began to discover that helping others brought meaning into my life. I was developing a solid spiritual path professionally but was still struggling to do so personally because of my drinking.

Alcohol: The Quick Fix

Past Journal Entry: December 17, 2002, Age 26—California Visit
The surf video I watched allowed viewers to feel and observe the surfer's spiritual quest through natural means. His reason for getting up each day was the hope of reaching a new plane and level of thinking and feeling. The waves symbolize God—a force greater than ourselves. Surfing is the combination of man's search for a higher level of existence matched with the force of the Higher Power. They complement each other and remind each surfer and observers that we are mortal and hanging on to life or death with each wave. The power of the ocean is being challenged in order to obtain a state of "flow."

Certain activities can provide a key to unlocking our spiritual path and often can counteract the negative effects of drugs and alcohol. In achieving "flow" through our own unique means, we can translate this into our everyday life and provide a spiritual guide to follow. It is those with a desire to find a spiritual utopia who often fall into the trap of alcohol and drugs because these substances falsely advertise a shortcut to spiritual clarity and to our true soul or essence. They are the master of disguise and can convince you they are "helping" you. However, when the buzz is gone, we are left in a stagnant state, no further advanced than when we began.

The challenge in life is to find a healthy way to experience spirituality. For some it is a relationship, others a career, and for others meditation. I feel that I have a source of it, but still get my high from alcohol. Abstaining for 6 months allowed me to hear my inner guide with clarity.

Watching a video about someone who pursued spirituality through natural means emphasized that I had been choosing the shortcut for a "high" in life through alcohol. I seemed to understand those concepts intellectually but was unable to apply them to my life. It also became clear that I would not be able to advance spiritually while alcohol was in my life. I was sensing a spiritual void that continued to deepen through drinking and then tried to figure out what would fill it. In trying to solve my own drinking problem, I set out on a quest for fulfillment that ironically led me right back to drinking—I could not fix myself.

Spiritual Experiences

Past Journal Entry: May 16, 2000, Age 23
I feel as though the truth has jumped out at me, a light has glimmered. From the day that I stopped drinking, a force greater than me has blessed me with an inner peace which has helped me to cope with life's obstacles from within. I feel a force pulling me down a path of helping others—I have lived an amazing and a full life thus far—but only by a stroke of luck.

When I abstained from alcohol for brief periods of time, I would have intense spiritual experiences, during which I saw the world in a different light. However, these experiences alone were not powerful enough to keep me sober—I needed a spiritually based recovery program.

Past Journal Entry: July 24, 2001, Age 24—Sitting on the Dock of the Charles . . .
I feel energized—like I am in the center of something great when I sit on this dock. The roar of the traffic on Storrow Drive is complemented by the gentle swishing sound of the Charles River gently hitting against the planks of the dock. Sailboats float weightlessly along, and kayaks rush back and forth intercepting the wave patterns and reflection of the sun upon my face.

No one on their boats seems to have a destination—just a mission to be at peace and enjoy the remaining hours of daylight. It seems to be the perfect place to honor a day that is ending. The water almost talks to me and soothes my mind and vision. The breeze is a relief from the humid and lazy summer day—nature's own air-conditioner. I have no thoughts that relate to people at home—for here I have a world that exists only within myself. . . it is my sanctuary.

Sometimes spiritual experiences were moments of deep mindfulness and heightened awareness of my senses. I had a sense of awe of my surroundings and a sense of internal peace that was not usually present. These sober experiences were powerful—I truly appreciated them and intended to take more time to be by myself and observe the world around me.

Past Journal Entry: July 2, 2004, Age 27—Sobriety
I truly have felt different since June 15th. I just remember sitting on my lawn and I just felt different—more content and complete. That feeling has pretty much stayed with me . . . I am slowly losing my longing to be drunk like those around me. I see the endless cycle as unappealing and an activity that ends up leaving me exactly where I began. I feel that I am making progress on my sober journey and growing. Drinking causes me to regress and set myself back. It takes away from my true essence. Maybe my content feeling is allowing me to resist the drinking urge. My sobriety feels normal in some ways. I feel such growth and connections with sober forces that I don't want to backtrack.

At this point, I am five months sober in a Twelve-Step Recovery Program, as opposed to my past periods of abstinence. Spiritual experiences in sobriety became longer lasting, and slowly, I started to crave these feelings of contentment more than the high of drinking. However, these types of experiences were not enough by themselves to keep me sober. Ultimately, it was working the Twelve Steps of recovery that allowed me to develop a strong relationship with my Higher Power, to have a spiritual awakening, and to enter into recovery from alcoholism.

9

TRANSFORMATION: THE TWELVE STEPS

The early A.A.s knew from their own experience that, for the alcoholic, nothing in this world is as reliable or as immediate as the magic of alcohol, and they also knew that alcohol's "magic" inevitably destroyed spirituality. And so they discovered that whatever spirituality they would find in sobriety would have to be "earned"—earned in the original sense of "made one's own" by the work, the building, the journey, the "toil, sweat and tears" that the ancients insisted was necessary if the soul was to "ripen."
—Ernest Kurtz and Katherine Ketcham, *The Spirituality of Imperfection*[1]

Alcoholism affects every aspect of an alcoholic's life, and therefore the process of recovery must be comprehensive. Alcoholics may feel afraid or cursed to have been diagnosed with this disease, but there is incredible hope for their recovery—unlike with many other diseases. Their prognosis is excellent if they follow the treatment: "We believe there is no middle-of-the-road solution. We were in a position where life was becoming impossible, and if we had passed into the region from which there is no return through human aid, we had but two alternatives: One was to go on to the bitter end, blotting out the consciousness of our intolerable situation as best we could; and the other, to accept spiritual help. This we did because we honestly wanted to, and were willing to make the effort."[2] The spiritual help referred to is working the Twelve Steps of recovery. It is imperative that those who begin this journey are willing and motivated to do the necessary work required for this solution to a life-or-death condition.

The Twelve Steps of recovery were developed in 1939 by the founders of Alcoholics Anonymous (A.A.). They have been used in a variety of twelve-step-based rehab facilities in this country, including, but not limited to, the Betty Ford Center, Hazelden, and Caron Treatment Services. In addition, the Steps have been a road map for millions of individuals in recovery from alcoholism, drug dependency, eating disorders, sexual compulsions, gambling, and other conditions.[3] Their origin is rooted in the foundation of many religious traditions, including, but not limited to, Catholicism, Buddhism, and Judaism. Written out, each Step is only one sentence, but the power and complexity of each is infinite.

To maintain long-term recovery, sober alcoholics are encouraged to work the Twelve Steps of recovery. The Steps are intended to lead sober alcoholics to have a spiritual awakening and to pass their recovery experience and the Steps on to other sober alcoholics. They are the catalyst for individuals to change who they were when drinking alcoholically, thereby allowing themselves to be content in a life without alcohol. Those who choose not to do the Steps are sometimes referred to as having *untreated alcoholism* or as *dry drunks* because although they are not drinking, they have not had the spiritual awakening or psychic change many deem necessary for recovery. Kevin Griffin, recovering alcoholic and author of *One Breath at a Time: Buddhism and the Twelve Steps*, believes that recovery "is not ordinary life with the drugs and alcohol cut out. It's a new way of living, of relating to ourselves and the world. It's not a different version of the life we are living; it's a completely new life, one that can't be imagined until you are there."[4]

Not everyone in a Twelve-Step Recovery Program works the Twelve Steps. In fact, some sober alcoholics admit that they waited years until their emotional pain was great enough to motivate them to do the work of the program. Reasons that sober alcoholics often state for not doing the Steps include not seeing the importance, fear of drudging up the past, fear in general, lack of motivation, no interest, pride, being too busy, believing they don't need the Steps to stay sober, and/or lack of exposure. Griffin believes that when sober alcoholics are resistant to doing the Twelve Steps or to a recovery program, "the problem isn't really the Steps or the program or the meetings or 'those people.' The problem is that getting clean and sober and rebuilding your life is difficult and painful work. Whether you use the Twelve Steps or some other system, it's going to be hard. Choose your poison—or I guess I should say, choose your antidote."[5]

Every sober alcoholic has a different experience when he or she works the Twelve Steps. However, sharing the common and differing patterns helps bring clarity to the process for those who are just starting out and for those who continue to work the Steps. Specific directions for the Steps are laid out in the *Big Book* and are expanded on in the book *Twelve Steps and Twelve Traditions*, commonly referred to as the *Twelve and Twelve*. If a sober alcoholic follows these directions with the help of a sponsor, there is no way that he or she can do them incorrectly. One recovering alcoholic refers to the Steps as "alcoholic-proof" in that they were created for every alcoholic and that "the only way to mess them up is not to do them." A male high-functioning alcoholic (HFA) explains that "I later realized that there are many 'right ways,' in fact a sincere desire to grow spiritually almost always lead to a 'right way.'"

Different variations and schools of thought on the format in which the Steps are done vary from person to person as well as in different geographic locations. In all cases, it is important to complete each of the Twelve Steps. One recovering alcoholic explains that "the Steps are the symphony—beautiful together—but imagine it without certain instruments—the music isn't as harmonious—they must work together." Individuals may use variations or shorter versions of the directions from the *Big Book* and may either feel satisfied with their work or then choose to follow the directions more specifically. The way the Steps lead individuals to a spiritual awakening continues to be a mystery for those who work them. Often sober alcoholics attempt to dissect them and "figure them out"; however, surrendering to the process is all part of the journey through the Twelve Steps.

Although it is an individual's choice whether or not to do the Twelve Steps, it is important to keep in mind that the Steps are the foundation on which Twelve-Step Recovery Programs are based. "The tremendous fact for every one of us [alcoholics] is that we have discovered a common solution. We have a way out on which we can absolutely agree, and upon which we can join in brotherly and harmonious action."[6]

This chapter is intended only as a brief overview of each Step as it is laid out in the *Big Book* and not as a substitute or recreation of working the Twelve Steps. For the sake of tradition, the original Twelve Steps of A.A. will be used.

STEP 1: WE ADMITTED WE WERE POWERLESS OVER ALCOHOL—THAT OUR LIVES HAD BECOME UNMANAGEABLE

Perhaps the greatest paradox in the story of spirituality is the mystical insight that we are able to experience release only if we ourselves "let go." . . . Surrender begins with the acceptance that we are not in control of the matter at hand—in fact, we are not in absolute control of anything. Thus the experience of surrender involves the "letting in" of reality that becomes possible when we are ready to let go of our illusions and pretensions.
—Ernest Kurtz and Katherine Ketcham, *The Spirituality of Imperfection*[7]

Step 1 is the beginning of the journey through the Twelve Steps, and moving past this Step is crucial to beginning the true work of recovery. Many HFAs report that this is one of the most challenging Steps. It is typically divided into two sections, the first being "we admitted we were powerless over alcohol." The term *powerless* is one that many HFAs react to—they have spent much of their lives proving that they were in control. The *Big Book* explains that alcoholics are powerless over alcohol because when they take one drink, whether they can stop is unpredictable. Alcoholics "have one symptom in common: they cannot stop drinking without developing the phenomenon of craving. This phenomenon, as we have suggested, may be the manifestation of an allergy which differentiates these people, and sets them apart as a distinct entity."[8] One female HFA recalls, "I thought I didn't qualify as 'powerless' because I had gone periods of time without a drink. I was finally able to admit it when I attempted the 'just have one drink' experiment which gave me an undeniable sense of the 'phenomenon of craving.'"

Caron has observed that this Step is a "surrender in control—and only then can you proceed." He believes that HFAs wear "the perfect mask," which hides them from reality and from appearing weak. This Step is difficult for them because "it is hard to take off the mask—to become normal, vulnerable and not in control." Therefore it is important for alcoholics to have hit some type of bottom—emotional or physical—that allows them to acknowledge that their drinking is out of their control. Alcoholics who have not hit some type of bottom may not see the necessity of abstaining from alcohol nor have the motivation to work the Twelve Steps to maintain long-term recovery.

Powerlessness, in terms of addiction, is part of a paradox that when alcoholics admit that they are powerless over alcohol, they begin the process of empowerment over their addiction. In some ways, our culture reinforces the notion that being out of control or surrendering is a sign of weakness—when just the opposite is true. It takes strength for individuals to admit their problems and to be completely honest with themselves and others. One male HFA reports that "admitting powerlessness was so difficult and was an initial barrier," and another HFA doctor stated, "Who wants to admit powerlessness—I make life-or-death decisions for a living." Other HFAs were able to admit that they were powerless over alcohol through identifying with others at meetings and because they had minimal denial.

The second part of Step 1—"that our lives had become unmanageable"—can also be difficult for HFAs to admit or even to realize. Many HFAs pride themselves on having their lives in control, even if their drinking is not. They often compare themselves to those whose lives are visibly falling apart to feel better about themselves. However, it is this command of the outside things that may mask the true internal problem of their alcoholism and result in emotional pain. One female HFA admits that "because I hadn't had the outside losses, maybe it was harder for me to admit how unmanageable my life was, but keeping the spotlight shining on Step 1 helped me keep coming back to how intolerable things had felt internally by the end of my drinking." Another female HFA recalls that this Step "was a challenge because I prided myself on managing the outside stuff fairly well despite how discontent and miserable I felt inside." In time, HFAs may realize that Step 1 includes emotional unmanageability as well. HFAs have utilized self-will, discipline, and control to succeed in many aspects of their lives. However, these characteristics could not "fix" their drinking, and therefore their lives are unmanageable.

"Hindsight" Reflections of the Author: Step 1

Past Journal Entry: May 13, 2004, Age 27—Four Months Sober
Am I an alcoholic? Am I truly powerless over alcohol? How can I ask these questions over and over? I experienced an internal battle in my mind for the first 3-4 weeks of sobriety. One day I was convinced that I was, but I would then think either of the times that I drank in control or of friends who question the severity of my problem and I would be back to square one.... There was a small part of me that felt I could learn to control it—even though I have spent the past

4 years trying to prove that I could and have failed miserably. The evidence is there, I just know I need to dig down deep and be really honest with myself.

Past Journal Entry: May 14, 2004

I began writing in my journal that I am an alcoholic and the true sign of acceptance was when I spoke at a meeting and stated, "Hi, I'm Sarah, and I am an alcoholic." I then said out loud that it was so hard for me to say that because I had been struggling the past few weeks to figure it out.... Once I spoke, I knew that I was ready to do Step 1. My sponsor and I read several sections of the *Big Book* out loud and discussed the intricacies. While reading it, many parts rang true and I knew in this moment of sanity that I was an alcoholic. Once I accepted this, the internal battle in my mind quieted. I also felt less of a need for those around me to say only what I needed to hear—I accepted it and that is what really mattered.

Step 1 was the most difficult as well as the most life-changing Step for me. Although it was obvious I was powerless over alcohol, based on years of trying to control and moderate my drinking, some part of my mind struggled to accept this fact. This battle within my mind was exhausting, and I came to the point where I wanted to accept I was powerless but could not completely. Finally, through the help of my sponsor, meeting other sober HFAs, prayer, and reading recovery material, I was able to move past this part of the Step.

I was successful professionally, and I had stable living conditions and a support system of friends and family. Therefore I wondered, what could possibly be unmanageable about my life? Over time, listening to speakers at meetings and talking with other sober alcoholics, I came to acknowledge that when I was drinking, my life was out of control, and because I was unable to stop drinking, my life was unmanageable.

STEP 2: CAME TO BELIEVE THAT A POWER GREATER THAN OURSELVES COULD RESTORE US TO SANITY

The Steps and the practices of Buddhism give us a way to gently "stop the war," "step out of the battle," to "cease fighting," to surrender. This surrender, which begins in Step One, means, in Step Two, that we are giving up our own attempt at incessant control and opening to what life offers.
      —Kevin Griffin, *One Breath at a Time: Buddhism and the Twelve Steps*[9]

Having admitted powerlessness over alcohol and that their lives were unmanageable, alcoholics move to Step 2, the essence of which is that an outside force can help them to recover. The *Big Book* states, "Lack of power, that was our dilemma. We had to find a power by which we could live, and it had to be a *Power greater than ourselves.*"[10] The challenge for sober alcoholics is to become willing to believe in a Higher Power. Several HFAs report preconceived notions of a Higher Power that made this Step particularly challenging. One male HFA reflected, "Based on my experiences and the evidence I saw around me at the time, I had long believed that if there was an omnipotent and omnipresent God, it was either incompetent or possessed a will of horrific evil. I have forced myself to let go of these thoughts and ideas in order to stay sober now." Others feared that they were going to be told what type of Higher Power to believe in. One female HFA explains that "I was full of fear that I was going to be forced to swallow somebody else's concept of a Higher Power in order to be able to get sober and have access to the tools of the Twelve-Step Recovery Program. I needed a lot of reassurance that that wasn't the case, and when I really felt free to embrace my own concept of a Higher Power, the spiritual tools really began to work for me." The truth of Twelve-Step Recovery Programs is that individuals are free to believe in whatever form of a Higher Power feels right for them, and this concept may change over time.

Many HFAs have been able to run aspects of their lives on self-will. Therefore surrendering this control to a Higher Power can be an enormous challenge. One HFA doctor recalls that for most of his life, he held the belief that if he had to ask for help, then that accomplishment did not count. He felt that if he could not do something on his own, then no one could, because "I am a doctor, people come to me for help, I don't go to people for help." The *Twelve and Twelve* addresses this type of thought process as it relates to Step 2 in stating,

> Now we come to another kind of problem: the intellectually self-sufficient man or woman. To these, many A.A.s can say, "Yes, we were like you—far too smart for our own good. We loved to have people call us precarious. We used our education to blow ourselves up into prideful balloons, though we were careful to hide this from others. Secretly, we felt we could float above the rest of the folks on our brainpower alone. Scientific progress told us there was nothing man couldn't do. Knowledge was all-powerful. Intellect could conquer nature... humility and intellect could be compatible, provided we place humility first. When we begin to do that, we received the gift of faith, a faith which works."[11]

The Step 2 phrase "restore us to sanity" may be confusing to alcoholics who do not consider themselves insane. However, the term *insane* can refer to alcoholic behavior such as "doing the same thing over and over and expecting different results."[12] One male HFA struggled with this idea at first but then was able to be honest with himself and stated, "Believing that a Higher Power would return us to sanity... I'm not insane—then I realized that my drinking was insane—like continuing to drink after five [driving under the influence charges]." Griffin believes that the phrase "return us to sanity" refers to the insanity of alcoholics destroying their lives with alcohol as well as the behaviors that go along with this addiction.[13]

"Hindsight" Reflections of the Author: Step 2

Past Journal Entry: May 24, 2004, Age 27
Ironically, I completed Step 2 just before I attended a wine tasting. I acknowledged that I believe in a Higher Power and read aloud more of the *Big Book*.

It is amazing that rereading this book impacts me differently each time. I relate to things now that I didn't fully grasp before.... I am learning that in order to live my life in a manner consistent with who I am, I must eliminate drinking and turn to God. I always knew that my connection with God would lead me to sobriety.... The sheer force of alcohol on my brain is not to be competed with by anything else. My only hope or guarantee is abstinence and a reliance on God for my life to be lived "happy, joyous and free." ... This Twelve-Step Recovery Program has been a cushion which softens the transition into sobriety. I don't feel the loss as much because I am filling that hole with spirituality that I could only half focus on when drinking.

Step 2 directly deals with the acknowledgment of a Higher Power, which I chose to call God, and for me, this Step was a natural and comfortable shift. I had tried to rely on God in the past to help me moderate my drinking and failed. I learned that I needed to be sober to feel spiritually connected. Even though I ran my life on self-will and credited that with my successes, I innately knew that the solution to my alcoholism was a reliance on God. Although I did not consider myself insane, I did identify with the definition of insanity of "doing the same thing over and over again and expecting different results" in terms of my drinking. I could admit that my alcoholic behavior was truly insane and that part of me needed to be brought back to "sanity." In contrast with my past solo attempts to abstain, in a Twelve-Step Recovery Program, I felt more support and spiritual fulfillment.

STEP 3: MADE A DECISION TO TURN OUR WILL AND OUR LIVES OVER TO THE CARE OF GOD AS WE UNDERSTOOD HIM

We are certain that our intelligence, backed by willpower, can rightly control our inner lives and guarantee us success in the world we live in. This brave philosophy wherein each man plays God, sounds good in the speaking, but still has to meet the acid test: how well does it actually work? One good look in the mirror ought to be answer enough for any alcoholic.

—The *Twelve and Twelve*[14]

Step 3 can be challenging spiritually for sober alcoholics as well as life-changing. While Step 2 involves "coming to believe," Step 3 is more drastic and involves trusting in a Higher Power and placing spirituality at the core of life. When alcoholics are hanging on to their self-will and are convinced that they know the way that life should go, they will constantly be in conflict with the "flow of life."[15] In a sense, alcoholics are making a conscious shift from turning their will over to a destructive power (alcohol) to turning their will over to a constructive power and to spiritual growth.[16] This Step requires saying the Third Step Prayer together with a sponsor: "God, I offer myself to Thee—to build with me and to do with me as Thou wilt. Relieve me of the bondage of self, that I may better do Thy will. Take away my difficulties, that victory over them may bear witness to those I would help of Thy Power, Thy

Love, and Thy Way of life. May I do Thy will always!"[17] This act symbolizes readiness to do the work of the Twelve Steps and the promise to carry this message to other alcoholics. Step 3 also reassures individuals that they are free to choose their own concept of "God *as we understood Him.*"

One male HFA has observed that many men "rely on their intellect and willpower to run their lives," and the thought of relinquishing some of this control can be a huge test. What at first may seem impossible—letting go—may actually become a relief. HFAs realize that they don't have to run the show, that they are not God. Several HFAs reported having spiritual experiences as a result of this Step. One HFA doctor found this Step to be the most challenging because "physicians are control freaks—they are taught to be. That's what we do—control—and we are not good at delegating. We believe that to do something right, you do it yourself." Through this Step, he was able to "turn it over—to let go and let God." One female HFA prayed daily to "turn it over" to her Higher Power and that "things went better" when she was able to surrender control.

"Hindsight" Reflections of the Author: Step 3

Past Journal Entry: July 6, 2004—Five Months Sober

It was a foggy and rainy day in Boston, and my sponsor and I went onto her porch high above the city and kneeled down next to each other. We held hands and recited the Third Step Prayer together. This Step symbolized my willingness to let God into my life and to pass the gift of the Steps on to other alcoholics once I had completed all Twelve Steps. Although the day was dreary, God's light was shining down on me.

STEP 4: MADE A SEARCHING AND FEARLESS MORAL INVENTORY OF OURSELVES

While working this Step, I gained a true appreciation, almost a sense of awe, for the wisdom of the twelve-step process. I could see how much I was learning about myself and the crucial understanding I was gaining about the reasons I drank in the first place. Most importantly, the Step 4 process forced me to really exercise the tools I had gained thus far in recovery. All those demons were rising to the surface, all those painful feelings, and instead of drinking over them, I was writing them down, calling my sponsor when I was overwhelmed . . . more than anything, this experience *proved* to me that my disease could throw its worst at me, and I could combat it with the help of a Twelve-Step Recovery Program and my Higher Power, instead of anesthetizing it with a drink.

—recovering female HFA

Step 4 is a change of pace from the "surrender" Steps 1 through 3 because it is concrete and involves clear directions. It is the beginning of a series of steps that involve investigating and taking responsibility.[18] This Step involves a written moral inventory that may vary in length. Individuals may take weeks, months, and even years to complete this Step—yet it is suggested to be as time-efficient as possible. An inventory can be defined as a "fact-finding and fact-facing process"[19] or as "a list, or description, of your personal history."[20] The purpose of the moral inventory is for sober alcoholics to discover past and present behavior patterns that negatively affect their lives. This Step requires rigorous honesty and challenges individuals to examine their past behaviors. Stephanie S. Covington, author of *A Woman's Way through the Twelve Steps*, conceptualizes this Step, stating, "Think of this Step as turning on a light in a pitch-dark room: If you continue to walk around in the dark, you'll probably keep tripping over the furniture and bruising yourself. But when you turn on the light, you can see where you're going. In the same way, the Step Four inventory sheds light on the obstacles in your path. By taking an inventory you'll be able to see what stands in the way of your recovery."[21]

Step 4 is highly structured. Individuals who like organization tend to enjoy the clear-cut directions, but HFAs who tend to be perfectionists may worry that they are not doing it perfectly and, as a result, fear the process may not work for them. One HFA found herself competing with others in terms of how long she was taking to write and felt "I should be done with this" and admits that she was "chasing the prize." Others may be so thorough that they struggle to complete the Step and sit in their writing for years. This can put the individual's sobriety in danger—sober alcoholics doing Steps 4 and 5 are thought by many to be the most vulnerable for relapse. Therefore finding a balance between being thorough in the inventory but not obsessive is recommended.

Step 4 is said to be both challenging and life-changing for sober alcoholics. Some individuals avoid this Step out of fear or lack of motivation but tend to report growth and insight once they complete it. One female HFA admitted that "I initially thought that the Fourth Step would point out all of my negative characteristics, when in fact it showed me both positive and negative." Some describe it as a "catharsis," "cleansing," and "cleaning my side of the street." This Step involves taking action toward recovery and is in some ways symbolic of this dedication, marking the beginning of "spiritual practice and discipline." Another recovering alcoholic stated that the inventory "opened a path to understanding myself. I came of age because of the inventory. My problems have been addressed and mostly dealt with due to the humility and honesty required in self-discovery."

"Hindsight" Reflections of the Author: Step 4

Past Journal Entry: July 9, 2004—Six Months Sober
My Fourth Step has left me confused. It is hard to see how this Step will help to keep me sober, but I am going to move forward and I have faith that it will eventually make sense.

While writing my Fourth Step, I constantly tried to figure out how it worked and why it was going to help me to recover from alcoholism. At this time, I was unable to see what this Step had to do with my alcoholism. In time, I learned that the Steps are a mystery and that it is not important why they work, but that they actually work.

Past Journal Entry: July 17, 2004
I don't know where the anger and hurt all came from.... I felt intense emotions and I am still trying to figure out why. I feel raw and vulnerable and I cannot control them.... My emotions were running through me like fire in my veins. But nothing really happened—something got stirred up—what though? I keep trying to rationalize it—but I am having trouble. Those around me think that I have lost it. In fact, one friend asked me how regularly I was seeing a therapist. I now feel like I've been on an emotional roller coaster.... But the feelings are there. I am angry—but at whom?

I learned through other sober alcoholics that when writing the Fourth Step, a lot of emotions get stirred up and moods can go up and down. It is as though the past and the subconscious come to haunt us. I began to feel extremely anxious, with randomly shifting moods. I felt intense fear that I would never feel "myself" again, but I was reassured by others who have been through the Steps that the way I felt was normal for this Step. I continued to have faith that when I was through Steps 4 and 5, I would be on the path to feeling more balanced.

Past Journal Entry: August 12, 2004
I have been procrastinating with my Fourth Step writing for several reasons—I have no time to myself, have forgotten to write and I have had a bit of resistance to the Steps. It is as though I need to see where everything is leading me instead of blindly moving forward. I also feel like I have examined myself so much throughout my life that I am unsure what else can be uncovered.... My sponsor sent me an e-mail while she was away on vacation stating, "You are living in the problem... there is a high chance that you will drink—you need to get through the Fourth Step writing so that you can begin to live in the solution."

The Fourth Step inventory writing process is often tedious and time consuming—to the point that many individuals may take breaks or stop altogether. I, too, lost motivation with this process at times, especially when I convinced myself that I had acquired enough self-knowledge through my own introspection, graduate school, and past therapy. However, it was impossible to see what I did not know about myself. My sponsor reminded me how important it was to finish the writing and how vulnerable I was in my current sobriety. The truths that I eventually realized about myself were the gifts of doing this work. With God's help and guidance from others, I was able to surpass my previous level of insight.

STEP 5: ADMITTED TO GOD, TO OURSELVES, AND TO ANOTHER HUMAN BEING THE EXACT NATURE OF OUR WRONGS

Provided you hold back nothing, your sense of relief will mount from minute to minute. The damned-up emotions of years break out of their confinement, and miraculously vanish as soon as they are exposed. As the pain subsides, a healing tranquility takes its place. And when humility and serenity are so combined, something else of great moment is apt to occur.

—The *Twelve and Twelve*[22]

Step 5 is the release of Step 4. In Step 5, the entire Fourth Step inventory is read out loud, generally to a sponsor and to a Higher Power. Individuals have a choice of reading their inventories to whomever they choose. This may be a priest, a rabbi, or a therapist—but ideally, it should be one's sponsor. This process can be broken up into sessions of several hours or may be done all at once. After the reading is complete, individuals are asked to return home and meditate for one hour and to contemplate if they have left anything out of their inventories. After this period of meditation, individuals are to call their sponsors and discuss anything that may have surfaced that was missed.

Many sober alcoholics initially fear sharing their inventories with another person. However, they tend to find that after this Step, they feel less stigma and shame about events in their past. Individuals feel less "terminally unique," and when they hesitate to share personal parts of their inventory out loud and their sponsors share that they had similar experiences, true healing occurs. One female HFA admitted, "I was filled with a lot of fear around Step 5 before I started it. I had kept thoughts, feelings, and behaviors to myself most of my life, so admitting the worst parts of myself to another person seemed impossible.... The fear was worse than the thing itself." A male HFA felt that this Step led to "release, I let go of secrets, I wasn't unique as my sponsor shared similar stories." It becomes clear that telling the truth can actually bring relief. Griffin concludes, "When you expose your hidden secrets and shame to your sponsor, you learn that you aren't alone. Your failings are common. Your shame, unnecessary."[23]

Some sober alcoholics report that after Step 5, they experience some form of a spiritual experience or spiritual awakening. Many feel for the first time since becoming sober that their minds are quiet, and they sense serenity. However, pressing on with the remaining Steps is necessary because more work needs to be done in healing the "wreckage of the past."

"Hindsight" Reflections of the Author: Step 5

My Fifth Step was done in about ten reading sessions, and I was determined to finish by reading quickly. After nine months of writing my Fourth Step, I was more than ready to move on with the process of the Steps. My sponsor gave me a beautiful candle that we lit each time before I read. I then said the Third Step prayer and would read my inventory for about two hours. My sponsor worked on some organizing projects while I was reading, responding minimally, except on a few occasions. This gave me the feeling that I was ultimately reading and releasing my inventory to God and that my sponsor was simply a witness.

Past Journal Entry: May 24, 2005, Age 28—One Year and Four Months Sober
I am scared about how I feel right now...it's a bad space. I am also feeling stuck in it. I could cry for I want to feel "me" again. I almost feel like I am imagining this. My stomach and head hurt, I feel horrible, sad, scared, and somewhat hopeless. I feel like it is taking so much work to feel "OK"—something is off and I have no idea how to figure out what.

I had hoped that I would feel better while reading Step 5 than how I felt when writing Step 4. However, I was still struggling emotionally and with my anxiety level. My sponsor shared with me that she had reached her emotional bottom during Step 5, and I felt comforted in knowing that I was not alone and that there was a reason I was feeling this way.

Past Journal Entry: June 5, 2005
I completed reading the Fifth Step today! *Relief*—on a warm sunny day, I am thrilled to leave the rain of the past week behind literally and metaphorically. For my hour of meditation I chose to sit outside in the courtyard of my apartment complex. The summer sun felt like God's rays hugging me. After the first thirty minutes, which included noise distractions from nearby construction, I concluded that peace involves both calm and distractions. I do harbor resentments at times of interruptions in life. I felt myself cringe a bit as my meditation was interrupted— but I decided to meditate on that thought and reaction. I also concluded that there is no perfect meditation.
I decided to spend the second half of the hour on the back porch, where it was quieter. After thirty minutes of uninterrupted meditation I allowed myself to feel serene and truly absorb the sun...I thought about how wonderful it would be to feel like this all of the time and for a moment I sensed worry about the peace slipping away. I realized that I also have fear about life's ups and downs and my mental health. One can miss the great moments by worrying about the future bad ones.
My entire day was great. I felt calm and content everywhere I went....I sensed the clouds floating away and the beginning of a new phase of moving past my problems into positive solutions.

Once I finished reading Step 5, I had a vivid and powerful spiritual experience during my hour of meditation. The chatter within my mind had quieted, and I felt true peace and stillness. This period of serenity lasted for months, and I was finally sensing that I was "recovering" from alcoholism.

STEP 6: WERE ENTIRELY READY TO HAVE GOD REMOVE ALL THESE DEFECTS OF CHARACTER AND STEP 7: HUMBLY ASKED HIM TO REMOVE OUR SHORTCOMINGS

When there is a behavior pattern that I dislike and feel is not beneficial for me or others, I can utilize these two Steps and continually ask my Higher Power for help in eliminating this behavior pattern. Miraculously, there have been some behaviors that I never thought I could give up, and after many prayers I finally found myself disengaging from them.

—recovering female HFA

Steps 6 and 7 are generally done together. Individuals learn what their character defects are by writing through their Fourth Step inventory and by reading their Fifth Step. The term *character defects* (dishonesty, anger, people pleasing, etc.) may also be referred to as *character patterns* or *old behaviors* and are thought to block individuals from connecting with their Higher Power. Steps 6 and 7 comprise a mere two paragraphs in the *Big Book*, unlike other Steps, which have pages and even chapters devoted to them. After all of the work and time spent on Steps 4 and 5, it is often perplexing that it is possible to complete two Steps in one day. However, it soon becomes clear that character defects do not disappear magically and that these Steps will be worked on for a lifetime.

Completing Step 6 represents one's willingness "to make a beginning on this lifetime job. This does not mean that we expect all our character defects to be lifted out of us as the drive to drink was. A few of them may be, but with most of them we shall have to be content with patient improvement."[24] One HFA viewed this Step as "the willingness to let go of some faulty beliefs and coping mechanisms which at one time served me well but are no longer appropriate or useful." Once this willingness is established, the individual moves on to Step 7 and says the Seventh Step Prayer out of the *Big Book*: "My Creator, I am now willing that you should have all of me, good and bad. I pray that you now remove from me every single defect of character which stands in the way of my usefulness to you and my fellows. Grant me strength, as I go out from here, to do your bidding. Amen."[25]

Step 7 emphasizes humility, which can be defined as "clear recognition of what and who we really are, followed by a sincere attempt to become what we could be,"[26] and is "about self-knowledge, self-acceptance, and knowing your place in the universe."[27] Humility allows an individual to realize that he or she can neither wish nor will certain character defects away, and therefore the individual must be able to admit when only his or her Higher Power can remove these shortcomings. An HFA in the military reported, "I had a problem with the concept of humility... because in military training, *humility* meant "humiliation."" However, over time, he was able to believe that "humility is seeking and doing God's will and that God's will is to be happy, joyous, and free."

The brief nature of these readings and the time initially spent doing these Steps does not accurately represent their difficulty. In fact, many HFAs indicate that these Steps proved to be the most challenging throughout their recovery. One HFA doctor explains that all of the character traits that allow people to be successful are "often counterintuitive to recovery." HFAs may cling to some of these traits that may harm themselves and others because they feel they are receiving some benefit. A recovering alcoholic found these Steps to be the most difficult because "I was really attached to my character defects." One male HFA found relief through these Steps in knowing that "God can help me with this selfishness, this ego, this fear. I am powerless over these like my alcohol usage."

"Hindsight" Reflections of the Author: Step 6 and Step 7

One Year and Five Months Sober
Progressing through Step 6 and Step 7 in several minutes was a surprise to me after the 11 months it took for me to complete Steps 4 and 5. I felt as though I was missing something or did not do them thoroughly. What I did not realize at the time was that I would continue to work these Steps throughout my recovery. I had expectations that all of the character defects that had become clear through my moral inventory would disappear after I said the Seventh Step Prayer. Some defects were eliminated, but over time different defects cropped up, causing me and others pain. Once again I needed to admit my powerlessness over them and then rework these Steps. I also realized that there were some character defects that I found pleasure in, but that I knew needed to be eliminated, such as gossiping and anger. However, I began to look at myself under a microscope and noticed that my conscience was now in overdrive. I felt guilt about things that I would say to others, thinking that I may have gossiped, and I would then "confess" to my sponsor. Over time I stopped beating myself up and developed confidence in my own ability to determine when a character defect was blocking me from my connection to God.

STEP 8: MADE A LIST OF ALL PERSONS WE HAD HARMED, AND BECAME WILLING TO MAKE AMENDS TO THEM ALL AND STEP 9: MADE DIRECT AMENDS TO SUCH PEOPLE WHENEVER POSSIBLE, EXCEPT WHEN TO DO SO WOULD INJURE THEM OR OTHERS

As we make our amends list, opening deeply to the pain we've caused ourselves and others, the heart begins to soften. The willingness to face pain—internally and externally—awakens love and compassion.
　　　—Kevin Griffin, *One Breath at a Time: Buddhism and the Twelve Steps*[28]

Steps 8 and 9 are listed together in the *Big Book* and deal with the amends process. An *amends* can be defined as setting right a wrong, and it involves courage in taking responsibility for one's actions and harms done. To continue to live on a spiritual path, sober alcoholics must eventually forgive even those who may have harmed them—for individuals suffer from holding on to resentments that block them from connecting to a Higher Power. Step 8 involves creating a list of those people and institutions that the individual has harmed. Step 9 is the actual process of making amends, and it requires guidance and support from one's sponsor. This Step involves an individual taking responsibility for his or her part and setting aside the other person's part in a matter. Amends can be done through face-to-face contact, a phone call, a letter, an e-mail, or simply praying for someone—depending on what is determined by a sponsor to be most appropriate. It is crucial that amends are not made for the purpose of relieving guilt at the expense of another person's feelings: "We are not to be the hasty and foolish martyr who would needlessly sacrifice others to save himself from the alcoholic pit." The *Big Book* gives examples and guides sober alcoholics through this process, but it is often suggested that each amends be discussed with a sponsor and specific directions agreed on. This Step may take years, but it is important to get started immediately on the process.

Many HFAs report that this Step is challenging for them in many ways. For HFAs who tend to be concerned about others' perceptions, it can be difficult to openly admit when they have been wrong and in a sense let others know that they are truly human. One female HFA explained, "I had always kept a very high-functioning persona—most people around me didn't know how bad things had gotten for me, and how many lies I was telling to keep up that facade.... But once I did actually make amends I found a lot of transformation of some really problematic relationships." Another female HFA admitted, "I have had a hard time admitting that I was at fault without completely wallowing in self-pity and thinking that I'm a horrible person. It's difficult for me to separate the person I was when active in my disease from the recovering person that I am now.... Ultimately I believe that working on Step 9 will contribute the most to my growth as a person and my reentry into the world." Another female HFA admits that this step was difficult because "there were people I was hesitant to approach because of lingering ill feelings, which I needed to pray for my Higher Power to remove and replace with willingness." Although some individuals may experience initial fear or resistance about making amends, they generally report gaining peace and spiritual growth as a result of their efforts. One male HFA stated, "The amount of fear I had going into it was immense, but I truly felt that after I had completed each amends, I had felt the presence of God and had a renewed faith in the work in this program."

"Hindsight" Reflections of the Author: Step 8 and Step 9

One Year and Six Months Sober until Present

Steps 8 and 9 did not intimidate me, and I quickly began to make amends to people in my life. In my mind, I had already said I was sorry so many times to friends for my drunken behavior, but this was my final apology with an explanation that I do not now live my life in the manner that I did as an active alcoholic. Most people tended to minimize my behavior and acted as though I did not really hurt them. However, one of the most powerful amends was with a friend who actually thought back in time to how she felt as a result of my drunken behaviors and admitted that she was affected negatively. In the beginning of this process, I sped through (because I am very task oriented), but over time I slowed down and faced several deeply emotional amends.

The amends that I made to several institutions were especially meaningful and healing. I went back to my college sorority and told my "drinking story" to the members at their weekly meeting. My message to the sorority members was that I had been just like them—having the time of my life in college with my many friends and earning good grades—but that did not mean I was not an alcoholic. I could see young women in the audience nodding their heads and identifying with what I was saying. I wondered if I had heard someone like myself speak about her story of being an HFA when I was in college, a seed would have been planted or my drinking habits would have changed.

Step 10: Continued to Take Personal Inventory and When We Were Wrong Promptly Admitted It

It is a spiritual axiom that every time we are disturbed, no matter what the cause, there is something wrong with us.

—The *Twelve and Twelve*[29]

Step 10 is often referred to as the "walking around Step," and it is the first of the three "maintenance" Steps: Step 10, Step 11, and Step 12. Step 10 allows individuals to continue the work that was originally done in previous Steps—Step 4, in particular. It is not enough to work the Steps and then return to old ways of thinking and behaving because alcoholics have only "a daily reprieve contingent on the maintenance of our spiritual condition."[30] Individuals who do not practice Step 10 in some form on a regular basis often report feeling blocked from their Higher Power, which can eventually lead to a relapse. The *Big Book* lays out specific instructions for this Step and suggests that "we continue to take personal inventory and continue to set right any new mistakes as we go along.... This is not an overnight matter. It should continue for our lifetime. Continue to watch for selfishness, dishonesty, resentment, and fear. When these crop up, we ask God at once to remove them. We discuss them with someone immediately and make amends quickly if we have harmed anyone. Then we resolutely turn our thoughts to someone we can help."[31]

Individuals can do a "Tenth Step" in a variety of ways, and they often figure out which method works best for them by working with their sponsor and by experimenting. Some prefer to do this Step verbally with their sponsor or another sober alcoholic, while others tend to write Tenth Steps. One male HFA explained, "I did the nightly inventory from the *Big Book*, each night asking myself if I'd been resentful, selfish, dishonest, or frightened. I initially did this written, now I do it in my head each night.... This helps me to watch my own behavior, and to look out for areas where I still have shortcomings."

Another HFA reports that she struggles with this Step and often forgets to do it or procrastinates. A female HFA observed, "Now, I can quickly realize when I behave in a way that is not true to myself or others. I have a working sober mind that can tell me when I've behaved in a way that is not congruent with my values. This Step allows me to quickly see the truth about any situation and then decide the best way to handle it."

"Hindsight" Reflections of the Author: Step 10

One Year and Seven Months Sober until Present
When I first began practicing Step 10, I was concerned that I was not doing it correctly, but over time I have learned that it is not as important to do the Steps perfectly as it is to just work them. I learned different ways to do this Step with the help of several sponsors. At one point, I read Step 10 out of the *Big Book* in the evening to review my day—but I was unable to maintain that practice. Other times I would call my sponsor and discuss difficult situations that came up and if I then needed to make an amends to anyone. The most effective suggestion I received for this Step was to make a Tenth Step notebook in which I reviewed my day and wrote down when "selfishness, dishonesty, resentment and fear" cropped up along with what corrective measures I was going to take—prayer, make an amends, speak with the person, etc. It has become important for me to live my life in a way in which I am being honest with myself and caring about people enough to tell them the truth.

STEP 11: SOUGHT THROUGH PRAYER AND MEDITATION TO IMPROVE OUR CONSCIOUS CONTACT WITH GOD *AS WE UNDERSTOOD HIM*, PRAYING ONLY FOR KNOWLEDGE OF HIS WILL FOR US AND THE POWER TO CARRY THAT OUT

In thinking about our day we may face indecision. We may not be able to determine which course to take. Here we ask God for inspiration, an intuitive thought or a decision. We relax and take it easy. We don't struggle. We are often surprised how the right answers come after we have tried this for a while. What used to be the hunch or the occasional inspiration gradually becomes a working part of the mind.

—The *Big Book*[32]

Step 11 is a lifelong practice that ebbs and flows with recovery. The clear-cut directions for this Step in the *Big Book* are divided into awakening, during the day and at night. However, it is up to the individual to choose how and when he or she chooses to pray and meditate. Griffin conceptualizes this Step by saying that "once we've weathered the storms of inventory and amends, this Step leads us to a safe harbor where we can begin to live the promises of peace and serenity" and adds that this Step is crucial to spiritual maintenance.[33]

The *Big Book* encourages individuals who have religious affiliations to incorporate their practices into recovery and states, "If we belong to a religious denomination which requires a definite morning devotion, we attend to that also. If not members of religious bodies, we sometimes select and memorize a few set prayers which emphasize the principles we have been discussing. There are many helpful books also. Suggestions about these may be obtained from one's priest, minister, or rabbi. Be quick to see where religious people are right. Make use of what they offer."[34] However, moderation is the key to recovery, and sober alcoholics who throw themselves into religious or spiritual practices in an extreme manner and drift away from their recovery program risk relapse.

HFAs report practicing this Step in different ways and with differing frequency. One male HFA stated that he practices "meditation on the coming day and asks God for direction—does prayer throughout the day and usually but not always, short periods of meditation and self-evaluation at night." A female HFA reports using this Step "in the heat of the moment—taking a breather to ask for help, to be shown what God would have me be, re-centers me and puts the situation into perspective." For many, this Step leads them to crave balance and harmony in their sober lives, in contrast to the chaos and intoxication they craved when actively drinking. This shift is often a sign that recovery has taken place. A female HFA captures the effect of this Step, stating, "Step 11 has given me permission to live a quieter life and not to get sucked into the fast-paced chaos that our modern-day society is living in. I was terrified that a life without booze would be so despicably boring that I wouldn't be able to handle it. This Step has shown me that a quieter life with a greater sense of peace is immensely rewarding and much preferred to a life filled with drama and overactivity."

"Hindsight" Reflections of the Author: Step 11

One Year and Seven Months Sober until Present
Step 11 has allowed me to truly sense God and allows me to access a sense of serenity in my life. At times I would focus on this Step and forget about Step 10. Throughout my sobriety I have practiced this step in a variety of ways, including praying upon waking and/or before going to bed on my meditation cushion, doing yoga, getting acupuncture treatments, praying while running and attending a weekly meditation group. I often practiced this Step throughout the day by taking deep diaphragmatic breaths and connecting with God. Later in recovery I discovered that I can connect with God through nature and by simply being mindful while gardening. I am able to practice this Step and sense "conscious contact with God" in a church, a synagogue, a Buddhist temple—I have felt a universal spiritual connection in all places of worship.

When I was an active alcoholic, I prayed for God to make circumstances in my life turn out the way "I" wanted. I learned through a Twelve-Step Recovery Program that prayer is not about telling God how things should be, but instead tapping into that source of power to gain acceptance of how things are meant to be. In sobriety, I began to pray for the strength to get through whatever life brings my way and to carry out God's will for me. I also prayed for others to have this same strength and to sense a spiritual connection to get through life's challenges.

This was a process of letting go and accepting that my life was happening in exactly the way God intended it.

STEP 12: HAVING HAD A SPIRITUAL AWAKENING AS THE RESULT OF THESE STEPS, WE TRIED TO CARRY THIS MESSAGE TO ALCOHOLICS, AND TO PRACTICE THESE PRINCIPLES IN ALL OUR AFFAIRS

In telling our story, we may see more deeply into ourselves. Sometimes we don't know who we are or how we got from here to there until we describe our journey to someone else. So our sharing continues the upward spiral. We gain more by giving it away. In mutually supportive environments of recovery, we depend on others as they depend on us, to constantly grow and evolve, to become our genuine selves. Having had a spiritual awakening, we become integrated and whole. We find new direction in our lives and the joy of balances and purposeful living.

—Stephanie S. Covington, *A Woman's Way through the Twelve Steps* [35]

Recovering alcoholics who are working Step 12 are proving that they are transcending the selfishness of their disease and thinking of how they can help others—a stark contrast to when they were active alcoholics focused mainly on their own needs. Each of the prior Steps is intended to lead to a spiritual awakening (described in Chapter 8), and Step 12 implies that at this point, the individual has had the type of awakening necessary to recover from alcoholism. However, this is just the beginning of the path toward maintaining recovery. Many believe that "carrying this message to alcoholics" or being of service is the key to long-term recovery. An entire chapter in the *Big Book* dedicated to Step 12 discusses the various ways to be of service and states that "life will take on new meaning. To watch people recover, to see a fellowship grow about you, to have a host of friends—this is an experience you must not miss.... Frequent contact with newcomers and with each other is the bright spot of our lives."[36] There are many ways to perform the work of the Twelve Steps that include, but are not limited to, being a sponsor, telling your story at a meeting, taking phone calls from other sober alcoholics, having a service position, making coffee or putting chairs away at a meeting, and so on. Being of service allows individuals to take the focus off of themselves and place the welfare of others first. In fact, this Step encourages individuals to "practice these principles in all of our affairs," including in our relationships, at work, and in society. One HFA explained how he applies this concept, stating, "In a broader sense, looking for opportunities to be useful and helpful to whomever I come in contact with throughout my day results in a sense of well-being, purposefulness, and better perspective."

For many, this Step is truly fulfilling and allows them to find meaning in their lives and in the experience of being a recovering alcoholic. The relationship between a sober alcoholic and his or her sponsor is mutually beneficial in that it enhances the recovery of the sponsor as much, if not more, than that of the sober alcoholic. One female HFA explains that sponsoring helps her to stay "on the beam.... If I'm telling someone how to do something, or guiding them on appropriate or spiritual behavior, then I better be following spiritual principles myself," and she adds that "each time I take a sponsee [a sober alcoholic who is sponsored] through the Steps, not only do I feel like I experience them all over again, but I also get to have a new loving relationship in my life. My own understanding of the Steps, my connection to God, and my love for others keeps growing." A male HFA finds Twelve-Step work satisfying and necessary, believing that "you don't keep it [recovery] if you don't give it away." A female HFA has found that "there are an infinite number of ways to be of service. I try to incorporate into my daily life an attitude of humility and service. Each day I ask myself, how can I help others? and what can I bring to this situation? This Step has helped me in interactions with other people. It has taken the focus off of me and my immediate needs and more onto what I can contribute. I believe that self-esteem comes from this sense of being able to contribute." One male HFA sensed a true change in himself by this Step and poetically described, "I'm different; something has happened as a result of the actions I have taken. This obsession has been lifted. I can't imagine a life with drinking.... I see, when I work with you, I forget about me. Love and service. I have a new way of life. I have a new way of seeing things. It's not about what I can achieve, it's about what I can experience."

"Hindsight" Reflections of the Author: Step 12

One Year and Seven Months Sober until Present
I intentionally waited until I completed the Twelve Steps before sponsoring anyone. Taking into consideration my professional capacity as a mental health counselor, I felt that I needed to learn the differences between sponsoring someone and counseling them. Over time, I began to fully understand the differences. As a sponsor, I led sober alcoholics through the Twelve Steps to help them develop a relationship with their Higher Power. I shared my personal experiences along the way and was open about my past as well. In contrast, as a counselor, I helped to guide clients to make the best life choices, learn coping skills and listened to their stories—but did not reveal my personal experiences and struggles. I have been blessed professionally to have the opportunity to help others as a counselor and have been graced personally in finding a variety of service work that has brought a true sense of purpose and fulfillment to my recovery.

10

THE CHALLENGE: LIFE IN RECOVERY

We become more accepting, and we experience a consistent inner peacefulness. We are available to the experience of finding pleasure in everyday things. We are released from the cycle of constant searching and seeking for the quick fix or the high to fill the emptiness. Fulfillment—the real "high"—comes from staying on the path and being present in the moment. We find pleasure in the simple.
—Stephanie S. Covington, *A Woman's Way through the Twelve Steps*[1]

The evolution from early sobriety into long-term recovery takes time, work, and effort in making the necessary life changes. The sober person, who began this journey years prior, has transformed into a recovered individual with different belief systems, behaviors, and thought patterns. These shifts may have never been thought possible while in the grip of alcoholism—the sober person now senses that some type of miracle has taken place. Many high-functioning alcoholics (HFAs) are suddenly amazed at how different their lives are after they emerge from the intense emotions and pain of early sobriety into more stable recovery. In addition, they may sense internal shifts and changes that allow them to almost feel reprogrammed in terms of their relationship to alcohol.

There is not just one way to recover from alcoholism. Although this book focuses mainly on recovery through Twelve-Step Recovery Programs, alcoholics have found other ways to maintain long-term recovery. Research indicates that alcoholics have a better recovery rate when affiliated with some type of treatment and/or recovery program (see Chapter 7). The key to a successful recovery program is leading alcoholics not only to initially become sober, but also to maintain sobriety. The statement "Quitting drinking is easy; I have done it a hundred times" sums up this challenge. Alcoholics who achieve long-term recovery have lower relapse rates and greater defenses against drinking. Alcoholism is a lifelong disease, chronic and progressive; therefore alcoholics need to nourish and tend to their recovery.

LONG-TERM RECOVERY

They said, "You only have to change one thing: everything." And I have done that... I've become a completely different person... everything is different. The way that I look at the world is different. The way that I look at life, the way that I look at me.

—recovering alcoholic[2]

Maintaining long-term recovery is the ultimate goal in the treatment for alcoholism, but it does not become a reality for everyone who wants it—relapse is always a possibility. Many factors determine if an individual will be able to achieve long-term recovery from alcoholism. These factors include, but are not limited to, access to treatment/recovery programs, willingness to get help, support of family and friends, effort put into recovering, spiritual beliefs, current age, age when drinking began, level of disease progression, co-occurring mental illness, and others. Mulligan has observed that HFAs often have a "better shot at having longer recovery because they often have a strong skill set and support system." However, only a minority of alcoholics enter into full recovery. Research from the National Institute on Alcohol Abuse and Alcoholism found that about 18% of alcohol-dependent individuals are abstinent and in recovery from alcohol for over a year. In addition, the results of this study concluded that "the likelihood of abstinent recovery increased over time and with age and was higher among women, individuals who were married or cohabitating, individuals with an onset of dependence at ages 18–24, and persons who had experienced a greater number of dependence symptoms."[3]

Most individuals in long-term recovery report dramatic changes in all areas of their lives compared with those in early sobriety. According to the Transtheoretical Model, those in long-term recovery have entered into the Maintenance stage—the final stage of change preceded by the Precontemplation, Contemplation, Preparation, and Action stages. A considerable amount of time and effort is required to reach this stage. Successful negotiation of this stage includes "1. actively countering any threats and temptations, 2. checking and renewing commitment, 3. making sure that the decisional balance remains negative for reengaging in the addictive behavior and 4. establishing a protective environment and a satisfying lifestyle."[4] In addition, individuals begin to expend less energy trying to stay sober—they are developing a sense of self-efficacy and belief in their ability to manage the ups and down of recovery without turning to alcohol. Being sober begins to feel normal, and the cravings to drink lessen in frequency and intensity—and are eliminated for some. Successful "maintainers" begin to see life as a big picture and not as a day-to-day struggle to fight triggers and to stay sober—allowing them to focus on other goals, such as getting an education, bettering their career, forming healthy relationships, and so on. Individuals have formed a new identity—one that is whole and complete without alcohol.[5] One recovering alcoholic declared, "I met myself in recovery."

Long-term recovery is different for each individual, but there are some common patterns and experiences. For those in Twelve-Step Recovery Programs, recovery most often occurs after they have worked the Twelve Steps. Many HFAs experience radical changes in their personal and spiritual belief systems to which they could not adhere when drinking alcoholically and even in early sobriety. They often rely less on their sponsor and more on a Higher Power for strength and peace of mind. One female HFA, sober for ten years, feels that her inner life has changed more than her outside life. She has "learned how to live according to values and spiritual principles.... I began to build a sense of self-esteem based on right living. I began to take responsibility for myself.... I learned about acceptance—not spending my life battling reality—and that has brought a lot of peace." Another female HFA, sober for over three years, explained, "I can be completely honest with myself and my sponsor; I have found self-esteem, peace of mind, and a true belief that things will be OK." One male HFA, sober for three years, tended to isolate as an active alcoholic. He explains the enormous changes in his behaviors and life, stating that "externally, my life is improved. I have resurrected old friendships and started new ones. I am confident and helpful in my professional role as a physician. I am not afraid to look people in the eye, because I make a habit of apologizing and setting right my new mistakes before they turn into feuds. People are no longer afraid of me! I am, more often than not, approachable, reasonable and predictable." One female recovering alcoholic, sober for over eight years, explains that life in recovery compared with that in early sobriety is "not comparable. My quality of life is different. The only things that are the same are that I live in the same physical vessel and that I am still an alcoholic."

Another characteristic of long-term recovery is that being sober becomes normal and alcohol cravings are minimal. One female HFA, sober over four years, explains that "sobriety seems pretty normal to me. When I first got sober, it was very strange not to be under the influence of something. Now, it's harder to remember what it was like to be drunk." Another female HFA, sober for over three years, adds, "I don't crave alcohol anymore—a miracle—and I can be around others drinking and not want to." HFAs who once struggled to accept that they were alcoholic because of comparisons to low-bottom alcoholics now tend to completely accept their alcoholism. A female HFA, sober for over three years, expands on this, stating, "The longer I'm sober, the stronger I feel about my status as a legitimate alcoholic. I like meeting people like myself [HFAs] who know what I mean when I say I don't have a *big* fat story to tell, that I cannot and will not compete for a juicy tale. There are probably more of us than low-bottom people, and it's the overemphasis on the Bowery stories that leaves out many who need help and convince themselves that they're just too lightweight to make the grade of belonging to a Twelve-Step Recovery Program or need support of such a group."

Long-term recovery also brings about a leveling of the highs of drinking and lows of the crash to which active alcoholics were accustomed. Recovery tends to balance out these fluctuations and may feel strange at first, but HFAs begin to acclimate over time. One female HFA, sober for over three years, admits, "I now feel fine a lot.... I no longer have those intense feelings as often and life is good. I am happy. Not the happiest, but not depressed either. I am just run-of-the-mill happy with life and feel fine, which sometimes I think is bad, but I'm learning is actually normal. I feel normal most of the time now... and that is a good thing." A male HFA, sober for over two years, stated, "I can honestly say my mood is fairly balanced and I am beginning to find pleasure in very simple acts of self-care, trust, and reliance upon God and service to others."

Many HFAs report that recovery allows them to handle their emotions well, in contrast to drinking in reaction to their feelings. In other words, they now have emotional sobriety as well as physical sobriety. A male HFA, sober for over twenty-five years, describes emotional sobriety, emphasizing that "destructive emotions keep us blocked, unplugged from a Higher Power, and with no Higher Power we are without defense from the insane thinking which leads to the first drink. It is so important that we stay on the beam emotionally." A female HFA, sober for ten years, adds, "I don't feel so afraid of feelings. I can see them for what they are, I know they won't kill me, I know they don't have to mean everything and I can let them pass." In addition, HFAs begin to truly believe that alcohol is not a solution for discomfort and pain. One female HFA going through a difficult time in her life stated, "I am convinced that all of the alcohol in the world cannot fix how I am feeling." She has learned different coping skills and developed spiritual beliefs that are helping her to deal with her feelings—no matter how painful—and to move forward. A male HFA, sober for three years, stated, "I now believe, deep inside in a way that I never forget, that escaping my feelings with alcohol is no longer an option, ever.... On the whole, I am happy and productive much more often than I am hopeless, bitter, or resentful—and that is a radical change from my previous mode of living." A recovering alcoholic, sober for over eight years, concurs that "it's important to me that I can feel anything—I spent a number of years not feeling and that's why I drank... to not feel anything, because I couldn't deal with it. It didn't matter if it was a bad feeling or a good feeling or anything. It was all too strong, or so I thought, for me to take. And so, I anesthetized myself frequently.... To me drinking... was a walking deadness, you know, and now it's not.... Those kinds of feelings are things I never had before. It's important to feel them."[6]

RELAPSE

It is easy to let up on the spiritual program of action and rest on our laurels. We are headed for trouble if we do, for alcohol is a subtle foe. We are not cured of alcoholism. What we really have is a daily reprieve contingent on the maintenance of our spiritual condition.

—The *Big Book*[7]

Getting sober and sustaining long-term recovery are enormous challenges for all alcoholics. No matter how long an alcoholic has been in recovery, he or she is always vulnerable to relapsing—no alcoholic is exempt.[8] HFAs face many of the same issues as low-bottom alcoholics in terms of relapse. A relapse can be defined as "the return to the problematic behavior."[9] There are different examples of relapse, but because this book explores abstinence-based recovery, a relapse is considered intentionally drinking any amount of alcohol or using other mood-altering substances (e.g., marijuana, cocaine). Just one alcoholic drink can stimulate the phenomenon of craving and reactivate the addiction. In addition, if an alcoholic uses another mood-altering drug, such as marijuana, his or her judgment will be impaired, which can lead back to drinking alcohol.

Although extensive addiction research has been conducted, there is not just one established relapse rate. Several reasons have been found for this, including that definitions of treatment success vary from one treatment center to another. Most studies of relapse are based on population samples from treatment facilities, and rates are affected by the follow-up times as well as the definition of relapse.[10] Some treatment centers report rates of alcoholics who continuously abstain, while others report rates of alcoholics who decrease their usage. While some research assesses all patients admitted to the treatment center, other research focuses only on those patients who completed their programs.[11] Research is limited on relapse rates of individuals attending recovery program support groups.

There is a range of relapse rates for individuals who went to a treatment center—40% to 60% of alcoholics relapse within the first few months after treatment, and up to 70% to 80% by the end of the first year. Studies with follow-up intervals of over two years indicate that only 30% of individuals are able to abstain—implying a 70% relapse rate.[12] Research is minimal on relapse rates for alcoholics in the general population who are not admitted into treatment centers. In one research study of a nationally representative sample of alcoholics in the general population, about 31% relapsed in a three-year follow-up period. This figure was higher for young adults aged eighteen to twenty-five, who had a relapse rate of over 40%.[13] The difference between the higher relapse rates of those alcoholics who were admitted into treatment centers and those in the general population may be explained by the severity of the cases seen in treatment centers.

Ideally, alcoholics would want to get sober and not relapse. However, that is not realistic given the chronic nature of this disease,[14] which is reflected in the high relapse rates. When an individual relapses, he or she generally has a shift in readiness to get sober again—this process can be referred to as "recycling" through the Transtheoretical Model stages of change. For example, one individual may relapse and then be ready for the Action stage and attempt to get sober again, while another may relapse and begin to question his or her readiness for change and recycle to the Contemplation stage. A relapse can affect an individual's motivation to press on with his or her sobriety, and if it happens repeatedly, he or she may feel defeated by the disease. Therefore the way an individual handles and interprets a relapse is crucial to his or her recovery. Relapse is a humbling experience and can lead some to become more committed to their recovery programs because they now have witnessed their vulnerability. They also may learn about emotional, spiritual, and physical triggers in their environment of which they need to be aware in the future. According to DiClemente, "The purpose of treatments, self-help, and other types of interventions is to make the learning more efficient.... The hope is that by understanding better this process of change we can facilitate movement and recycling through the stages and reduce the time needed to achieve successfully established and maintained change."[15]

There are some common patterns of those who relapse. The following are warning signs and triggers that many alcoholics report precipitated their relapse:

- Social isolation
- Extreme negative thinking
- Negative mood states (e.g., angry, sad)
- Positive mood states (e.g., euphoric, excited)
- Lack of spiritual connectedness
- Loss of personal values and/or morals
- Feeling overconfident in one's sobriety
- Feeling invincible and lacking humility
- False security in believing he or she is "cured" of alcoholism
- Being convinced of personal control or ability to moderate if he or she drinks again
- Lack of involvement in a recovery program
- Recurring thoughts of not having hit a low enough bottom
- Persistent denial
- Spending a lot of unnecessary time around alcohol and/or heavy drinkers
- Intense reminiscing, romanticizing alcohol, and extreme focus on the positive aspects of drinking
- Lack of day-to-day routine and structure (e.g., on vacation, retired, unemployed)
- Negative life events (e.g., death of loved one, divorce)
- Untreated mental illness
- Failure to make life changes necessary for recovery
- Interpersonal conflict(s)
- The holidays and other celebratory occasions (e.g., weddings, birthdays)

The preceding list illustrates the importance of attaining recovery from alcoholism, for the triggers for relapse are endless. Treatment centers and/or recovery programs help alcoholics recover and develop resistance against the temptations and catalysts for relapse. HFAs may have a higher risk of experiencing several of the previously listed warning signs and triggers for relapse such as "recurring thoughts of not having hit a low enough bottom" and "persistent denial," because these are issues that many struggled with initially when getting sober. In addition, they may also be more prone to "intense reminiscing, romanticizing alcohol, and extreme focus on the positive aspects of drinking," for alcohol may not have led to many losses for them, as it usually does for low-bottom alcoholics. HFAs also need to be vigilant about maintaining humility as well as challenging their thinking that they have been "cured" of alcoholism—they are accustomed to using their self-will to fix problems and to succeed. Griffin expands on this point, stating, "The trouble with 'I got it,' is that, like every other experience, it's impermanent. Many people have similar moments in meditation, therapy, sobriety, and other psycho/spiritual practices. If they fall under the illusion that what they got is good for all time, they are setting themselves up for disappointment at least, and possibly worse."[16] In addition, some HFAs may not involve themselves in a recovery program nor do the work required to recover because they may not feel a sense of desperation to get help. Therefore they may be vulnerable to relapse in ways that other low-bottom alcoholics are not.

Relapse can happen for different reasons and at various times in an individual's sobriety. Many alcoholics report that they experienced an emotional relapse well before the actual physical relapse of taking a drink. When sober alcoholics behave in ways that compromise their values (e.g., dishonesty, lashing out at others, etc.), they often become blocked spiritually and emotionally. Over time, this disconnect may bring negative thought and behavior patterns back to the surface—triggering them to drink. DiClemente explains that "'apparently irrelevant decisions' represent shifts in thinking and in decisional considerations that promote a return to the addictive behavior. The shifts include the slow erosion of the commitment to change and a subtle increase in the positive valence of the addictive behavior. After the passage of time or intervening events, the commitment to change can be undermined.... In fact, for most people it will always be easier to return to the addictive behavior."[17] This is particularly true when they have not established stable long-term recovery. Caron explains that a relapse can start off slowly when an alcoholic does not do the necessary work of recovery (e.g., not attending meetings, spending time with unhealthy friends) and then quickly take over. He uses the metaphor of the spinning vortex of water during a toilet flush to illustrate a relapse in that "it is a slow tailspin at the top, but as the water begins to exit there is a fast spin that will suck you down—you can't get out."

Relapse is considered by many to be part of recovery from an addiction. This can be encouraging to those who struggle to stay sober, but it does not detract from the danger that relapse poses. Because so many alcoholics relapse, there may be a false impression that relapse is simply a setback in an individual's recovery. Far more important than just being a discouraging regression, relapse can ultimately be deadly.

MAINTAINING RECOVERY

The absence of the addictive behavior is not sufficient to successfully maintain the change and become an ex-addict. In order to sustain recovery, new behaviors and reinforcing experiences must become part of a new way of living in the world.
—Carlo C. DiClemente, *Addiction and Change: How Addictions Develop and Addicted People Recover*[18]

Recovery is not something that an individual does once and then is finished. In fact, the largest challenge for alcoholics is not in initially getting sober, but in maintaining recovery. One male HFA, sober for over thirty years, lightheartedly admits, "I want a diploma from recovery.... I am still waiting." Foster explains that because alcoholism is a chronic disease, "you don't actually get better.... It's a disease that needs to be managed over the long-term. And so recovery is this issue of how do you manage this disease? And there are many ways you can do that."[19] Recovery does not become a permanent state without continued efforts by the individual. DiClemente concurs: "The challenge of human behavior change is to make change permanent."[20]

Researchers, addiction experts, and recovering alcoholics can all agree that there are many approaches to maintaining recovery. Duda believes that recovering alcoholics need to "take responsibility for every aspect of their lives." Maintenance is as necessary for HFAs as it is for low-bottom alcoholics and involves putting effort into actual recovery program work, personal self-care, spiritual pursuits, mental health, and interpersonal relationships. Those who have achieved long-term recovery tend to have a balance between these aspects of recovery and life. In addition, they are continuously striving to grow emotionally and spiritually. Regardless, the most basic, but most essential aspect of maintaining long-term recovery is to not drink alcohol.

HFAs in a Twelve-Step Recovery Program take basic actions to sustain their recovery. Most important is that they place recovery first in their lives— for without it, alcoholics risk losing everything. One recovering alcoholic, sober for seven years, has observed that "the difference between individuals who attain long-term sobriety and those who do not is the action of recommitting themselves to their recovery, to a Higher Power, and to being of service to others." It is easy for sober alcoholics to begin feeling better emotionally, physically, and spiritually, and then to lose their incentive. Pain often motivates, and the absence of pain can lead to stagnation. Long-term recovery entails continuing to take action through both the difficult and joyful times in life.

Many HFAs report that working the Twelve Steps is their main recovery tool and the core of maintenance. Most report some form of a daily routine that involves prayer and/or meditation. One male HFA, sober for over twenty-five years, explains that "morning coffee and meditation is a must. One hour a day." Another male HFA, sober for four years, reports, "I rise in the morning and spend most of my first hour reading, praying, meditating, and writing in a journal. I review my day before I retire at night and thank my Higher Power for another day free from addictions." Some HFAs report praying or reading daily reflections for a few minutes in the morning, at night, or both. Others choose to pray throughout the day or focus on their breathing when they are stressed or need to clear their minds. The specific length of time given to prayer or meditation is not important—finding a way to tap into a spiritual connection is what matters.

Another necessity of recovery for those in a Twelve-Step Recovery Program is attending meetings. HFAs report attending meetings at different frequencies.

The key is for an individual to figure out how often attending a meeting works for him or her—there are no rules, only suggestions. In addition, HFAs report that phone calls and spending time with other sober alcoholics are crucial to their recovery. Most find that helping another alcoholic through sponsoring is imperative, and one female HFA, sober for three years, believes, "I need to give it away and carry this message of hope to others like me."

In terms of personal self-care, HFAs report that managing their stress in a healthy manner is essential. A female HFA, sober for four years, reports, "I exercise regularly, I eat well and I don't smoke anymore. I work really hard to care for myself, to stay balanced because I know that a lot of my drinking functioned in part to relieve anxiety, stress, feelings of insecurity, etc." Another female HFA, sober for two years, reports, "I eat healthy food that keeps me strong, stay away from other addictive things [caffeine, cigarettes], and try to get enough sleep each night." Many HFAs report practicing yoga, which combines exercise with meditation and prayer, creating a sense of serenity. In general, HFAs describe having some type of consistent daily routine that creates structure and purpose.

In addition to physical self-care, psychological self-care is equally important. Some HFAs report that they attend therapy to deal with outside mental health issues or as a supplement to their recovery program. A female HFA, sober for two years, adds, "I also go to therapy with an addictions counselor as needed. In stressful times in my life I go weekly, but generally two times a month." Another female HFA, sober for four years, adds, "I also work to stay secure and happy with myself—I believe that therapy, my meditation practice, and my work in my Twelve-Step Recovery Program all help with this." Psychological self-care can also include doing activities and hobbies that are pleasurable and bring joy into an individual's life such as hiking, gardening, socializing, reading, dancing, and so on. Life in recovery should involve living, and individuals should be encouraged to find and participate in things about which they are passionate.

Healthy interpersonal friendships and romantic relationships are also an important aspect of maintaining recovery. One male HFA, sober for twenty years, reports that "friendship with those in my recovery program has been the truest form of support after all these years." Recovering alcoholics often notice that they attract healthier people into their lives when they are sober and balanced, compared with when they were drinking and living in chaos. A female HFA, sober for four years, reports, "I make an effort to keep good, sober people in my life. I make an effort to take responsibility for my actions. I make an effort to remove myself from and avoid drama." One male HFA, sober for two years, reports, "I try to give myself a little more space these days to decompress, but I also like to be around friends in the recovery program a lot." In contrast, the ability of an individual to "decompress" while alone is a sign that he or she no longer needs constant distraction. For many, part of drinking alcoholically was constant socializing. Therefore recovery entails finding a balance between being with others and being alone.

"Hindsight" Reflections of the Author

Long-Term Recovery

Past Journal Entry: March 14, 2006, Age 29—Two Years Sober

I feel able to see beyond my own distorted thoughts around alcohol. My recovery program has helped me to challenge the distorted thoughts that alcoholism created within my mind.

Throughout my life struggles, I had some part of my soul connected to my future path. I prayed and waited for the time to come when I could look back on my pain and help others to cope. That time has finally come and I have arrived here "one day at a time." I can finally look back on what was once me. I felt shame about the alcoholic part of my life and now I feel pride in sharing it with others. I felt fear about people knowing I am an alcoholic, but I now feel strength and liberation. I can honestly say that I have something to offer others—sobriety, wisdom and serenity.

Through completing the Steps, my past has healed. I am living more in the present. A sense of the truth in my life has become clear and I have found the strength to live in it.

Past Journal Entry: February 2, 2007, Age 30—Three Years Sober

I got married, I am sober, I have a home, I am content . . . so much has changed. . . . Through all of the ups and downs, I have transcended with God as my guide. I am not perfect. I am still working on myself and falling at times—but I get back up with love and support.

Some of the pain of the past has scarred me—but the guilt has lifted. For today I see the truth—my truth . . . and the thing that I am most proud of is that I went "any length for my sobriety." My life has come a long way from my last drink, the bar and the blackout—by the grace of God.

There have been dramatic internal and external shifts in my life from early sobriety, through the Steps, and into longer-term recovery. I have emerged from the tunnel of early sobriety and am amazed at the clarity I now have regarding my alcoholism and how it has impacted my life and relationships. Recovery has allowed me to find my true self—and I have discovered my true self, who was hidden behind the drinking, the socializing, and the chaos of my addiction. I cannot compare my drinking life to my life in recovery—they feel like separate existences.

The growth process of recovery never ends. Just as one obstacle is faced and lessons are learned, another may arise. Though challenges constantly occur and uncomfortable feelings still crop up, they pass, and I have the tools to get through them. I may be afraid at times, but I am always reassured that no matter what happens in my life, I will be all right—I have a source of Power to tap into: God.

Relapse

I had my own forms of relapse many times before getting sober again. For four years I had abstained for brief periods and attempted to moderate my drinking. I repeatedly promised myself and others that I would never have a blackout episode again—and I would break these promises over and over again. These drunken episodes led me to experience intense feelings of shame and defeat, and then I would repeat the cycle. Since joining a Twelve-Step Recovery Program, I have been fortunate not to have had a relapse. However, I believe the only reason I have not relapsed is that I had failed at every possible experiment to control my drinking before joining the program.

Past Journal Entry: August 4, 2006, Age 29—Two Years and Seven Months Sober

I had a great time in Martha's Vineyard. However, when I was out to dinner in an area on the water with beach bars and boats docked nearby I suddenly found myself jealous of those who were out drinking. I began fixating on a young woman who was hardly able to stand up, hanging on the shoulders of a male near her and embarrassing herself. I actually wished I was her—wasted and in that numb state. These obsessive thoughts and cravings took me by surprise and I felt embarrassed about them.... When I called my sponsor I received some insight and felt that this wasn't some huge regression on my part—just a reminder that I am still an alcoholic!

In recovery, I have never felt immune from relapse. I sense the disease of alcoholism lingering in the back of my mind—dormant, but never gone. A part of me, at times, romanticizes alcohol, and I find this to be a strange blessing, for it is a humbling reminder that I am an alcoholic. After all the pain and danger that drinking has caused me and others in my life, the fact that I can at times think fondly of drinking alcohol is a symptom of the disease. Today I am able to recognize these thoughts and feelings for what they are: motivation to continue doing the work of recovery, not reasons to drink.

Maintaining Recovery

Past Journal Entry: July 19, 2005, Age 28—One Year and Six Months Sober

I am at a yoga retreat center for several days. This center is located above a peaceful lake in the rolling hills of western Massachusetts. There are services offered including yoga, meditation, massage and many other spiritual practices. It is my reward instead of the bars! I have come so far—I am in awe of the peace here and feel blessed to pass through. I feel God's presence here and sense that this trip will benefit me mentally, physically and spiritually. The visual beauty of this place and the spiritual nature of the community here have stimulated all of my senses.

I am even noticing that things that once annoyed me are flowing through me. I see the big picture and feel peace—why should small dramas inhibit that?

I see those around me spinning their wheels and realize how effortlessly I am "riding the wave." Faith brings us comfort when our minds can't. I am able to appreciate nature, the small things, calm—everything that I knew my soul craved, but alcohol had gotten in the way. I choose sobriety over being drunk, peace over chaos, harmony over drama, and love not anger.

Past Journal Entry: September 2, 2006, Age 29—Two Years and Seven Months Sober
Sometimes I want to stagnate—I feel like I am always on this sobriety treadmill—"I need to do this, do that, do this more, etc."—I just want to "be."...Maybe a part of me is passively rebelling. I just don't want to deal.

Maintaining my recovery has evolved over time. My Twelve-Step Recovery Program helped me to recover from alcoholism and led me onto a spiritual path. However, it was not designed to cure all outside issues. Therefore I made this distinction and have been proactive in my self-care, incorporating a variety of other practices into my life. Acupuncture, massage, yoga, running, and therapy have all been crucial at various times in helping me to maintain a sense of balance in my life. In early sobriety, I devoted a great deal of time to recovery and self-care. At times, I felt like staying sober was a full-time job: Twelve-Step Recovery Program meetings, working the Steps, service work, and self-care. I was working so hard just to be OK, and at times, I wanted to do nothing, to stop analyzing myself and to be carefree again. However, over time, I reached a more stable place emotionally, physically, and spiritually, allowing me to cut back on some aspects of self-care. Throughout most of my recovery, I have found it necessary to take time to be alone to quiet my mind and recharge myself—something that I never desired or needed to do before getting sober.

My battle against alcoholism has evolved into a journey of spiritual and emotional growth. What started as a need for chaos has been transformed into a desire for serenity. I have shared my experiences in their raw form, and I pray that my life lessons and growth will help others. May the torch of God's light be passed on.

APPENDICES

APPENDIX A: DSM-IV TR—SUBSTANCE DEPENDENCE DIAGNOSTIC CRITERIA[1]

A maladaptive pattern of substance use, leading to clinically significant impairment or distress, as manifested by three (or more) of the following, occurring at any time in the same 12-month period:

1. tolerance, as defined by either of the following:
   a. a need for markedly increased amounts of the substance to achieve desired effect
   b. markedly diminished effect with continued use of the same amount of the substance
2. withdrawal, as manifested by either of the following:
   a. the characteristic syndrome for the substance
   b. the same (or closely related) substance is being taken to relieve or avoid withdrawal symptoms
3. the substance is taken in larger amounts over a longer period than was intended
4. there is a persistent desire or unsuccessful efforts to cut down or control substance use
5. a great deal of time is spent in activities necessary to obtain the substance, use the substance or recover from its effects
6. important social, occupational or recreational activities are given up or reduced because of the substance use
7. the substance use is continued despite the knowledge of having a persistent or recurrent physical or psychological problem that is likely to have been caused or exacerbated by the substance

Appendix B: DSM-IV TR—Substance Abuse Diagnostic Criteria[2]

A. A maladaptive pattern of substance use leading to clinically significant impairment or distress, as manifested by one (or more) of the following within a 12-month period:
   1. recurrent substance use resulting in a failure to fulfill major role obligations at work, school or home
   2. recurrent substance use in situations in which it is physically hazardous
   3. recurrent substance-related legal problems
   4. continued substance use despite having persistent or recurrent social or interpersonal problems caused or exacerbated by the effects of the substance
B. The symptoms have never met the criteria for Substance Dependence for this class of substance

Appendix C: Alcohol Screening Test[3]

Check "Yes" or "No" in Response to the Following Questions

1. Have you ever decided to stop drinking for a week or so, but only lasted for a couple of days? Yes _____ No _____
2. Do you wish people would mind their own business about your drinking—stop telling you what to do? Yes _____ No _____
3. Have you ever switched from one kind of drink to another in the hope that this would keep you from getting drunk? Yes _____ No _____
4. Have you had to have an eye-opener upon awakening during the past year? Yes _____ No _____
5. Do you envy people who can drink without getting into trouble? Yes _____ No _____
6. Have you had problems connected with drinking during the past year? Yes _____ No _____
7. Has your drinking caused trouble at home/school? Yes _____ No _____
8. Do you ever try to get "extra" drinks at a party because you do not get enough? Yes _____ No _____
9. Do you tell yourself you can stop drinking any time you want to, even though you keep getting drunk when you don't mean to? Yes _____ No _____
10. Have you missed days of work or school because of your drinking? Yes _____ No _____
11. Do you have blackouts? Yes _____ No _____
12. Have you ever felt that your life would be better if you did not drink? Yes _____ No _____

TOTAL # "Yes" responses _____

Did you answer YES 4 or more times? If so, then you may have a problem with alcohol.

Appendix D: Alcohol Recovery Programs
Contact Information

Alcoholics Anonymous World Headquarters

Mailing address:
A.A. World Services Inc.
P.O. Box 459
Grand Central Station
New York, NY 10163
Location:
A.A. World Services Inc.
11th Floor
475 Riverside Drive at West 120th Street
New York, NY 10115
General Service Office: (212) 870-3400
National Web site: http://www.aa.org
Local meeting finder (United States and Canada): http://www.aa.org/en_find_meeting.cfm

Secular Organization for Sobriety/Save Our Selves (SOS)

Mailing address and location:
4773 Hollywood Boulevard
Hollywood, CA 90027
Telephone: (323) 666-4295
Web site: http://www.sossobriety.org
E-mail: SOS@CFIWest.org

SMART Recovery

National office:
7537 Mentor Avenue, Suite 306
Mentor, OH 44060
Telephone: (440) 951-5357
Web site: http://www.smartrecovery.org
E-mail: info@smartrecovery.org

Women for Sobriety Inc. (WFS)

Mailing address:
WFS Inc.
P.O. Box 618
Quakertown, PA 18951-0618
Contact number for meeting places and times: (215) 536-8026
Web site: http://www.womenforsobriety.org (meetings are not listed on Web site)
E-mail: NewLife@nni.com

APPENDIX E: TWELVE STEPS OF ALCOHOLICS ANONYMOUS[4]

1. We admitted we were powerless over alcohol—that our lives had become unmanageable.
2. Came to believe that a Power greater than ourselves could restore us to sanity.
3. Made a decision to turn our will and our lives over to the care of God *as we understood Him.*
4. Made a searching and fearless moral inventory of ourselves.
5. Admitted to God, to ourselves, and to another human being the exact nature of our wrongs.
6. Were entirely ready to have God remove all these defects of character.
7. Humbly asked Him to remove our shortcomings.
8. Made a list of all persons we had harmed, and became willing to make amends to them all.
9. Made direct amends to such people wherever possible, except when to do so would injure them or others.
10. Continued to take personal inventory and when we were wrong promptly admitted it.
11. Sought through prayer and meditation to improve our conscious contact with God, *as we understood Him*, praying only for knowledge of His will for us and the power to carry that out.
12. Having had a spiritual awakening as the result of these steps, we tried to carry this message to alcoholics, and to practice these principles in all our affairs.

APPENDIX F: "NEW LIFE" ACCEPTANCE PROGRAM OF WOMEN FOR SOBRIETY, INC.—THIRTEEN STATEMENTS[5]

1. I have a life-threatening problem that once had me. *I now take charge of my life. I accept the responsibility.*
2. Negative thoughts destroy only myself. *My first conscious act must be to remove negativity from my life.*
3. Happiness is a habit I will develop. *Happiness is created, not waited for.*
4. Problems bother me only to the degree I permit them to. *I now better understand my problems and do not permit problems to overwhelm me.*
5. I am what I think. *I am a capable, competent, caring, compassionate woman.*
6. Life can be ordinary or it can be great. *Greatness is mine by a conscious effort.*
7. Love can change the course of my world. *Caring becomes all important.*
8. The fundamental object of life is emotional and spiritual growth. *Daily I put my life into a proper order, knowing which are the priorities.*
9. The past is gone forever. *No longer will I be victimized by the past, I am a new person.*
10. All love given returns. *I will learn to know that others love me.*
11. Enthusiasm is my daily exercise. *I treasure all moments of my new life.*
12. I am a competent woman and have much to give life. *This is what I am and I shall know it always.*
13. I am responsible for myself and for my actions. *I am in charge of my mind, my thoughts, and my life.*

NOTES

CHAPTER 1

1. Caroline Knapp, *Drinking: A Love Story* (New York: Delta, 1996), 30.

2. B. F. Grant et al., "The 12-Month Prevalence and Trends in DSM-IV Alcohol Abuse and Dependence: United States, 1991–1992 and 2001–2002," *Drug and Alcohol Dependence* 74, no. 3 (2004): 223–234, quoted in National Institute of Alcohol Abuse and Alcoholism, "Surgeon General Calls on Americans to Face Facts about Drinking: Transportation Safety Leaders Join Alcohol Research, Prevention, and Treatment Leaders to Recommend Screening on April 8, National Screening Day, 2004," *NIH News*, http://www.niaaa.nih.gov/NewsEvents/NewsReleases/Screenday04.htm.

3. Knapp, *Drinking*, 12–13.

4. H. B. Moss, C. M. Chen, and H. Yi, "Subtypes of Alcohol Dependence in a Nationally Representative Sample," *Drug and Alcohol Dependence* 91, no. 2–3 (2007): 149–158.

5. T. J. Berger, "Alcohol Abuse in Medical School," *Journal of the American Medical Association* 258, no. 9 (1987): 1173.

6. J.-B. Daeepen, T. L. Smith, and M. A. Schuckit, "How Would You Label Your Own Drinking Pattern Overall? An Evaluation of Answers Provided by 181 High-Functioning Middle-Aged Men," *Alcohol and Alcoholism* 34, no. 5 (1999): 767–772.

7. Knapp, *Drinking*.

8. Betty Ford Center, "A Brief History of the Betty Ford Center," Betty Ford Center, http://www.bettyfordcenter.org/welcome/ourhistory.php.

9. Meg Grant, "On Her Own Terms: Beating Breast Cancer and Alcoholism, Betty Ford Found That Her Greatest Strength Lay in Helping Others by Being Herself (First Ladies)," *People Weekly*, May 15, 2000, p. 169.

10. Jane Nicolls, "Sunny Side Down," *People Weekly*, October 30, 1995, p. 71.

11. Robert Epstein, "Buzz Aldrin: Down to Earth (Interview)," *Psychology Today*, May 2001, p. 68.

12. "Boy Interrupted With A. J. McLean Fighting Depression and Alcoholism, the Backstreet Boys Take an Unscheduled De-Tour," *People Weekly*, July 23, 2001, p. 60.

13. "Pat O'Brien Comes Clean about Rehab," *People Online*, May 5, 2005, http://www.people.com/people/article/0,,1057723,00.html.

14. John E. Mulligan, "Patrick Kennedy Finds Much to Celebrate after a Year of Sobriety," *Providence Journal*, May 6, 2007, p. A1.

15. "But Seriously . . . ," *People Weekly*, October 16, 2006, p. 91.

16. Steve Serby, "His Sobering Experience," *New York Post*, November 17, 2006, p. 128.

17. Mark Dagostino, "I'm an Alcoholic," *People Weekly*, February 12, 2007, p. 71.

18. Associated Press, "He'll Skip the Complimentary Drink," *Boston Globe*, May 22, 2007, p. F3.

19. Alan Light, "A Guitar God's Memories, Demons and All," *New York Times*, October 7, 2007, Music sec. 23–24.

20. Associated Press, "Bush Says Reliance on Faith Helped Him Beat 'Addiction' to Alcohol," *MSNBC.com*, http://www.msnbc.msn.com/id/22898644/#storyContinued, (para. 1).

21. American Psychiatric Association, *Diagnostic and Statistical Manual of Mental Disorders*, 4th ed., text rev. (Washington, DC: American Psychiatric Press, 2000), 213–214.

22. Alcoholics Anonymous, *Alcoholics Anonymous*, 4th ed. (New York: Alcoholics Anonymous World Services Inc., 2001).

23. American Psychiatric Association, *Diagnostic and Statistical Manual*, 213.

24. Dan Williams, "Addiction Information," Peace and Healing, http://www.peaceandhealing.com/addiction/index.asp.

25. American Psychiatric Association, *Diagnostic and Statistical Manual*, 214.

26. National Institute of Alcohol Abuse and Alcoholism, "FAQs for the General Public," National Institute on Alcohol Abuse and Alcoholism, http://www.niaaa.nih.gov/FAQs/General-English/.

27. Roundtable on Religion and Social Welfare Policy, "An Interview with Susan Foster of CASA," Nelson A. Rockefeller Institute of Government, http://www.religionandsocialpolicy.org/interviews/interview.cfm?id=152.

28. Alcoholics Anonymous, *Alcoholics Anonymous*, xxx.

29. Ibid., xxviii.

30. Ibid., 34.

31. Ibid., 21.

32. Ibid., xxx.

33. Melinda Beck, "Are You an Alcoholic?" *Wall Street Journal*, January 8, 2008, p. D1.

34. News-Medical.Net, "Five Distinct Subtypes of Alcoholism Identified," News-Medical.Net, http://www.news-medical.net/?id=27074 (para. 1).

35. Ibid. (para. 7).

36. Ibid.

CHAPTER 2

1. J. A. McDonald, "Confessions from a Quarter Bounce (Voices of Youth)," *Reclaiming Children and Youth* 11, no. 3 (2002): 135(2).

2. U.S. Department of Health and Human Services, "News Release: Acting Surgeon General Issues National Call to Action on Underage Drinking," U.S. Department of Health and Human Services, http://www.hhs.gov/news/press/2007pres/20070306.html (para. 6).

3. Office of the Surgeon General, *The Surgeon General's Call to Action to Prevent and Reduce Underage Drinking: What It Means to You: A Guide to Action for Families*, Washington, DC: U.S. Department of Health and Human Services, 2007, http://www.surgeongeneral.gov/topics/underagedrinking/FamilyGuide.pdf.

4. Substance Abuse and Mental Health Services Administration, *Results from the 2005 National Survey on Drug Use and Health: National Findings*, NSDUH Series H-30, DHHS Publ. No. 06-4194 (Rockville, MD: SAMHSA Office of Applied Studies, 2006), quoted in Office of the Surgeon General, *The Surgeon General's Call to Action to Prevent and Reduce Underage Drinking*, Washington, DC: U.S. Department of Health and Human Services, 2007, http://www.surgeongeneral.gov/topics/underagedrinking/calltoaction.pdf.

5. Mary Pipher, *Reviving Ophelia: Saving the Selves of Adolescent Girls* (New York: Ballantine, 1994), 190, quoted in Devon Jersild, *Happy Hours: Alcohol in a Woman's Life* (New York: Perennial, 2001), 96.

6. David C. Treadway, *Before It's Too Late: Working with Substance Abuse in the Family* (New York: W. W. Norton, 1989), 136.

7. Jersild, *Happy Hours*, 104–105.

8. Lori Aratani, "Surveys Say Girls' Drug Use Is Rising," *Boston Globe*, February 11, 2008, p. A2.

9. Office of the Surgeon General, *Surgeon General's Call to Action*.

10. S. Gabel et al., "Personality Dimensions and Substance Misuse: Relationships in Adolescents, Mothers and Fathers," *American Journal on Addictions* 8 (1999): 101–113, quoted in Office of the Surgeon General, *Surgeon General's Call to Action*.

11. McDonald, "Confessions," 135.

12. S. H. Rhee et al., "Genetic and Environmental Influences on the Onset of Heavier Drinking among Adolescents," *Archives of General Psychiatry* 60 (2003): 1256–1264, quoted in Office of the Surgeon General, *Surgeon General's Call to Action*.

13. National Center on Addiction and Substance Abuse at Columbia University, "CASA 2007 Teen Survey Reveals America's Schools Infested with Drugs," National Center on Addiction and Substance Abuse at Columbia University, http://marketwire.com/mw/release.do?id=761295.

14. Deirdre M. Kirke, *Teenagers and Substance Abuse: Social Networks and Peer Influence* (New York: Palgrave Macmillan, 2006), 69.

15. L. Franks, "The Sex Lives of Your Children," *Talk* (February 2000): 102–107, quoted in S. S. Luthar and B. E. Becker, "Privileged but Pressured? A Study of Affluent Youth," *Child Development* 73, no. 5 (2002): 1593–1610.

16. P. Belluck, "Parents Try to Reclaim Their Children's Time," *New York Times*, June 13, 2000, p. A18, and B. Kantrowitz, "Busy around the Clock," *Newsweek*, July 17, 2000, p. 136, quoted in Luthar and Becker, "Privileged but Pressured?"

17. Luthar and Becker, "Privileged but Pressured?"

18. Susan Schindehette, "Dying for a Drink," *People Weekly*, September 4, 2006, p. 143.

19. Office of Applied Studies, Substance Abuse and Mental Health Services Administration, "The National Survey on Drug Use and Health Report: Academic Performance and Substance Use among Students Aged 12 to 17: 2002, 2003, and 2004," *NSDUH Report* 18 (2006), http://www.oas.samhsa.gov/2k6/academics/academics.pdf.

20. W. W. Hartup, "The Company They Keep: Friendships and Their Developmental Significance," *Child Development* 67 (1996): 1–13, quoted in E. A. P. Poelen, R. C. M. E. Engels, H. Van Der Vorst, R. H. J. Scholte, and A. A. Vermulst, "Best Friends and

Alcohol Consumption in Adolescence: A Within-Family Analysis," *Drug and Alcohol Dependence* 88 (2007): 163–173.

21. Kirke, *Teenagers and Substance Abuse*, 86.

22. National Center on Addiction and Substance Abuse at Columbia University, "CASA 2007 Teen Survey."

23. Ibid.

24. Poelen et al., "Best Friends."

25. National Center on Addiction and Substance Abuse at Columbia University, "CASA 2007 Teen Survey."

26. National Center for Injury Prevention and Control, "Web-Based Injury Statistics Query and Reporting System (WISQARS) 2004," Center for Disease Control and Prevention, http://www.cdc.gov/ncipc/wisqars/default.htm; R. Hingson and D. Kenkel, "Social Health and Economic Consequences of Underage Drinking," in *Reducing Underage Drinking: A Collective Responsibility*, ed. R. J. Bonnie and M. E. O'Connell (Washington D.C.: National Academies Press, 2004), 351–382; D. T. Levy, T. R. Miller, and K. C. Cox, *Costs of Underage Drinking* (Washington D.C.: U.S. Department of Justice, Office of Justice Programs, Office of Juvenile Justice and Delinquency Prevention, 1999); National Highway Traffic Safety Administration, *Traffic Safety Facts 2002: Alcohol*, DOT Publ. No. HS-809-606 (Washington D.C.: NHTSA, National Center for Statistics and Analysis, 2003); and G. S. Smith, C. C. Branas, and T. R. Miller, "Fatal Nontraffic Injuries Involving Alcohol: A Meta-analysis," *Annals of Emergency Medicine* 33 (1999): 659–668, quoted in Office of the Surgeon General, *Surgeon General's Call to Action*.

27. M. L. Cooper and H. K. Orcutt, "Drinking and Sexual Experience on First Dates among Adolescents," *Journal of Abnormal Psychology* 106 (1997): 191–202, and M. L. Cooper, R. S. Pierce, and R. F. Huselid, "Substance Use and Sexual Risk Taking among Black Adolescents and White Adolescents," *Health Psychology* 13 (1994): 251–262, quoted in Office of the Surgeon General, *Surgeon General's Call to Action*.

28. Jersild, *Happy Hours*, 116.

29. Office of the Surgeon General, *Surgeon General's Call to Action*.

30. Sam Spady Foundation, "The Wallet Card Every Student Needs," Sam Spady Foundation, http://www.samspadyfoundation.org/cards.html.

31. S. A. Brown et al., "Neurocognitive Functioning of Adolescents: Effects of Protracted Alcohol Use," *Alcoholism: Clinical and Experimental Research* 24 (2000): 164–171; F. T. Crews et al., "Binge Ethanol Consumption Causes Differential Brain Damage in Young Adolescent Rats Compared with Adult Rats," *Alcoholism: Clinical and Experimental Research* 24 (2000): 1712–1723; M. D. De Bellis et al., "Hippocampal Volume in Adolescent-Onset Alcohol Use Disorders," *American Journal of Psychiatry* 157 (2000): 737–744; H. S. Swartzwelder, W. A. Wilson, and M. I. Tayyeb, "Age-Dependent Inhibition of Long-Term Potentiation by Ethanol in Immature Versus Mature Hippocampus," *Alcoholism: Clinical and Experimental Research* 19 (1995): 1480–1485; H. S. Swartzwelder, W. A. Wilson, and M. I. Tayyeb, "Differential Sensitivity of NMDA Receptor-Mediated Synaptic Potentials to Ethanol in Immature Versus Mature Hippocampus," *Alcoholism: Clinical and Experimental Research* 19 (1995): 320–323; S. F. Tapert and S. A. Brown, "Neuropsychological Correlates of Adolescent Substance Abuse: Four Year Outcomes," *Journal of the International Neuropsychological Society* 5 (1999): 481–493; and A. M. White and H. S. Swartzwelder, "Age-Related Effects of Alcohol on Memory and Memory-Related Brain Function in Adolescents and Adults," in *Recent Developments in Alcoholism*, vol. 17, *Alcohol Problems in Adolescents and Young Adults: Epidemiology, Neurobiology, Prevention, Treatment*, ed. M. Galanter (New York: Springer,

2005), 161–176, quoted in Office of the Surgeon General, *Surgeon General's Call to Action.*

32. J. D. Hawkins et al., "Exploring the Effects of Age of Alcohol Initiation and Psychosocial Risk Factors on Subsequent Alcohol Misuse," *Journal of Studies on Alcohol* 58 (1997): 280–290, and J. E. Schulenberg et al., "Adolescent Risk Factors for Binge Drinking during the Transition to Young Adulthood: Variable- and Pattern-Centered Approaches to Change," *Developmental Psychology* 32 (1996): 659–674, quoted in Office of the Surgeon General, *Surgeon General's Call to Action.*

33. "Alcohol and Disease Interactions," *Alcohol Research and Health* 25, no. 4 (2001), 230–306, quoted in Office of the Surgeon General, *Surgeon General's Call to Action.*

34. U.S. Department of Transportation, "Fatality Analysis Reporting System 2004," U.S. Department of Transportation, http://www-fars.nhtsa.dot.gov, quoted in Office of the Surgeon General, *Surgeon General's Call to Action.*

35. Jersild, *Happy Hours*, 105.

36. Treadway, *Before It's Too Late*, 141.

37. Schindehette, "Dying for a Drink."

38. Will Dunham, "Study Links Teen Smoking, Drinking, Younger They Start, the Higher the Risk" *Boston Globe*, October 24, 2007, p. A13. A report by CASA indicates that teenage smokers ages twelve to seventeen are five times more likely to drink alcohol.

CHAPTER 3

1. Amy Kamm, "'From Binge to Blackout' Program," *Gloucester Daily Times*, April 27, 2007, letter to the editor sec.

2. Samuel G. Freedman, "Calling the Folks about Campus Drinking," *New York Times*, September 12, 2007, p. A21.

3. Pauline Vu, "Colleges Go on Offense against Binge Drinking," Pew Research Center, http://www.stateline.org/live/details/story?contentId=245335.

4. National Institute on Alcohol Abuse and Alcoholism, "What Is a Standard Drink?," National Institute on Alcohol Abuse and Alcoholism, http://pubs.niaaa.nih.gov/publications/Practitioner/pocketguide/pocket_guide2.htm. A standard drink can be defined as a twelve-ounce can or bottle of beer, eight to nine ounces of malt liquor, a four-ounce glass of wine, a twelve-ounce wine cooler, or a one and a half ounce shot of 80-proof alcohol.

5. Vu, "Colleges Go on Offense."

6. National Center on Addiction and Substance Abuse at Columbia University, "High Society: How Substance Abuse Ravages and What to Do about It," National Center on Addiction and Substance Abuse at Columbia University, http://www.casacolumbia.org/absolutenm/templates/Publications.aspx?articleid=472 &zoneid=52.

7. J. R. Knight et al., "Alcohol Abuse and Dependence among U.S. College Students," *Journal of Studies on Alcohol* 63, no. 3 (2002): 253–270, quoted in Task Force of the National Advisory Council on Alcohol Abuse and Alcoholism, *A Call to Action: Changing the Culture of Drinking at U.S. Colleges* (Rockland, MD: National Institute on Alcohol Abuse and Alcoholism, 2002), http://www.collegedrinkingprevention.gov/media/TaskForceReport.pdf.

8. Bert Plutmen, *The Thinking Person's Guide to Sobriety* (New York: St. Martin's Press, 1999), 116.

9. Sean Flynn, "Should the Drinking Age Be Lowered?" *New York Times Parade Magazine*, August 12, 2007, p. 4.

10. Richard Kadison and Theresa Foy DiGeronimo, *College of the Overwhelmed: The Campus Mental Health Crisis and What to Do about It* (San Francisco: Jossey-Bass, 2004), 115.

11. Vu, "Colleges Go on Offense."

12. Ibid., 99–100.

13. Todd Zwillich, "Rise in Alcohol Abuse by College Women," MedicineNet Inc., http://www.medicinenet.com/script/main/art.asp?articlekey=79828.

14. Ibid.

15. Justin Pope, "Substance Abuse Called Growing Threat at Colleges," *Boston Globe*, March 15, 2007, p. A7.

16. B. F. Grant et al., "The 12-Month Prevalence and Trends in DSM-IV Alcohol Abuse and Dependence: United States, 1991–1992 and 2001–2002," *Drug and Alcohol Dependence* 74 (2004): 223–234, quoted in Office of the Surgeon General, *The Surgeon General's Call to Action to Prevent and Reduce Underage Drinking* (Washington D.C.: U.S. Department of Health and Human Services, 2007), http://www.surgeongeneral.gov/topics/underagedrinking/calltoaction.pdf.

17. J. Schulenberg et al., "The Problem of College Drinking: Insights from a Developmental Perspective," *Alcoholism: Clinical and Experimental Research* 25, no. 3 (2001): 473–477, quoted in Task Force of the National Advisory Council on Alcohol Abuse and Alcoholism, *A Call to Action*.

18. K. M. Jackson , K. J. Sher, and A. Park, "Drinking among College Students: Consumption and Consequences," in *Recent Developments in Alcoholism,* vol. 17, *Alcohol Problems in Adolescents and Young Adults: Epidemiology, Neurobiology, Prevention, Treatment,* ed. M. Galanter (New York: Springer, 2005), 85–117, quoted in H. R. White and K. Jackson, "Social and Psychological Influences on Emerging Adult Drinking Behavior," *National Institute on Alcohol Abuse and Alcoholism* 28, no. 4 (2004–2005), http://pubs.niaaa.nih.gov/publications/arh284/182-190.htm.

19. C. A. Presley, P. W. Meilman, and J. S. Leichliter, "College Factors That Influence Drinking," *Journal of Studies on Alcohol* 14 (2002, Suppl.): 82–90, quoted in National Institute on Alcohol Abuse and Alcoholism, "Changing the Culture of Campus Drinking," *Alcohol Alert* 58 (October 2002), http://pubs.niaaa.nih.gov/publications/aa58.htm.

20. Harvard School of Public Health, "Binge Drinking on American College Campuses: A New Look at an Old Problem, August 1995," http://www.hsph.harvard.edu/cas/rpt1994/CAS1994rpt.shtml (para. 10).

21. B. Borsari and K. B. Carey, "Peer Influence on College Drinking: A Review of the Research," *Journal of Substance Abuse* 13 (2001): 391–424, quoted in H. R. White and K. Jackson, "Social and Psychological Influences."

22. Flynn, "Should the Drinking Age Be Lowered?"

23. Borsari and Carey, "Peer Influence"; B. Borsari and K. B. Carey, "Descriptive and Injunctive Norms in College Drinking: A Meta-Analytic Integration," *Journal of Studies on Alcohol* 64 (2003): 331–341; and H. W. Perkins, "Social Norms and the Prevention of Alcohol Misuse in Collegiate Contexts," *Journal of Studies on Alcohol* 14 (2002, Suppl.): 164–172, quoted in White and Jackson, "Social and Psychological Influences."

24. White and Jackson, "Social and Psychological Influences."

25. Harvard School of Public Health, "Binge Drinking."

26. Ibid.

27. H. Wechsler et al., "Changes in Binge Drinking and Related Problems among American College Students between 1993 and 1997," *Journal of the American College of Health* 7, no. 2 (1998): 57–68, quoted in Devon Jersild, *Happy Hours: Alcohol in a Woman's Life* (New York: Perennial, 2001), 99–100.

28. Kamm, "From Binge to Blackout."

29. J. E. Wells, L. J. Horwood, and D. M. Fergusson, "Stability and Instability in Alcohol Diagnosis from Ages 18 to 21 and Ages 21 to 25 Years," *Drug and Alcohol Dependence* 81 (2006): 157–165.

30. Melinda Beck, "Are You an Alcoholic?," *Wall Street Journal*, January 8, 2008, Health sec.

31. Wechsler et al., "Changes in Binge Drinking."

32. Marcia Russell, "Prevalence of Alcoholism among Children of Alcoholics," in *Children of Alcoholics: Critical Perspectives*, ed. Michael Windle and John S. Searles (New York: Guilford Press, 1990), 9–38, quoted in Task Force of the National Advisory Council on Alcohol Abuse and Alcoholism, *A Call to Action.*

33. Wechsler et al., "Changes in Binge Drinking."

34. Paul Joseph Barriera, "The State of College Mental Health," series lecture, Grand Rounds 2006–2007, Brigham and Women's Hospital, Boston, October 25, 2007.

35. R. W. Hingson et al., "Magnitude of Alcohol-Related Mortality and Morbidity among U.S. College Students Ages 18–24," *Journal of Studies on Alcohol* 63, no. 2 (2002): 136–144, quoted in Task Force of the National Advisory Council on Alcohol Abuse and Alcoholism, *A Call to Action.*

36. Ibid.

37. Ibid.

38. Phoenix House, "Facts on Tap: Here Are Some Stone-Cold Sobering Statistics about the College Sex-and-Alcohol Cocktail," Phoenix House, http://www.factsontap. org/factsontap/risky/the_facts.htm.

39. G. M. Boyd and V. Fadan, "Overview (Statistical Data Included)," *Journal of Studies on Alcohol* 63, no. 2 (2002): S6(8).

40. Phoenix House, "Facts on Tap."

41. Hingson et al., "Magnitude of Alcohol-Related Mortality."

42. R. Hingson et al., "Magnitude of Alcohol-Related Mortality and Morbidity among U.S. College Students Age 18–24: Changes from 1998–2001," *Annual Review of Public Health* 26 (2005): 259–279, quoted in Office of the Surgeon General, *Surgeon General's Call to Action.*

43. Robert Davis and Anthony DeBarros, "Students Get Firm Warning on Fire Danger, New Report Cites On-Campus Stats," *USA Today*, August 21, 2007, p. D6.

44. C. A. Presley, M. A. Leichliter, and P. W. Meilman, *Alcohol and Drugs on American College Campuses: A Report to College Presidents: Third in a Series, 1995, 1996, 1997* (Carbondale: Core Institute, Southern Illinois University, 1998), quoted in Task Force of the National Advisory Council on Alcohol Abuse and Alcoholism, *A Call to Action.*

45. M. Lynne Cooper et al., "Gender, Stress, Coping and Alcohol Use," in *Gender and Alcohol: Individual and Social Perspectives,* ed. Richard W. Wilsnack and Sharon C. Wilsnack (New Brunswick, NJ: Rutgers Center of Alcohol Studies, 1997), 199–224, quoted in Jersild, *Happy Hours,* 104.

46. Hingson et al., "Magnitude of Alcohol-Related Mortality."

47. National Institute on Alcohol Abuse and Alcoholism, "College Students and Drinking," *Alcohol Alert* 29 (July 1995), http://pubs.niaaa.nih.gov/publications/A.A. 29.htm, quoted in Substance Abuse and Mental Health Services Administration, "Binge

Drinking in Adolescents and College Students," Substance Abuse and Mental Health Services Administration, http://ncadi.samhsa.gov/govpubs/rpo995/.

48. Crews, F. T., C. J. Braun, B. Hoplight, R. C. Switzer 3rd, and D. J. Knapp, "Binge Ethanol Consumption Causes Differential Brain Damage in Young Adolescent Rats Compared with Adult Rats," *Alcoholism: Clinical and Experimental Research* 24 (2000): 1712–1723; M. D. De Bellis and others, "Hippocampal Volume in Adolescent-Onset Alcohol Use Disorders, *American Journal of Psychiatry* 157 (2000): 737–744; A. M. White and H. S. Swartzwelder, "Age-Related Effects of Alcohol on Memory and Memory-Related Brain Function in Adolescents and Adults, in M. Galanter, ed., *Recent Developments in Alcoholism, Vol. 17: Alcohol Problems in Adolescents and Young Adults: Epidemiology, Neurobiology, Prevention, Treatment* (New York: Springer, 2005), 161–176; and L. P. Spear and E. I. Varlinskaya "Adolescence: Alcohol Sensitivity, Tolerance, and Intake, in M. Galanter, ed., *Recent Developments in Alcoholism, Vol. 17: Alcohol Problems in Adolescents and Young Adults: Epidemiology, Neurobiology, Prevention, Treatment* (New York: Springer, 2005), 143–159, quoted in Office of the Surgeon General, *Surgeon General's Call to Action*.

49. Rodd, Z. A., R. L. Bell, H. J. K. Sable, J. M. Murphy, and W. J. McBride, "Recent Advances in Animal Models of Alcohol Craving and Relapse," *Pharmacology, Biochemistry, and Behavior* 79, no. 3 (2004): 439–450, and Siciliano, D. and R. F. Smith, "Periadolescent Alcohol Alters Adult Behavioral Characteristics in the Rat," *Physiology and Behavior* 74, no. 4–5 (2001): 637–643, quoted in Office of the Surgeon General, *Surgeon General's Call to Action*.

50. R. C. Engs, B. A. Diebold, and D. J. Hansen, "The Drinking Patterns and Problems of a National Sample of College Students, 1994," *Journal of Alcohol and Drug Education* 41, no. 3 (1996): 13–33; C. A. Presley, P. W. Meilman, and J. R. Cashin, *Alcohol and Drugs on American College Campuses: Use, Consequences, and Perceptions of the Campus Environment*, vol. IV, 1992–1994 (Carbondale: Core Institute, Southern Illinois University, 1996); C. A. Presley et al., *Alcohol and Drugs on American College Campuses: Use Consequences and Perceptions of the Campus Environment*, vol. III, 1991–1993 (Carbondale: Core Institute, Southern Illinois University, 1996); and H. Wechsler et al., "Trends in College Binge Drinking during a Period of Increased Prevention Efforts: Findings from Four Harvard School of Public Health Study Surveys, 1993–2001," *Journal of the American College of Health* 50, no. 5 (2002): 203–217, quoted in Task Force of the National Advisory Council on Alcohol Abuse and Alcoholism, *A Call to Action*.

51. H. W. Perkins, "Surveying the Damage: A Review of Research on Consequences of Alcohol Misuse in College Populations," *Journal of Studies on Alcohol* 14 (2002): 91–100.

52. Arnold E. Kaplan and Philip E. Garfinkel, *Medical Issues and the Eating Disorders: An Interface* (New York: Brunner/Mazel, 1993), quoted in Jersild, *Happy Hours*, 103.

53. Harvard School of Public Health, "Binge Drinking."

54. Task Force of the National Advisory Council on Alcohol Abuse and Alcoholism, *A Call to Action*.

55. Chi Omega Sorority, "The State of the Chi Omega Sorority," *Eleusis of Chi Omega* 110, no. 3 (2007): 38–42.

56. Vu, "Colleges Go on Offense."

57. Eric Tucker, "Brown U. Aims to Curb Student Drinking," *Boston Globe*, March 11, 2006, p. B3.

58. Vu, "Colleges Go on Offense."

59. *New Dictionary of Cultural Literacy*, s.v. "In loco parentis."

60. Freedman, "Calling the Folks."

61. Barriera, "State of College Mental Health."

62. Harvard University Health Services, "Alcohol and Other Drug Services," Harvard University Health Services, http://www.huhs.harvard.edu/OurServices/CounselingMentalHealthSupport/AlcoholAndOtherDrugServices.aspx.

63. Rebecca O'Brien, "Countering Alcohol," *Harvard Magazine,* January–February 2005, pp. 75,78.

64. Flynn, "Should the Drinking Age Be Lowered?", 4.

65. Vu, "Colleges Go on Offense."

66. Office of the Surgeon General, *Surgeon General's Call to Action.*

67. Office of the Surgeon General, *The Surgeon General's Call to Action to Prevent and Reduce Underage Drinking: What It Means to You: A Guide to Action for Families* (Washington D.C.: U.S. Department of Health and Human Services, 2007), http://www.surgeongeneral.gov/topics/underagedrinking/FamilyGuide.pdf.

68. Task Force of the National Advisory Council on Alcohol Abuse and Alcoholism, *A Call to Action.*

CHAPTER 4

1. Alexandra Robbins and Abby Wilner, *Quarterlife Crisis: The Unique Challenges of Life in Your Twenties* (New York: Jeremy P. Tarcher/Putnam, 2001), 53.

2. Jeffrey Jensen Arnett, *Emerging Adulthood: The Winding Road from the Late Teens through the Twenties* (New York: Oxford University Press, 2004), 3.

3. Ibid., 5.

4. M. Mogelonsky, "The Rocky Road to Adulthood," *American Demographics* 56 (May 1996): 26–36, quoted in Arnett, *Emerging Adulthood,* 6.

5. S. M. Bianchi and D. Spain, "Women, Work, and Family in America," *Population Bulletin* 51, no. 3 (1996): 1–48, and Eric L. Dey and Sylvia Hurtado, "Students, Colleges, and Society: Considering the Interconnections," in *American Higher Education in the Twenty-first Century: Social, Political, and Economic Challenges,* ed. Philip G. Altbach, Robert O. Berndahl, and Patricia J. Gumport (Baltimore: Johns Hopkins University Press, 1999), 298–322, quoted in Arnett, *Emerging Adulthood,* 7.

6. Arnett, *Emerging Adulthood,* 8.

7. Ibid., 6.

8. John Schulenberg et al., "Early Adult Transitions and Their Relation to Well-being and Substance Abuse," in *On the Frontier of Adulthood: Theory Research and Public Policy,* ed. Richard A. Settersten Jr., Frank F. Furstenberg Jr., and Rubén G. Rumbaut (Chicago: University of Chicago Press, 2005), 417–453.

9. Sandra Whitehead, "Emerging Adulthood, No Longer Adolescents, but Not Yet Fully Adult, Today's Older Teens and 20-Somethings Are Charting a New Path to Maturity–Quite Different from the One Taken by Previous Generations. What's Behind This New Life Stage, and What Does It Mean for Parents of Today's Teens and Tweens?", http://www.parenthood.com/articles.html?article_id=9153.

10. B. Borsari and K. B. Carey, "Peer Influences on College Drinking: A Review of the Research," *Journal of Substance Abuse* 13 (2001): 391–424, quoted in Helene Raskin White and Kristina Jackson, "Social and Psychological Influences on Emerging Adult Drinking Behavior," *National Institute on Alcohol Abuse and Alcoholism* 28, no. 4 (2004–2005), http://pubs.niaaa.nih.gov/publications/arh284/182–190.htm.

11. M. E. Bennet et al., "Problem Drinking from Young Adulthood to Adulthood: Patterns, Predictors and Outcomes," *Journal of Studies on Alcohol* 60 (1999): 605–614.

12. John E. Helzer, Audrey Burnam, and Lawrence T. McEvoy, "Alcohol Abuse and Dependence," in *Psychiatric Disorders in America*, ed. L. N. Robins and D. A. Regier (New York: Free Press, 1991), 53–80, quoted in H. D. Chilcoat and N. Breslau, "Alcohol Disorders in Young Adulthood: Effects of Transitions into Adult Roles," *Journal of Health and Social Behavior* 37 (1996): 339–349.

13. Al-Anon/Alateen, "What Is Al-Anon?," Al-Anon Group Headquarters Inc., http://www.al-anon.alateen.org/about.html; "The Al-Anon Family Groups are a fellowship of relatives and friends of alcoholics who share their experience, strength, and hope in order to solve their common problems. They believe alcoholism is a family illness and that changed attitudes can aid recovery" (para. 1).

14. Devon Jersild, *Happy Hours: Alcohol in a Woman's Life* (New York: Perennial, 2001), 130–131.

15. David C. Clark et al., "Alcohol-Use Patterns through Medical School," *Journal of the American Medical Association* 257, no. 21 (1987): 2921–2926.

16. Laurent Belsie, "A Stronger Link between Degrees and Dollars," *Christian Science Monitor*, July 18, 2002, http://www.csmonitor.com/2002/0718/p01s04-ussc.html (para. 18).

17. Judith Woods, "Young, Professional and Hungover," *Telegraph*, January 9, 2003, http http://www.telegraph.co.uk/news/uknews/1440242/Young-professional-and-hungover.html (para. 20).

18. Christopher Munsey, "Emerging Adults: The In-Between Age. A New Book Makes the Case for a Phase of Development between Adolescence and Adulthood," American Psychological Association, http://www.apa.org/monitor/jun06/emerging.html (para. 16).

19. "Turbulent Twenties," *The Oprah Winfrey Show*, VHS (Chicago, IL: Harpo Productions Inc., 2001).

20. Whitehead, "Emerging Adulthood."

21. Robbins and Wilner, *Quarterlife Crisis*, 53.

22. "Turbulent Twenties," *The Oprah Winfrey Show*.

23. Frank F. Furstenberg Jr., Rubén G. Rumbaut, and Richard A. Settersten, "On the Frontier of Adulthood: Emerging Themes and New Directions," in Settersten et al., *On the Frontier of Adulthood*, 3–25.

24. Keturah Gray, "Quarterlife Crisis Hits Many in Late 20's: Settling on a Real, Grown-Up Job Is Harder for a New Generation of College Grads," *ABC News*, April 21, 2005, http://abcnews.go.com/Business/Careers/story?id=688240&page=1.

25. Robbins and Wilner, *Quarterlife Crisis*, 102–103.

26. Ibid., 104.

27. John Mayer, "Why Georgia," http://www.sing365.com/music/lyric.nsf/Why-Georgia-lyrics-John-Mayer/0F0B7CF8EB68FB3448256BA00031291D.

28. "Turbulent Twenties," *The Oprah Winfrey Show*.

29. Ibid.

30. Borsari and Carey, "Peer Influences."

31. Robbins and Wilner, *Quarterlife Crisis*, 99–100.

32. J. J. Arnett, "Emerging Adulthood: A Theory of Development from the Late Teens through the Twenties," *American Psychologist* 55 (2000): 469–480, quoted in White and Jackson, "Social and Psychological Influences."

33. L. D. Johnston, P. M. O'Malley, and J. G. Bachman, *National Survey Results on Drug Use from the Monitoring the Future Study, 1975–1994,* vol. 1, *Secondary School Students* (Rockville, MD: National Institute on Drug Abuse, 1995); Michael E. Hilton, "The Demographic Distribution of Drinking Problems in 1984," in *Alcohol in America: Drinking Practices and Problems,* ed. Walter B. Clark and Michael E. Hilton (Albany: State University of New York Press, 1991), 87–101; and R. W. Wilsnack, S. C. Wilsnack, and A. Klassen, "A Woman's Drinking and Drinking Problems: Patterns from a 1981 National Survey," *American Journal of Public Health* 74 (1984): 1231–1238, quoted in J. Schulenberg et al., "Getting Drunk and Growing Up: Trajectories of Frequent Binge Drinking during the Transition to Young Adulthood," *Journal of Studies on Alcohol* 57 (1996): 289–304.

34. Schulenberg et al., "Getting Drunk and Growing Up."

35. M. T. Temple et al., "A Meta-Analysis of Change in Marital and Employment Status as Predictors of Alcohol Consumption on a Typical Occasion," *British Journal of Addiction* 86 (1991): 1268–1281, quoted in Chilcoat and Breslau, "Alcohol Disorders."

36. Henry David Thoreau, *Walden: The Writings of Henry David Thoreau* (Princeton, NJ: Princeton University Press, 1971).

CHAPTER 5

1. Joseph P. Cahn, "Caroline Knapp, Columnist–Wrote 'Drinking: A Love Story,'" *Boston Globe,* June 5, 2002, p. F14.

2. Caroline Knapp, *Drinking: A Love Story* (New York: Delta, 1996), 12, quoted in Harold E. Doweiko, *Concepts of Chemical Dependency* (Pacific Grove, CA: Brooks/Cole, 2002).

3. Marcia Dunn, "Don't Neglect Alcohol Study, Chief Doctor Tells NASA," *Boston Globe,* September 7, 2007, p. A8.

4. Jonathan Salzman and Frank Phillips, "Autopsies Find Alcohol, Some Cocaine, 2 Officials Say," *Boston Globe,* October 4, 2007, pp. A1, B7.

5. Donavan Slack and Jonathan Salzman, "Menino to Review City Fire Agency," *Boston Globe,* October 5, 2007, p. A10.

6. Ibid.

7. Michael Levenson, "More Random Drug Tests Required," *Boston Globe,* October 5, 2007, p. A10.

8. Ibid.

9. Ibid.

10. Douglas A. Moser, "Teacher Guilty of Drunken Driving," *Gloucester Daily Times,* July 21, 2007, pp. A1, A3.

11. Jacques Steinberg, "HBO's Chief Agrees to Quit TV Network," *New York Times,* May 10, 2007, p. C4.

12. Colleen Heild, "Under the Influence: The New Mexico Medical Board Is the Public's Link to Finding Out about Impaired Physicians. But the Board Isn't Always Notified When a Doctor Has a Drug or Alcohol Problem," *Albuquerque Journal,* October 1, 2007, pp. A1, A8.

13. Knapp, *Drinking,* 61.

14. G. Ames and C. Cunradi, "Alcohol Use and Preventing Alcohol-Related Problems among Young Adults in the Military," *Alcohol Research and Health* 28, no. 4 (2004–2005): 254.

15. Devon Jersild, *Happy Hours: Alcohol in a Woman's Life* (New York: Perennial, 2001), 129–132.

16. Al C. Peters, "Responsibilities of Educational Institutes towards Chemical Dependence in Dentistry," lecture, Northeast Regional Board Meeting of Educators and Examiners, Washington D.C., 1986, quoted in A. C. Peters, "Chemical Dependency in Dentistry: The Massachusetts Response," *Journal of the Massachusetts Dental Society* 35, no. 4 (1986): 185–190.

17. LeClair Bissell and Paul W. Haberman, *Alcoholism in the Professions* (New York: Oxford University Press, 1984), quoted in A. C. Peters, "Chemical Dependency in Dentistry."

18. CDAD-Dentist Health and Wellness Committee, "Fact Sheet," CDAD-Dentist Health and Wellness Committee, http://www.cdad.org/facts.htm.

19. Jersild, *Happy Hours*, 233.

20. Slack and Salzman, "Menino to Review City Fire Agency."

21. Melinda Beck, "Are You an Alcoholic?," *Wall Street Journal*, January 8, 2008, p. D1.

22. G. A. H. Benjamin, E. J. Darling, and B. Sales, "The Prevalence of Depression, Alcohol Abuse, and Cocaine Abuse among United States Lawyers," *International Journal of Law and Psychiatry* 13, no. 3 (1990): 233–246.

23. R. G. Frances, V. Alexopoulos, and V. Yandow, "Lawyers' Alcoholism," *Advances in Alcohol and Substance Abuse* 4, no. 2 (1984): 59–66, quoted in Jeffrey Lynn Speller, *Executives in Crisis: Recognizing and Managing the Alcoholic, Drug-Addicted or Mentally Ill Executive* (San Francisco: Jossey-Bass, 1989), 23.

24. American Bar Association, "For Students in Recovery," *Highlights* 10, no. 4 (2008), http://www.abanet.org/legalservices/colap/.

25. Office of the Inspector General, *Evaluation Report on the Economic Impact of Alcohol Misuse in DOD* (Arlington, VA: U.S. Department of Defense, 1997), quoted in Ames and Cunradi, "Alcohol Use."

26. U.S. Navy, *PREVENT: Personal Responsibilities and Values: Education and Training, Knowledge to Action,* 2004, http://www.preventonline.org, quoted in Ames and Cunradi, "Alcohol Use."

27. Speller, *Executives in Crisis*, 23.

28. J. H. LaRosa, "Executive Women and Health: Perceptions and Practices," *American Journal of Public Health* 80 (1990): 1450–1454, quoted in Jersild, *Happy Hours*, 137.

29. Speller, *Executives in Crisis*, 3.

30. Ibid., xiv–xv, 3–5.

31. Pete Hamill, *A Drinking Life* (New York: Little, Brown, 1994), 244.

32. Ibid., 212.

33. Augusten Burroughs, *Dry: A Memoir* (New York: Picador, 2003).

34. Lev Grossman, "Drinking Out Loud: Addiction and Advertising Can Be Funny. Who Knew?," *Time*, May 26, 2003.

35. Jersild, *Happy Hours*, 135–136.

36. Ibid., 129.

37. Bert Plutmen, *The Thinking Person's Guide to Sobriety* (New York: St. Martin's Press, 1999), 73.

38. Ibid., 96–97.

39. Irene Sege, "Her Time in a Bottle: Caroline Knapp's Memoir Recounts Her Painful Love Affair with Alcohol," *Boston Globe*, May 1, 1996, Living sec., p. 61.

40. Knapp, *Drinking*, 90.

41. Speller, *Executives in Crisis*, 33–35.

42. Sege, "Her Time in a Bottle," Living sec., p. 61.

43. Ibid.

44. Jersild, *Happy Hours*, 138–139.

45. Ibid., 153.

46. Alcoholics Anonymous, *Alcoholics Anonymous*, 4th ed. (New York: Alcoholics Anonymous World Services Inc., 2001), xxviii.

CHAPTER 6

1. Steven Gans, "Hitting Bottom: Usually It Must Get Worse before It Gets Better," About Inc., http://alcoholism.about.com/cs/support/a/aa031997.htm, (para. 2).

2. Merriam-Webster Online Dictionary, s.v. "Control."

3. Alcoholics Anonymous, *Alcoholics Anonymous*, 4th ed. (New York: Alcoholics Anonymous World Services Inc., 2001), 21.

4. Ibid., 22.

5. Ibid., 31.

6. Archive of editorials on the Moderation Management controversy, http://doctordeluca.com/documents/primarydocuments.htm, quoted in K. Humphreys, "Alcohol and Drug Abuse: A Research Based Analysis of the Moderation Management Controversy," *Psychiatric Services* 54 (May 2003): 621, http://psychservices.psychiatryonline.org/cgi/content/full/54/5/621.

7. Audrey Kishline, "Here's What Audrey Kishline Told Moderation Management Listserv on January 20, 2000," http://www.doctordeluca.com/Documents/KishlineToldMM.htm (para. 4).

8. Anne Koch, "'Moderate Drinking' Author Has Decided to Abstain," *Seattle Times*, June 20, 2000.

9. Audrey Kishline, *Moderate Drinking: The Moderation Management Guide for People Who Want to Reduce Their Drinking* (New York: Crown, 1994).

10. Ibid., 21.

11. Humphreys, "Alcohol and Drug Abuse."

12. Alcoholics Anonymous, *Alcoholics Anonymous*, 30.

13. E. Klaw, S. Luft, and K. Humphreys, "Characteristics and Motives of Problem Drinkers Seeking Help from Moderation Management Self-Help Groups," *Cognitive and Behavioral Practice* 10, no. 4 (2003): 384–389.

14. Moderation Management, "Assumptions of MM," Moderation Management Network Inc., http://www.moderation.org/assumptions.shtml (para. 1).

15. Alcoholics Anonymous World Services Inc., *Alcoholics Anonymous 2001: Membership Survey* (New York: Alcoholics Anonymous World Services Inc., 1999), quoted in A. Kosok, "The Moderation Management Programme in 2004: What Type of Drinker Seeks Controlled Drinking?," *International Journal of Drug Policy* 17, no. 4 (2006): 295–303.

16. Kosok, "Moderation Management Programme."

17. Kishline, *Moderate Drinking*, 115.

18. Ibid.

19. J. E. Helzer et al., "The Extent of Long-Term Moderate Drinking among Alcoholics Discharged from Medical and Psychiatric Treatment Facilities," *New England Journal of Medicine* 312 (1985): 1678–1685, quoted in George Vaillant, *The Natural*

History of Alcoholism Revisited (Cambridge, MA: Harvard University Press, 1995), 297–298.

20. M. B. Sobell and L. C. Sobell, "Alcoholics Treated by Individualized Behavior Therapy: One Year Outcomes," *Behavior Research and Therapy* 11 (1973): 599–617, and M. B. Sobell and L. C. Sobell, "Second Year Treatment Outcomes of Alcoholics Treated by Individualized Behavior Therapy: Results," *Behavior Research and Therapy* 14 (1976): 195–215, quoted in A. C. Peters, "Chemical Dependency: An Overview and Position," *Journal of the Massachusetts Dental Society* 36, no. 2 (1987): 73–77, 92.

21. M. L. Pendery, I. M. Malzman, and L. J. West, "Controlled Drinking by Alcoholics? New Findings and a Reevaluation of a Major Affirmative Study," *Science* 217 (1982): 169–175, quoted in Peters, "Chemical Dependency," 73–77, 92.

22. S. Hamberg, "Behavior Therapy in Alcoholism: A Critical Review of Broad-Spectrum Approaches," *Journal of Studies on Alcohol* 36 (1975): 69–87, quoted in Vaillant, *Natural History of Alcoholism Revisited,* 303.

23. Vaillant, *Natural History of Alcoholism Revisited,* 303.

24. D. A. Dawson et al., "Recovery from DSM-IV Alcohol Dependence, United States 2001–2002," *Alcohol Research and Health* 29, no. 2 (2006): 131–142.

25. Koch, "Moderate Drinking."

26. Alcoholics Anonymous, *Alcoholics Anonymous,* 20.

27. "From Top to Bottom: Demonstrating Again that Alcoholism Is No Respecter of Position or Power," *A.A.Grapevine.org: The International Journal of Alcoholics Anonymous* 18, no. 1 (1961).

28. Melinda Beck, "Are You an Alcoholic?" *Wall Street Journal,* January 8, 2008, Health sec.

29. Caroline Knapp, *Drinking: A Love Story* (New York: Delta, 1996), 213.

30. L. H. Clever, "A Checklist for Making Good Choices in Trying—or Tranquil—Times," *Western Journal of Medicine* 174, no. 1 (2001): 41–43.

31. Knapp, *Drinking,* 217.

32. Beck, "Are You An Alcoholic?," Health sec.

CHAPTER 7

1. Words and music by Marv Green, Troy Verges, and Hillary Lindsey © 2005 Warner-Tamerlane Publishing Corp., Raylene Music, Songs from the Engine Room and Songs of Universal, Inc. All Rights for Raylene Music administered by BPJ Administration. All Rights Reserved. Used by Permission of Alfred Publishing Co., Inc.

2. Kitty Dukakis and Larry Tye, *Shock: The Healing Power of Electroconvulsive Therapy* (New York: Penguin Group, 2006), 76–77.

3. M. E. McCaul and J. Furst, "Alcoholism Treatment in the United States," *Alcohol Health and Research World* 18, no. 4 (1994): 253–260, quoted in Devon Jersild, *Happy Hours: Alcohol in a Woman's Life* (New York: Perennial, 2001), 285–286.

4. Jersild, *Happy Hours,* 286–287.

5. Substance Abuse and Mental Health Services Administration, "Results from the 2005 National Survey on Drug Use and Health: National Findings," U.S. Department of Health and Human Services, http://www.oas.samhsa.gov/NSDUH/2k5NSDUH/2k5results.htm.

6. Roundtable on Religion and Social Welfare Policy, "An Interview with Susan Foster of CASA," Nelson A. Rockefeller Institute of Government, http://www.religionandsocialpolicy.org/interviews/interview.cfm?id=152.

7. C. Timko et al., "Long-Term Outcomes of Alcohol Use Disorders: Comparing Untreated Individuals with Those in Alcoholics Anonymous and Formal Treatment," *Journal of Studies on Alcohol* 61 (2001): 529–540, quoted in Butler Center for Research, "Alcoholics Anonymous," *Hazelden Foundation Butler Center for Research: Research Update* (December 2004).

8. "Interview: A Doctor Speaks," *A.A. Grapevine Magazine* 57, no. 12 (2001), http://www.divisiononaddictions.org/html/reprints/vaillant.htm.

9. Alcoholics Anonymous, *Alcoholics Anonymous*, 4th ed. (New York: Alcoholics Anonymous World Services Inc., 2001), xv–xvi.

10. Alcoholics Anonymous World Services Inc., "The A.A. Preamble: Background Information," Alcoholics Anonymous World Services Inc., http://www.alcoholics-anonymous.org/en_services_for_members.cfm?PageID=98&SubPage=110 (para. 6).

11. William R. Miller and Barbara S. McCrady, "The Importance of Research on Alcoholics Anonymous," in *Research on Alcoholics Anonymous*, ed. Barbara S. McCrady and William R. Miller (New Brunswick, NJ: Publication Division Rutgers Center of Alcohol Studies, 1993), 3–11.

12. Alcoholics Anonymous World Services Inc., *44 Questions* (New York: Alcoholics Anonymous World Services Inc., 1984), http://www.aa.org/en_pdfs/p-2_44questions.pdf.

13. Miller and McCrady, "Importance of Research."

14. General Service Office of Alcoholics Anonymous, *A.A. Fact File* (New York: Alcoholics Anonymous World Services Inc., 1956), 6, http://www.alcoholics-anonymous.org/en_pdfs/m-24_aafactfile.pdf.

15. Alcoholics Anonymous World Services Inc., *This Is A.A.: An Introduction to the A.A. Recovery Program* (New York: Alcoholics Anonymous World Services Inc., 1984), 7, http://www.aa.org/pdf/products/p-1_thisisaa1.pdf.

16. General Service Office, *A.A. Fact File*, 6.

17. "What We Were Like: Fragments of A.A. History," *A.A.Grapevine.org: the International Journal of Alcoholics Anonymous* 46, no. 5 (1989).

18. Alcoholics Anonymous, *Alcoholics Anonymous*, xx.

19. Alcoholics Anonymous World Services Inc., *Alcoholics Anonymous 2007 Membership Survey* (New York: Alcoholics Anonymous World Services Inc., 2008).

20. SOS Clearinghouse, "Welcome to SOS," SOS Clearinghouse, http://www.secularsobriety.org/ (para. 2).

21. SOS Clearinghouse, "An Overview of SOS," SOS Clearinghouse, http://www.secularsobriety.org/overview.html.

22. Save Our Selves, "The SOS Story, Jim Christopher—A Brief Biography," Save Our Selves, http://www.sosbehindbars.org/jameschristopher.htm.

23. SOS Clearinghouse, "Welcome to SOS."

24. SOS Clearinghouse, "An Overview of SOS."

25. Rational Recovery Systems Inc., "Frequently Asked Questions," Rational Recovery Systems Inc., http://www.rational.org/faq.html.

26. SMART Recovery, "Frequently Asked Questions about SMART Recovery," SMART Recovery, http://www.smartrecovery.org/resources/faq.htm.

27. SMART Recovery, "Welcome," SMART Recovery, http://www.smartrecovery.org/.

28. SMART Recovery, "Frequently Asked Questions."

29. SMART Recovery, "Welcome."

30. Ibid.

31. Anne M. Fletcher, *Sober for Good: New Solutions for Alcohol Problems—Advice from Those Who Have Succeeded* (New York: Houghton Mifflin, 2002), 276–277.

32. Women for Sobriety Inc., *Who We Are* (Quakertown, PA) Women for Sobriety Inc., http://www.womenforsobriety.org/brochure/Brochure-%20Who%20We%20Are.pdf, 2.

33. Women for Sobriety Inc., *Women and Addictions* (Quakertown, PA) Women for Sobriety Inc., http://www.womenforsobriety.org/brochure/Brochure-%20Women%20&%20Addictions.pdf.

34. NYS Work-Life Services, Employee Assistance Program, "History of EAP," NYS Employee Assistance Program and NYS Family Benefits Program, http://worklife.state.ny.us/eap/history.html.

35. Marion, Allison McClintic, and Brian Rabold, eds., "Employee Assistance Programs," *Encyclopedia of Business and Finance* (New York: Macmillan Reference USA. 2001).

36. NYS Work-Life Services, "History of EAP."

37. T. C. Blum and P. M. Roman, "A Description of Clients Using Employee Assistance Programs," *Alcohol and Health Research World* 16, no. 2 (Spring 1992): 120–129.

38. J. C. Erfurt and A. Foote, "Who Is Following the Recovering Alcoholic?—Follow-up Employee Assistance Programs," *Alcohol and Health Research World* 16, no. 2 (Spring 1992): 154–156.

39. Federation of State Physician Health Services Inc., "History," Federation of State Physician Health Services Inc., http://www.fsphp.org/History.html.

40. N. Chesanow, "Why Is It So Hard to Report a Problem Doctor?," *Medical Economics* 7 (2001): 94.

41. Federation of State Physician Health Services Inc., "History."

42. Chesanow, "Why Is It So Hard," 94.

43. American Bar Association, "For Students in Recovery," http://www.abanet.org/legalservices/colap/.

44. Paul J. Virgo, "From Disciplinary Action to Recovery: ADPs and LAPs," *GPSolo Magazine*, 23, no. 7 (October–November 2006).

45. CDAD-Dentist Health and Wellness Committee, "Fact Sheet," CDAD-Dentist Health and Wellness Committee, http://www.cdad.org/facts.htm (para. B).

46. Ibid.

47. "Primetime: Family Secrets," first episode of six-part series, produced by David Sloan (ABC, aired June 26, 2007).

48. Stephanie D. Brown, "Therapeutic Process in Alcoholics Anonymous," in McCrady and Miller, *Research on Alcoholics Anonymous*, 137–152.

49. Dale Mitchel, *A Ghost in the Closet: Is There an Alcoholic Hiding?* (Center City, MN: Hazelden-Pittman Archives Press, 2001), 191–192.

50. *USA Today*, "'Big Lag' in Treatment for Alcoholism Grows," July 3, 2007, p. 9D.

51. Roundtable on Religion and Social Welfare Policy, "An Interview with Susan Foster of CASA."

52. Jersild, *Happy Hours*, 228–230.

53. B. F. Grant, "Barriers to Alcoholism Treatment: Reasons for Not Seeking Treatment in a General Population Sample," *Journal of Studies on Alcohol* 58, no. 4 (1997): 366.

54. Jersild, *Happy Hours*, 227.

55. Grant, "Barriers to Alcoholism Treatment."

56. J.-B. Daeppen, T. L. Smith, and M. A. Schuckit, "How Would You Label Your Own Drinking Pattern Overall? An Evaluation of Answers Provided by 181 High-Functioning Middle-Aged Men," *Alcohol and Alcoholism* 34, no. 5 (1999): 767–772.

57. Carlo C. DiClemente, *Addiction and Change: How Addictions Develop and Addicted People Recover* (New York: Guilford Press, 2003), 25–29.

58. Substance Abuse and Mental Health Services Administration, "Results from the 2005 National Survey."

59. Grant, "Barriers to Alcoholism Treatment."

CHAPTER 8

1. National Center on Addiction and Substance Abuse at Columbia University, *So Help Me God: Substance Abuse, Religion and Spirituality–November 2001* (New York: National Center on Addiction and Substance Abuse at Columbia University, 2001), http://www.casacolumbia.org/absolutenm/articlefiles/379-So%20Help%20Me%20God.pdf.

2. George H. Gallop Jr., *Religion in America: 1990* (Princeton, NJ: Princeton Religious Research Center, 1990), quoted in Herbert Benson, *Timeless Healing* (New York: Fireside, 1996), 173.

3. Benson, *Timeless Healing*, 235.

4. M. E. Buxton, D. E. Smith, and R. B. Seymour, "Spirituality and Other Points of Resistance to the 12-Step Recovery Process," *Journal of Psychoactive Drugs* 19, no. 3 (1987): 279–280, quoted in Ernest Kurtz and Katherine Ketcham, *The Spirituality of Imperfection* (New York: Bantam, 1992), 31.

5. Ibid.

6. Kurtz and Ketcham, *Spirituality of Imperfection*, 146.

7. Marion Woodman, "Worshipping Illusions," *Parabola* 12, no. 2 (1987): 64, quoted in Kurtz and Ketcham, *Spirituality of Imperfection*, 29.

8. M. E. McCullough et al., "Religious Involvement and Mortality: A Meta-Analytic Review," *Health Psychology* 19, no. 3 (2000): 211–222, quoted in National Center on Addiction and Substance Abuse, *So Help Me God*.

9. D. B. Larson, S. S. Larson, and H. G. Koenig, "The Patient's Spiritual/Religious Dimension: A Forgotten Factor in Mental Health," *Directions in Psychiatry* 21, no. 4 (2001): 10–15, and H. G. Koenig and D. B. Larson, "Use of Hospital Services, Religious Attendance, and Religious Affiliation," *Southern Medicine Journal* 91, no. 10 (1998): 925–932, quoted in National Center on Addiction and Substance Abuse, *So Help Me God*.

10. Herbert Benson, *Beyond the Relaxation Response* (New York: Berkley Books, 1984), 5.

11. Bernard Spilka et al., *The Psychology of Religion: An Empirical Approach* (New York: Guilford Press, 2003), 82.

12. Benson, *Timeless Healing*, 216–217.

13. D. Spiegel et al., "Effect of Psychosocial Treatment on Survival of Patients with Metastatic Breast Cancer," *Lancet* 2 (1989): 888–891, quoted in Benson, *Timeless Healing*, 180.

14. L. F. Berkel and S. L. Syme, "Social Networks, Host Resistance, and Mortality: A Nine-Year Follow-up Study of Alameda County Residents," *American Journal of Epidemiology* 19 (1979): 186–204, quoted in Benson, *Timeless Healing*, 180.

15. R. Fiorentine and M. P. Hillhouse, "Drug Treatment and 12-Step Program Participation: The Additive Effects of Integrated Recovery Activities," *Journal of Substance Abuse Treatment* 18, no. 1 (2000): 65–74, quoted in National Center on Addiction and Substance Abuse, *So Help Me God.*

16. Ibid.

17. Kurtz and Ketcham, *Spirituality of Imperfection,* 120.

18. E. M. Jellinek, "The Symbolism of Drinking: A Cultural-Historical Approach," *Journal of Studies on Alcohol* 38, no. 5 (1977): 849–866, quoted in Kurtz and Ketcham, *Spirituality of Imperfection,* 120.

19. Kurtz and Ketcham, *Spirituality of Imperfection,* 121.

20. William James, *Varieties of Religious Experience* (New York: Barnes and Noble, 2004), 334–335.

21. University Health Services, "Understanding Blood Alcohol Content (BAC)," University of Rochester, http://www.rochester.edu/uhs/healthtopics/Alcohol/bac. html.

22. Alcoholics Anonymous, *Alcoholics Anonymous,* 4th ed. (New York: Alcoholics Anonymous World Services Inc., 2001), xxviii–xxix.

23. Kurtz and Ketcham, *Spirituality of Imperfection,* 114–115.

24. A.A. Grapevine Inc., *Spiritual Awakenings: Journeys of the Spirit from the Pages of the A.A. Grapevine* (New York: A.A. Grapevine Inc., 2003), 18.

25. Kurtz and Ketcham, *Spirituality of Imperfection,* 120.

26. National Center on Addiction and Substance Abuse, *So Help Me God,* i.

27. George E. Vaillant, *The Natural History of Alcoholism* (Cambridge, MA: Harvard University Press, 1983), 193.

28. National Center on Addiction and Substance Abuse, *So Help Me God.*

29. Ibid., 13.

30. D. A. Matthews, D. B. Larson, and C. P. Barry, *The Faith Factor: An Annotated Bibliography of Clinical Research on Spiritual Subjects,* vol. 1 (West Conshohocken, PA: John Templeton Foundation, 1993), quoted in Benson, *Timeless Healing,* 173–174.

31. Herbert Benson and Robert K. Wallace, "Decreased Drug Abuse with Transcendental Meditation—A Study of 1,862 Subjects," in *Drug Abuse—Proceedings of the International Conference,* ed. C. J. D. Zarafonetis (Philadelphia: Lea and Febiger, 1972), 369–376, quoted in H. Benson, J. F. Beary, and M. P. Carol, "The Relaxation Response," *Psychiatry* 37 (1974): 37–46.

32. J. M. Simoni and M. Z. Ortiz, "Mediational Models of Spirituality and Depressive Symptomatology among HIV-Positive Puerto Rican Women," *Cultural Diversity and Ethnic Minority Psychology* 9 (2003): 3–15, quoted in A. W. Carrico, E. V. Gifford, and R. H. Moos, "Spirituality/Religiosity Promotes Acceptance-Based Responding and 12-Step Involvement," *Drug and Alcohol Dependence* 89 (2007): 70.

33. R. D. Weiss et al., "Predictors of Self Help Group Attendance in Cocaine Dependent Patients," *Journal of Studies on Alcohol* 61 (2000): 714–719, quoted in Carrico et al., "Spirituality/Religiosity."

34. R. C. Sterling et al., "Levels of Spirituality and Treatment Outcome: A Preliminary Examination," *Journal of Studies on Alcohol* 67, no. 4 (2006): 600–606.

35. Ibid.

36. Kurtz and Ketcham, *Spirituality of Imperfection,* 110–111.

37. Alcoholics Anonymous, *Alcoholics Anonymous,* 567–568.

38. Elizabeth Gilbert, *Eat, Pray, Love* (New York: Penguin, 2006), 199.

39. R. S. Johnson, "Lloyd Advances to Open Semifinal," *New York Times*, September 4, 1986, quoted in Benson, *Timeless Healing*, 167.

40. Ibid.

41. S. R. Dean, "Metapsychiatry: The Confluence of Psychiatry and Mysticism," in *Psychiatry and Mysticism*, ed. S. R. Dean (Chicago: Nelson-Hall, 1975), quoted in Benson, *Timeless Healing*, 167.

42. Barbara Kantrowitz et al., "In Search of the Sacred," *Newsweek*, November 28, 1994, pp. 52–62, quoted in Benson, *Timeless Healing*, 154, 167–168.

43. Alcoholics Anonymous, *Alcoholics Anonymous*, 567.

44. Alcoholics Anonymous, *Twelve Steps and Twelve Traditions*. New York: Alcoholics Anonymous World Services Inc., 1981, 106.

45. Herbert Benson, *The Breakout Principle* (New York: Scribner, 2003), 18–19.

46. Ibid.

47. Ibid.

48. Ibid., 241–243.

49. James, *Varieties of Religious Experience*, 177.

50. Ibid., 198–199.

CHAPTER 9

1. Ernest Kurtz and Katherine Ketcham, *The Spirituality of Imperfection* (New York: Bantam, 1992), 121.

2. Alcoholics Anonymous, *Alcoholics Anonymous*, 4th ed. (New York: Alcoholics Anonymous World Services Inc., 2001), 25–26.

3. Stephanie S. Covington, *A Woman's Way through the Twelve Steps* (Center City, MN: Hazelden, 1994), 2.

4. Kevin Griffin, *One Breath at a Time: Buddhism and the Twelve Steps* (New York: Rodale Books, 2004), x.

5. Ibid., 167.

6. Alcoholics Anonymous, *Alcoholics Anonymous*, 17.

7. Kurtz and Ketcham, *Spirituality of Imperfection*, 168.

8. Alcoholics Anonymous, *Alcoholics Anonymous*, xxx.

9. Griffin, *One Breath at a Time*, 35–36.

10. Alcoholics Anonymous, *Alcoholics Anonymous*, 45.

11. Alcoholics Anonymous, *Twelve Steps and Twelve Traditions* (New York: Alcoholics Anonymous World Services Inc., 1981), 29–30.

12. Covington, *A Woman's Way*, 37.

13. Griffin, *One Breath at a Time*, 42.

14. Alcoholics Anonymous, *Twelve Steps and Twelve Traditions*, 37.

15. Covington, *A Woman's Way*, 51.

16. Griffin, *One Breath at a Time*, 52.

17. Alcoholics Anonymous, *Alcoholics Anonymous*, 63.

18. Griffin, *One Breath at a Time*, vi–vii.

19. Alcoholics Anonymous, *Alcoholics Anonymous*, 64.

20. Covington, *A Woman's Way*, 60.

21. Ibid.

22. Alcoholics Anonymous, *Twelve Steps and Twelve Traditions*, 62.

23. Griffin, *One Breath at a Time*, 120.

24. Alcoholics Anonymous, *Twelve Steps and Twelve Traditions*, 65.

25. Alcoholics Anonymous, *Alcoholics Anonymous*, 76.

26. Alcoholics Anonymous, *Twelve Steps and Twelve Traditions*, 58.

27. Covington, *A Woman's Way*, 110.

28. Griffin, *One Breath at a Time*, 186.

29. Alcoholics Anonymous, *Twelve Steps and Twelve Traditions*, 90.

30. Alcoholics Anonymous, *Alcoholics Anonymous*, 85.

31. Ibid., 84.

32. Ibid., 86–87.

33. Griffin, *One Breath at a Time*, 225.

34. Alcoholics Anonymous, *Alcoholics Anonymous*, 87.

35. Covington, *A Woman's Way*, 189.

36. Alcoholics Anonymous, *Alcoholics Anonymous*, 89.

CHAPTER 10

1. Stephanie S. Covington, *A Woman's Way through the Twelve Steps* (Center City, MN: Hazelden, 1994), 239.

2. James W. Fowler, "Alcoholics Anonymous and Faith Development," in *Research on Alcoholics Anonymous*, ed. Barbara S. McCrady and William R. Miller (New Brunswick, NJ: Publication Division Rutgers Center of Alcohol Studies, 1993), 131.

3. National Institute on Alcohol Abuse and Alcoholism, "2001–2002 Survey Finds That Many Recover from Alcoholism: Researchers Identify Factors Associated with Abstinent and Non-abstinent Recovery," *NIH News*, January 18, 2005, http://www.nih.gov/news/pr/jan2005/niaaa-18.htm (para. 6).

4. Carlo C. DiClemente, *Addiction and Change: How Addictions Develop and Addicted People Recover* (New York: Guilford Press, 2003), 190.

5. Ibid., 192, 195.

6. Fowler, "Alcoholics Anonymous and Faith Development," 130.

7. Alcoholics Anonymous, *Alcoholics Anonymous*, 4th ed. (New York: Alcoholics Anonymous World Services Inc., 2001), 85.

8. C. C. DiClemente et al., "Process Assessment in Treatment Matching Research," *Journal of Studies on Alcohol* 12 (1994, Suppl.): 156–162, and R. H. Moos, J. W. Finney, and R. C. Cronkite, *Alcoholism Treatment: Context, Process and Outcome* (New York: Oxford University Press, 1990), quoted in DiClemente, *Addiction and Change*, 191.

9. DiClemente, *Addiction and Change*, 181.

10. C. M. Bradizza, P. R. Stasiewicz, and N. D. Paas, "Relapse to Alcohol and Drug Use among Individuals Diagnosed with Co-occurring Mental Health and Substance Use Disorders: A Review," *Clinical Psychology Review* 26 (2006): 162–178; J. R. McKay et al., "Conceptual, Methodological and Analytical Issues in the Study of Relapse," *Clinical Psychology Review* 26 (2006): 109–127; J. R. McKay, "Studies of Factors to Relapse in Alcohol and Drug Use: A Critical Review of Methodologies and Findings," *Journal of Studies on Alcohol* 60 (1999): 566–576; A. Tonneato, L. C. Sobell, and M. B. Sobell, "Gender Issues in the Treatment of Abusers of Alcohol, Nicotine and Other Drugs," *Journal of Substance Abuse* 4 (1992): 209–218; and K. S. Walitzer and R. L. Dearling, "Gender Differences in Alcohol and Substance Abuse Relapse," *Clinical Psychology Review* 26 (2006): 128–148, quoted in D. A. Dawson, R. B. Goldstein, and B. F. Grant, "Rates and Correlates of Relapse among Individuals in Remission from DSM-IV Alcohol Dependence: A 3-Year Follow-up," *Alcoholism: Clinical and Experimental Research* 31, no. 12 (2007): 2036–2045.

11. Val Slaymaker, "Understanding the Whole Story of Addiction Treatment Outcomes," *The Voice*, Winter 2004, http://www.hazelden.org/web/public/vcwin4story. page.

12. K. Mann et al., "The Long-Term Course of Alcoholism, 5, 10 and 16 Years after Treatment," *Addiction* 100 (2005): 797–805; W. R. Miller, S. T. Walters, and B. E. Bennet, "How Effective Is Alcoholism Treatment in the United States?" *Journal of Studies on Alcohol* 62 (2001): 211–220; and Project MATCH Research Group, "Matching Alcoholism Treatments to Client Heterogeneity: Project MATCH Three-Year Drinking Outcomes," *Alcoholism: Clinical and Experimental Research* 22 (1998): 1300–1311, quoted in Dawson et al., "Rates and Correlates of Relapse."

13. Dawson et al., "Rates and Correlates of Relapse."

14. Roundtable on Religion and Social Welfare Policy, "An Interview with Susan Foster of CASA," Nelson A. Rockefeller Institute of Government, http://www. religionandsocialpolicy.org/interviews/interview.cfm?id=152.

15. DiClemente, *Addiction and Change*, 185.

16. Kevin Griffin, *One Breath at a Time: Buddhism and the Twelve Steps* (New York: Rodale Books, 2004), 211.

17. DiClemente, *Addiction and Change*, 196–197.

18. Ibid., 190.

19. Roundtable on Religion and Social Welfare Policy, "An Interview with Susan Foster of CASA" (para. 24).

20. DiClemente, *Addiction and Change*, 190.

APPENDICES

1. American Psychiatric Association, *Diagnostic and Statistical Manual of Mental Disorders*, 4th ed., text revision (Washington D.C.: American Psychiatric Press, 2000), 197.

2. Ibid., 199.

3. Alcoholics Anonymous World Services Inc., *Is AA for You? Twelve Questions Only You Can Answer* (New York: Alcoholics Anonymous World Services Inc., 1973), 2–5.

4. Alcoholics Anonymous, *Alcoholics Anonymous*, 4th ed. (New York: Alcoholics Anonymous World Services Inc., 2001), 59–60.

5. Women for Sobriety Inc., "'New Life' Acceptance Program," http://www. womenforsobriety.org/.

BIBLIOGRAPHY

A.A. Grapevine Inc. *Spiritual Awakenings: Journeys of the Spirit from the Pages of the AA Grapevine.* New York: A.A. Grapevine Inc., 2003.

Al-Anon/Alateen. "What Is Al-Anon?" Al-Anon Group Headquarters Inc. http://www.al-anon.alateen.org/about.html.

Alcoholics Anonymous. *Alcoholics Anonymous.* 4th ed. New York: Alcoholics Anonymous World Services Inc., 2001.

———. *Twelve Steps and Twelve Traditions.* New York: Alcoholics Anonymous World Services Inc., 1981.

Alcoholics Anonymous World Services Inc. "The A.A. Preamble: Background Information." Alcoholics Anonymous World Services Inc. http://www.alcoholics-anonymous.org/en_services_for_members.cfm?PageID=98&SubPage=110.

———. *Alcoholics Anonymous 2007 Membership Survey.* New York: Alcoholics Anonymous World Services Inc., 2008.

———. *44 Questions.* New York: Alcoholics Anonymous World Services Inc., 1984. http://www.aa.org/en_pdfs/p-2_44questions.pdf.

———. *Is A.A. for You? Twelve Questions Only You Can Answer.* New York: Alcoholics Anonymous World Services Inc., 1973.

———. *This is A.A.: An Introduction to the A.A. Recovery Program.* New York: Alcoholics Anonymous World Services Inc., 1984. http://www.aa.org/pdf/products/p-1_thisisaa1.pdf.

American Bar Association. "For Students in Recovery." http://www.abanet.org/legalservices/colap/.

American Psychiatric Association. *Diagnostic and Statistical Manual of Mental Disorders.* 4th ed., text rev. Washington, DC: American Psychiatric Press, 2000.

Ames, G., and C. Cunradi. "Alcohol Use and Preventing Alcohol-Related Problems among Young Adults in the Military." *Alcohol Research and Health* 28, no. 4 (2004–2005): 252–257.

Aratani, Lori. "Surveys Say Girls' Drug Use Is Rising." *Boston Globe,* February 11, 2008.

Arnett, Jeffrey Jensen. *Emerging Adulthood: The Winding Road from the Late Teens through the Twenties.* New York: Oxford University Press, 2004.

Associated Press. "Bush Says Reliance on Faith Helped Him Beat 'Addiction' to Alcohol." *MSNBC.com.* http://www.msnbc.msn.com/id/22898644/#storyContinued.

————. "He'll Skip the Complimentary Drink." *Boston Globe*, May 22, 2007.

Barriera, Paul Joseph. "The State of College Mental Health." Series lecture, Grand Rounds 2006–2007, Brigham and Women's Hospital, Boston, October 25, 2007.

Beck, Melinda. "Are You an Alcoholic?" *Wall Street Journal*, January 8, 2008.

Belsie, Laurent. "A Stronger Link between Degrees and Dollars." *Christian Science Monitor*, July 18, 2002. http://www.csmonitor.com/2002/0718/p01s04-ussc.html.

Benjamin, G. A. H., E. J. Darling, and B. Sales. "The Prevalence of Depression, Alcohol Abuse, and Cocaine Abuse among United States Lawyers." *International Journal of Law and Psychiatry* 13, no. 3 (1990): 233–246.

Bennet, M. E., B. S. McCrady, V. Johnson, and R. J. Pandina. "Problem Drinking from Young Adulthood to Adulthood: Patterns, Predictors and Outcomes." *Journal of Studies on Alcohol* 60 (1999): 605–614.

Benson, Herbert. *Beyond the Relaxation Response*. New York: Berkley Books, 1984.

————. *The Breakout Principle*. New York: Scribner, 2003.

————. *Timeless Healing*. New York: Fireside, 1996.

Benson, H., J. F. Beary, and M. P. Carol. "The Relaxation Response." *Psychiatry* 37 (1974): 37–46.

Berger, Thomas J. "Alcohol Abuse in Medical School." *Journal of the American Medical Association* 258, no. 9 (1987): 1173.

Betty Ford Center. "A Brief History of the Betty Ford Center." Betty Ford Center. http://www.bettyfordcenter.org/welcome/ourhistory.php.

Blum, T. C., and P. M. Roman. "A Description of Clients Using Employee Assistance Programs." *Alcohol Health and Research World* 16, no. 2 (Spring 1992): 120–129.

"Boy Interrupted With A. J. McLean Fighting Depression and Alcoholism, the Backstreet Boys Take an Unscheduled De-Tour." *People Weekly*, July 23, 2001.

Boyd, G. M., and V. Fadan. "Overview. (Statistical Data Included)." *Journal of Studies on Alcohol* 63, no. 2 (March 2002): S6(8).

Brown, Stephanie D. "Therapeutic Process in Alcoholics Anonymous." In *Research on Alcoholics Anonymous*, edited by Barbara S. McCrady and William R. Miller, 137–152. New Brunswick, NJ: Publication Division Rutgers Center of Alcohol Studies, 1993.

Burroughs, Augusten. *Dry: A Memoir*. New York: Picador, 2003.

"But Seriously . . ." *People Weekly*, October 16, 2006.

Butler Center for Research. "Alcoholics Anonymous." *Hazelden Foundation Butler Center for Research: Research Update*, December 2004.

Cahn, Joseph P. "Caroline Knapp, Columnist—Wrote 'Drinking: A Love Story.'" *Boston Globe*, June 5, 2002.

Carrico, A. W., E. V. Gifford, and R. H. Moos. "Spirituality/Religiosity Promotes Acceptance-Based Responding and 12-Step Involvement." *Drug and Alcohol Dependence* 89 (2007): 66–73.

CDAD-Dentist Health and Wellness Committee. "Fact Sheet." CDAD-Dentist Health and Wellness Committee. http://www.cdad.org/facts.htm.

Chesanow, N. "Why Is It So Hard to Report a Problem Doctor?" *Medical Economics* 7 (2001): 94.

Chi Omega Fraternity. "The State of the Chi Omega Fraternity." *Eleusis of Chi Omega* 110, no. 3 (2007): 38–42.

Chilcoat, H. D., and N. Breslau. "Alcohol Disorders in Young Adulthood: Effects of Transitions into Adult Roles." *Journal of Health and Social Behavior* 37 (1996): 339–349.

Clark, D. C., E. J. Eckenfels, S. R. Daugherty, and J. Fawcett. "Alcohol-Use Patterns through Medical School." *Journal of the American Medical Association* 257, no. 21 (1987): 2921–2926.

Clever, L. H. "A Checklist for Making Good Choices in Trying—or Tranquil—Times." *Western Journal of Medicine* 174, no. 1 (2001): 41–43.

Covington, Stephanie S. *A Woman's Way through the Twelve Steps*. Center City, MN: Hazelden, 1994.

Daeepen, J.-B., T. L. Smith, and M. A. Schuckit. "How Would You Label Your Own Drinking Pattern Overall? An Evaluation of Answers Provided by 181 High-Functioning Middle-Aged Men." *Alcohol and Alcoholism* 34, no. 5 (1999): 767–772.

Dagostino, Mark. "I'm an Alcoholic." *People Weekly,* February 12, 2007.

Davis, Robert, and Anthony DeBarros. "Students Get Firm Warning on Fire Danger, New Report Cites On-Campus Stats." *USA Today,* August 21, 2007.

Dawson, D. A., R. B. Goldstein, and B. F. Grant. "Rates and Correlates of Relapse among Individuals in Remission from DSM-IV Alcohol Dependence: A 3-Year Follow-up." *Alcoholism: Clinical and Experimental Research* 31, no. 12 (2007): 2036–2045.

Dawson, D. A., B. F. Grant, F. S. Stinson, P. S. Chou, B. Huang, and W. J. Ruan. "Recovery from DSM-IV Alcohol Dependence, United States 2001–2002." *Alcohol Research and Health* 29, no. 2 (2006): 131–142.

DiClemente, Carlo C. *Addiction and Change: How Addictions Develop and Addicted People Recover*. New York: Guilford Press, 2003.

Doweiko, Harold E. *Concepts of Chemical Dependency*. Pacific Grove, CA: Brooks/Cole, 2002.

Dukakis, Kitty, and Larry Tye. *Shock: The Healing Power of Electroconvulsive Therapy*. New York: Penguin, 2006.

Dunham, Will. "Study Links Teen Smoking, Drinking." *Boston Globe,* October 24, 2007.

Dunn, Marcia. "Don't Neglect Alcohol Study, Chief Doctor Tells NASA." *Boston Globe,* September 7, 2007.

Epstein, Robert. "Buzz Aldrin: Down to Earth. (Interview)." *Psychology Today,* May 2001.

Erfurt, J. C., and A. Foote. "Who Is Following the Recovering Alcoholic?—Follow-up Employee Assistance Programs." *Alcohol Health and Research World* 16, no. 2 (Spring 1992): 154–156.

Federation of State Physician Health Services Inc. "History." Federation of State Physician Health Services Inc. http://www.fsphp.org/History.html.

Fletcher, Anne M. *Sober for Good: New Solutions for Alcohol Problems—Advice from Those Who Have Succeeded*. New York: Houghton Mifflin, 2002.

Flynn, Sean. "Should the Drinking Age Be Lowered?" *New York Times Parade Magazine,* August 12, 2007.

Fowler, James W. "Alcoholics Anonymous and Faith Development." In *Research on Alcoholics Anonymous*, edited by Barbara S. McCrady and William R. Miller, 113–135. New Brunswick, NJ: Publication Division Rutgers Center of Alcohol Studies, 1993.

Freedman, Samuel G. "Calling the Folks about Campus Drinking." *New York Times,* September 12, 2007.

"From Top to Bottom: Demonstrating Again That Alcoholism Is No Respecter of Position or Power." *AAGrapevine.org: The International Journal of Alcoholics Anonymous* 18, no. 1 (1961). Available from http://www.aagrapevine.org.

Furstenberg, Frank F., Jr., Rubén G. Rumbaut, and Richard A. Settersten Jr. "On the Frontier of Adulthood: Emerging Themes and New Directions." In *On the Frontier of Adulthood: Theory, Research, and Public Policy*, edited by Richard A. Settersten Jr., Frank F. Furstenberg Jr., and Rubén G. Rumbaut, 3–25. Chicago: University of Chicago Press, 2005.

Gans, Steven. "Hitting Bottom: Usually It Must Get Worse Before It Gets Better." About Inc. http://alcoholism.about.com/cs/support/a/aa031997.htm.

General Service Office of Alcoholics Anonymous. *A.A. Fact File.* New York: Alcoholics Anonymous World Services Inc., 1956. http://www.alcoholics-anonymous.org/en_pdfs/m-24_aafactfile.pdf.

Gilbert, Elizabeth. *Eat, Pray, Love.* New York: Penguin, 2006.

Grant, B. F. "Barriers to Alcoholism Treatment: Reasons for Not Seeking Treatment in a General Population Sample." *Journal of Studies on Alcohol* 58, no. 4 (1997): 365–371.

Grant, Meg. "On Her Own Terms: Beating Breast Cancer and Alcoholism, Betty Ford Found That Her Greatest Strength Lay in Helping Others by Being Herself (First Ladies)."*People Weekly*, May 15, 2000.

Gray, Keturah. "Quarterlife Crisis Hits Many in Late 20's: Settling on a Real, Grown-Up Job Is Harder for a New Generation of College Grads." *ABC News*, April 21, 2005. http://abcnews.go.com/Business/Careers/story?id=688240&page=1.

Griffin, Kevin. *One Breath at a Time: Buddhism and the Twelve Steps.* New York: Rodale Books, 2004.

Grossman, Lev. "Drinking Out Loud: Addiction and Advertising Can Be Funny. Who Knew?" *Time*, May 26, 2003.

Hamill, Pete. *A Drinking Life.* New York: Little, Brown, 1994.

Harvard School of Public Health. "Binge Drinking on American College Campuses: A New Look at an Old Problem, August 1995." Harvard School of Public Health. http://www.hsph.harvard.edu/cas/rpt1994/CAS1994rpt.shtml.

Harvard University Health Services. "Alcohol and Other Drug Services." Harvard University Health Services. http://www.huhs.harvard.edu/OurServices/CounselingMentalHealthSupport/AlcoholAndOtherDrugServices.aspx.

Heild, Colleen. "Under the Influence: The New Mexico Medical Board Is the Public's Link to Finding Out about Impaired Physicians. But the Board Isn't Always Notified When a Doctor Has a Drug or Alcohol Problem." *Albuquerque Journal*, October 1, 2007.

Hingson, W. R., T. Heeren, R. C. Zakocs, A. Kopstein, and H. Wechsler. "Magnitude of Alcohol-Related Mortality and Morbidity among U.S. College Students Ages 18–24." *Journal of Studies on Alcohol* 63, no. 2 (2002): 136–144.

Hirsch, E. D., Jr., Joseph F. Kett, and James Trefil, eds. *The New Dictionary of Cultural Literacy*, 3rd ed. Boston: Houghton Mifflin, 2002.

Humphreys, Keith. "Alcohol and Drug Abuse: A Research Based Analysis of the Moderation Management Controversy." *Psychiatric Services* 54 (May 2003): 621–622. http://psychservices.psychiatryonline.org/cgi/content/full/54/5/621.

"Interview: A Doctor Speaks." *A.A. Grapevine Magazine* 57, no. 12 (2001). http://www.divisiononaddictions.org/html/reprints/vaillant.htm.

James, William. *Varieties of Religious Experience.* New York: Barnes and Noble, 2004.

Jersild, Devon. *Happy Hours: Alcohol in a Woman's Life.* New York: Perennial, 2001.

Kadison, Richard, and Theresa Foy DiGeronimo. *College of the Overwhelmed: The Campus Mental Health Crisis and What to Do about It.* San Francisco: Jossey-Bass, 2004.

Kamm, Amy. "'From Binge to Blackout' Program." *Gloucester Daily Times,* April 27, 2007.

Kirke, Deirdre M. *Teenagers and Substance Abuse: Social Networks and Peer Influence.* New York: Palgrave Macmillan, 2006.

Kishline, Audrey. "Here's What Audrey Kishline Told Moderation Management Listserv on January 20, 2000." http://www.doctordeluca.com/Documents/KishlineToldMM.htm.

———. *Moderate Drinking: The Moderation Management Guide for People Who Want to Reduce Their Drinking.* New York: Crown, 1994.

Klaw, E., S. Luft, and K. Humphreys. "Characteristics and Motives of Problem Drinkers Seeking Help from Moderation Management Self-Help Groups." *Cognitive and Behavioral Practice* 10, no. 4 (2003): 384–389.

Knapp, Caroline. *Drinking: A Love Story.* New York: Delta, 1996.

Koch, Anne. "'Moderate Drinking' Author Has Decided to Abstain." *Seattle Times,* June 20, 2000.

Kosok, A. "The Moderation Management Programme in 2004: What Type of Drinker Seeks Controlled Drinking?" *International Journal of Drug Policy* 17, no. 4 (2006): 295–303.

Kurtz, Ernest, and Katherine Ketcham. *The Spirituality of Imperfection.* New York: Bantam, 1992.

Levenson, Michael. "More Random Drug Tests Required." *Boston Globe,* October 5, 2007.

Light, Alan. "A Guitar God's Memories, Demons and All." *New York Times,* October 7, 2007, Sec. 2, 23–24.

Luthar, S. S., and B. E. Becker. "Privileged but Pressured? A Study of Affluent Youth." *Child Development* 73, no. 5 (2002): 1593–1610.

Marion, Allison McClintic, and Brian Rabold, eds. *Encyclopedia of Business and Finance.* New York: Macmillan Reference USA, 2001.

Mayer, John. "Why Georgia." http://www.sing365.com/music/lyric.nsf/Why-Georgia-lyrics-John-Mayer/0F0B7CF8EB68FB3448256BA00031291D.

McDonald, J. A. "Confessions from a Quarter Bounce. (Voices of Youth)." *Reclaiming Children and Youth* 11, no. 3 (2002): 135(2).

Merriam-Webster Inc. "Merriam-Webster Online." http://www.m-w.com.

Miller, William R., and Barbara S. McCrady. "The Importance of Research on Alcoholics Anonymous." In *Research on Alcoholics Anonymous,* edited by Barbara S. McCrady and William R. Miller, 3–11. New Brunswick, NJ: Publication Division Rutgers Center of Alcohol Studies, 1993.

Mitchel, Dale. *A Ghost in the Closet: Is There an Alcoholic Hiding?* Center City, MN: Hazelden-Pittman Archives Press, 2001.

Moderation Management. "Assumptions of MM." Moderation Management Network Inc. http://www.moderation.org/assumptions.shtml.

———. "Suggested Readings at MM Meetings." Moderation Management Network Inc. http://www.moderation.org/readings.shtml.

Moser, Douglas A. "Teacher Guilty of Drunken Driving." *Gloucester Daily Times,* July 21, 2007.

Moss, H. B., C. M. Chen, and H. Yi. "Subtypes of Alcohol Dependence in a Nationally Representative Sample." *Drug and Alcohol Dependence* 91, no. 2–3 (2007): 149–158.

Mulligan, John E. "Patrick Kennedy Finds Much to Celebrate after a Year of Sobriety." *Providence Journal*, May 6, 2007.

Munsey, Christopher. "Emerging Adults: The In-Between Age. A New Book Makes the Case for a Phase of Development between Adolescence and Adulthood." American Psychological Association. http://www.apa.org/monitor/jun06/emerging.html.

National Center on Addiction and Substance Abuse at Columbia University. "CASA 2007 Teen Survey Reveals America's Schools Infested with Drugs." National Center on Addiction and Substance Abuse at Columbia University. http://marketwire. com/mw/release.do?id=761295.

———. "High Society: How Substance Abuse Ravages and What to Do about It." National Center on Addiction and Substance Abuse at Columbia University. http://www.casacolumbia.org/absolutenm/templates/Publications.aspx? articleid=472&zoneid=52.

———. *So Help Me God: Substance Abuse, Religion and Spirituality–November 2001.* New York: National Center on Addiction and Substance Abuse at Columbia University, 2001. http://www.casacolumbia.org/absolutenm/articlefiles/379-So% 20Help%20Me%20God.pdf.

National Institute on Alcohol Abuse and Alcoholism. "Changing the Culture of Campus Drinking." *Alcohol Alert* 58 (October 2002). http://pubs.niaaa.nih.gov/ publications/aa58.htm.

———. "Diagnostic Criteria for Alcohol Abuse and Dependence." *Alcohol Alert* 30 (October 1995). http://pubs.niaaa.nih.gov/publications/aa30.htm.

———. "FAQ for the General Public." National Institute on Alcohol Abuse and Alcoholism. http://www.niaaa.nih.gov/FAQs/General-English/.

———. "Surgeon General Calls on Americans to Face Facts about Drinking: Transportation Safety Leaders Join Alcohol Research, Prevention, and Treatment Leaders to Recommend Screening on April 8, National Screening Day, 2004." *NIH News*, April 1, 2004. http://www.niaaa.nih.gov/NewsEvents/NewsReleases/ Screenday04.htm.

———. "2001–2002 Survey Finds That Many Recover from Alcoholism: Researchers Identify Factors Associated with Abstinent and Non-abstinent Recovery." *NIH News*, January 18, 2005. http://www.nih.gov/news/pr/jan2005/niaaa-18.htm.

———. "What Is a Standard Drink?" National Institute on Alcohol Abuse and Alcoholism. http://pubs.niaaa.nih.gov/publications/Practitioner/pocketguide/pocket_ guide2.htm.

News-Medical.Net. "Five Distinct Subtypes of Alcoholism Identified." News-Medical.Net. http://www.news-medical.net/?id=27074.

Nicolls, Jane. "Sunny Side Down." *People Weekly*, October 30, 1995.

NYS Work-Life Services, Employee Assistance Program. "History of EAP." NYS Employee Assistance Program and NYS Family Benefits Program. http://worklife. state.ny.us/eap/history.html.

O'Brien, Rebecca. "Countering Alcohol." *Harvard Magazine*, January–February 2005.

Office of Applied Studies, Substance Abuse and Mental Health Services Administration. "The National Survey on Drug Use and Health Report: Academic Performance and Substance Use among Students Aged 12 to 17: 2002, 2003, and 2004." *NSDUH Report* 18 (2006). http://www.oas.samhsa.gov/2k6/academics/academics.pdf.

Office of the Surgeon General. *The Surgeon General's Call to Action to Prevent and Reduce Underage Drinking.* Washington, DC: U.S. Department of Health and Human Services, 2007. http://www.surgeongeneral.gov/topics/underagedrinking/calltoaction.pdf.

———. *The Surgeon General's Call to Action to Prevent and Reduce Underage Drinking: What It Means to You: A Guide to Action for Families.* Washington, DC: U.S. Department of Health and Human Services. 2007. http://www.surgeongeneral.gov/topics/underagedrinking/FamilyGuide.pdf.

"Pat O'Brien Comes Clean about Rehab." *People Online,* May 5, 2005. http://www.people.com/people/article/0,,1057723,00.html.

Perkins, H.W. "Surveying the Damage: A Review of Research on Consequences of Alcohol Misuse in College Populations." *Journal of Studies on Alcohol* 14 (2002): 91–100.

Peters, A.C. "Chemical Dependency: An Overview and Position." *Journal of the Massachusetts Dental Society* 36, no. 2 (1987): 73–77, 90.

———. "Chemical Dependency in Dentistry: The Massachusetts Response." *Journal of the Massachusetts Dental Society* 35, no. 4 (1986): 185–190.

Phoenix House. "Facts on Tap: Here Are Some Stone-Cold Sobering Statistics about the College Sex-and-Alcohol Cocktail." Phoenix House. http://www.factsontap.org/factsontap/risky/the_facts.htm.

Plutmen, Bert. *The Thinking Person's Guide to Sobriety.* New York: St. Martin's Press, 1999.

Poelen, E. A. P., R. C. M. E. Engels, H. Van Der Vorst, R. H. J. Scholte, and A. A. Vermulst. "Best Friends and Alcohol Consumption in Adolescence: A Within-Family Analysis." *Drug and Alcohol Dependence* 88 (2007): 163–173.

Pope, Justin. "Substance Abuse Called Growing Threat at Colleges." *Boston Globe,* March 15, 2007.

"Primetime: Family Secrets." First episode of 6-part series. Produced by David Sloan. *ABC,* Aired June 26, 2007.

Rational Recovery Systems Inc. "Frequently Asked Questions." Rational Recovery Systems Inc. http//www.rationalrecovery.org/faq.html.

Robbins, Alexandra, and Abby Wilner. *Quarterlife Crisis: The Unique Challenges of Life in Your Twenties.* New York: Jeremy P. Tarcher/Putnam, 2001.

Roundtable on Religion and Social Welfare Policy. "An Interview with Susan Foster of CASA." Nelson A. Rockefeller Institute of Government. http://www.religionandsocialpolicy.org/interviews/interview.cfm?id=152.

Salzman, Jonathan, and Frank Phillips. "Autopsies Find Alcohol, Some Cocaine, 2 Officials Say." *Boston Globe,* October 4, 2007.

Sam Spady Foundation. "The Wallet Card Every Student Needs." Sam Spady Foundation. http://www.samspadyfoundation.org/cards.html.

Save Our Selves. "The SOS Story: Jim Christopher—A Brief Biography." Save Our Selves. http://www.sosbehindbars.org/jameschristopher.htm.

Schindehette, Susan. "Dying for a Drink." *People Weekly,* September 4, 2006.

Schulenberg, John, Patrick M. O'Malley, Jerald G. Bachman, and Lloyd D. Johnston. "Early Adult Transitions and Their Relations to Well-being and Substance Abuse." In *On the Frontier of Adulthood: Theory, Research, and Public Policy,* edited by Richard A. Settersten Jr., Frank F. Furstenberg Jr., and Rubén G. Rumbert, 417–453. Chicago: University of Chicago Press, 2005.

Schulenberg, J., P. M. O'Malley, J. G. Bachman, K. N. Wadsworth, and L. D. Johnston. "Getting Drunk and Growing Up: Trajectories of Frequent Binge Drinking during the Transition to Young Adulthood." *Journal of Studies on Alcohol* 57 (1996): 289–304.

Sege, Irene. "Her Time in a Bottle: Caroline Knapp's Memoir Recounts Her Painful Love Affair with Alcohol." *Boston Globe*, May 1, 1996.

Serby, Steve. "His Sobering Experience." *New York Post*, November 17, 2006.

Slack, Donavan, and Jonathan Saltzman. "Menino to Review City Fire Agency." *Boston Globe*, October 5, 2007.

Slaymaker, Val. "Understanding the Whole Story of Addiction Treatment Outcomes." *The Voice*, Winter 2004. http://www.hazelden.org/web/public/vcwin4story. page.

SMART Recovery. "Frequently Asked Questions about SMART Recovery." SMART Recovery. http://www.smartrecovery.org/resources/faq.htm.

———. "Welcome." SMART Recovery. http://www.smartrecovery.org/.

SOS Clearinghouse. "An Overview of SOS." SOS Clearinghouse. http://www.secularsobriety.org/overview.html.

———. "Welcome to SOS." SOS Clearinghouse. http://www.secularsobriety.org/.

Speller, Jeffrey Lynn. *Executives in Crisis: Recognizing and Managing the Alcoholic, Drug-Addicted or Mentally Ill Executive*. San Francisco: Jossey-Bass, 1989.

Spilka, Bernard, Ralph W. Hood Jr., Bruce Hunsberger, and Richard Gorsuch. *The Psychology of Religion: An Empirical Approach*. New York: Guilford Press, 2003.

Steinberg, Jacques. "HBO's Chief Agrees to Quit TV Network." *New York Times*, May 10, 2007.

Sterling, R. C., S. Weinstein, P. Hill, E. Gottheil, S. M. Gordon, and K. Shorie. "Levels of Spirituality and Treatment Outcome: A Preliminary Examination." *Journal of Studies on Alcohol* 67, no. 4 (2006): 600–606.

Substance Abuse and Mental Health Services Administration. "Results from the 2005 National Survey on Drug Use and Health: National Findings." U.S. Department of Health and Human Services. http://www.oas.samhsa.gov/NSDUH/2k5NSDUH/2k5results.htm.

Task Force of the National Advisory Council on Alcohol Abuse and Alcoholism. *A Call to Action: Changing the Culture of Drinking at U.S. Colleges*. Rockland, MD: National Institute on Alcohol Abuse and Alcoholism, 2002. http://www.collegedrinkingprevention.gov/media/TaskForceReport.pdf.

Thoreau, Henry David. *Walden: The Writings of Henry David Thoreau*. Princeton, NJ: Princeton University Press, 1971.

Treadway, David C. *Before It's Too Late: Working with Substance Abuse in the Family*. New York: W.W. Norton, 1989.

Tucker, Eric. "Brown U. Aims to Curb Student Drinking." *Boston Globe*, March 11, 2006.

"Turbulent Twenties." *The Oprah Winfrey Show*. VHS. Chicago: Harpo Productions, 2001.

University Health Services. "Understanding Blood Alcohol Content (BAC)." University of Rochester. http://www.rochester.edu/uhs/healthtopics/Alcohol/bac.html.

U.S. Department of Health and Human Services. "News Release: Acting Surgeon General Issues National Call to Action on Underage Drinking." U.S. Department of Health and Human Services. http://www.hhs.gov/news/press/2007pres/20070306.html.

USA Today. "'Big Lag' in Treatment for Alcoholism Grows." July 3, 2007.

Vaillant, George E. *The Natural History of Alcoholism.* Cambridge, MA: Harvard University Press, 1983.

———. *The Natural History of Alcoholism Revisited.* Cambridge, MA: Harvard University Press, 1995.

Virgo, Paul J. "From Disciplinary Action to Recovery: ADPs and LAPs." *GPSolo Magazine* 23, no. 7 (October–November 2006).

Vu, Pauline. "Colleges Go on Offense against Binge Drinking." Pew Research Center. http://www.stateline.org/live/details/story?contentId=245335.

Wells, E. J., J. L. Horwood, and D. M. Fergusson. "Stability and Instability in Alcohol Diagnosis from Ages 18 to 21 and Ages 21 to 25 Years." *Drug and Alcohol Dependence* 81 (2006): 157–165.

"What We Were Like: Fragments of A.A. History." *AAGrapevine.org: The International Journal of Alcoholics Anonymous* 46, no. 5 (1989). Available from http://www.aagrapevine.org.

White, H. R., and K. Jackson. "Social and Psychological Influences on Emerging Adult Drinking Behavior." *National Institute on Alcohol Abuse and Alcoholism* 28, no. 4 (2004–2005). http://pubs.niaaa.nih.gov/publications/arh284/182-190.htm.

Whitehead, Sandra. "Emerging Adulthood, No Longer Adolescents, but Not Yet Fully Adult, Today's Older Teens and 20-Somethings Are Charting a New Path to Maturity—Quite Different from the One Taken by Previous Generations. What's Behind This New Life Stage, and What Does It Mean for Parents of Today's Teens and Tweens?" http://www.parenthood.com/articles.html?article_id=9153.

Williams, Dan. "Addiction Information." Peace and Healing. http://www.peaceandhealing.com/addiction/index.asp.

Women for Sobriety Inc. "'New Life' Acceptance Program." Women for Sobriety Inc. http://www.womenforsobriety.org/.

———. *Who We Are.* Quakertown, PA: Women for Sobriety Inc. http://www.womenforsobriety.org/brochure/Brochure-%20Who%20We%20Are.pdf.

———. *Women and Addictions.* Quakertown, PA: Women for Sobriety Inc. http://www.womenforsobriety.org/brochure/Brochure-%20Women%20&%20Addictions.pdf.

Woods, Judith. "Young, Professional and Hungover." *Telegraph,* January 9, 2003. http://www.telegraph.co.uk/news/uknews/1440242/Young-professional-and-hungover.html.

Zwillich, Todd. "Rise in Alcohol Abuse by College Women." MedicineNet Inc. http://www.medicinenet.com/script/main/art.asp?articlekey=79828.

INDEX

About the Author

SARAH ALLEN BENTON is a Licensed Mental Health Counselor in Boston, where she is co-leader of an alcohol skills training program directed to help problem drinkers. She previously held several counselor positions at McLean Psychiatric Hospital, which is affiliated with Harvard Medical School and Massachusetts General Hospital. In an earlier career, in television, Benton produced segments for the Disney Channel in California, a CBS affiliate in Denver, and an NBC affiliate in Boston. Benton is a member of a 12-Step Recovery Program and has remained sober since 2004. She earned her Master of Science in Counseling Psychology from Northeastern University.